Reef Sharks
and
Rays of the World

A Guide to their Identification,
Behavior and Ecology

by
Scott W. Michael

SEA CHALLENGERS • MONTEREY, CALIFORNIA
1993

A SEA CHALLENGERS PUBLICATION

Copy Editors, Kenneth Hashagen, Dr. Hans Bertsch, Dr. Joe Hancock
Technical Editor, Dr. Tim Tricas

FRONT COVER

Spotted Wobbegong, *Orectolobus maculatus* (upper left)
Photograph by Rudie Kuiter

Caribbean reef sharks, *Carcharhinus perezi* (middle left)
Photograph by Scott W. Michael

Necklace carpet shark, *Parascyllium variolatum* (lower left)
Photograph by Rudie Kuiter

Marbled torpedo ray, *Torpedo marmorata* (upper right)
Photograph by Avi Klapfer

Bluespotted ribbontail ray, *Taeniura lymma* (middle right)
Photograph by Avi Klapfer

Manta ray, *Manta birostris* (lower right)
Photograph by Avi Klapfer

Library of Congress Cataloging-in-Publication Data

Michael, Scott W.
   Reef sharks and rays of the world: a guide to their identification, ecology, and behavior/ by Scott W. Michael.   p.   cm.
      Includes bibliographical references (p. 99) and indexes.
      ISBN 0-930118-18-9
      1. Sharks.   2. Rays (Fishes)   3. Coral reef fauna—Ecology.
   I. Title.
QL638.9.M525   1993
597.3—dc20

92-46402
CIP

SEA CHALLENGERS
4 Somerset Rise • Monterey, CA 93940
Printed in Hong Kong through Inter Print
Petaluma, CA, U.S.A.

Typography and prepress production by Colorgraphics, Pacific Grove, CA U.S.A.

TABLE OF CONTENTS

ACKNOWLEDGMENTS

This book was made possible by the support and contributions of many. Most noteworthy was the photographic contribution of Rudie Kuiter; without Rudie's beautiful pictures the book would have been sorely lacking. Many other great photographers kindly provided transparencies and information (see listing below). Stewart Cove's UnderSea Adventures (Nassau, Bahamas), the Stella Maris Inn (Long Island, Bahamas), FantaSea Divers (Phuket, Thailand), Kia Ora Resort and Ives Lefevre of Manta Ray Divers (Rangiroa, French Polynesia), Jais Aben Resort (Madang, New Guinea), the UnderSea Hunter (Cocos Island, Costa Rica), Manley Marineland (Sydney, Australia), Taronga Zoo and Aquarium (Sydney, Australia), the Sydney Aquarium (Sydney, Australia), and Kelly Tarlton's Underwater World (Auckland, New Zealand) assisted in the acquisition of shark and ray photographs. Michael DeGruy and Mimi Armstrong, Dr. Janine Caira, Dr. A. Peter Klimley, Wes Pratt, Marty Snyderman, Chuck Stilwell, and Dr. Kenneth Williams provided opportunities to gather field observations. Michael Brogan, Geremy Cliff, Dr. Leonard Compagno, Michael DeGruy, Dr. David Ebert, Glen Edney, Dr. A. Peter Klimley, Rudie Kuiter, Dr. Peter Last, Dr. Donald Nelson, Richard Pyle, Dr. Thomas Thorson, Michael Shaw, Mark Strikland, Wesley Strong, Dr. Timothy Tricas, John West and many others shared elasmobranch observations and anecdotes with me, while my friend Dr. Timothy Tricas edited and provided valuable suggestions and my "dive buddy" Dr. Joe Hancock acted as shark bait and also as a manuscript editor. For logistical support I extend thanks to my family and to my friends Gary Barth and Bill Zarnick. Finally, my dearest wife Janine has put up with, and even encouraged, my obsession with these animals since the day she met me! She helped in acquiring field data and photos for this book, typed and layed out the copy, and has given constant moral support throughout. Sincere thanks to all of these individuals and everyone else that made this effort possible.

PHOTOGRAPHIC CREDITS

PHOTOGRAPHER / SPECIES NUMBER

Dr. Gerald Allen 31
William J. Arzbaecher appendix
Michael Bacon 77, 103, 124, 140, 148
Gary Bell 22
S. Chater (ORI) 53, 55
Gary L. Chesnut 94
Michael Cufer 36
Neville Coleman 16, 23, 24, 47, 125, 136
Mark Conlin (Howard Hall Productions) 11, 14, 64 (lower)
CSIRO 56, 71, 74, 76, 108, 157
Helmut Debelius (IKAN) 50, 80, 111
Malcom Francis 156
Daniel Gotshall 1, 5, 49, 104, 106, 107, 119 (lower), 120, 144, 149, 161
Soichi Hagiwara 52 (upper, lower), 123, appendix
Wayne Hasson 35, 116
Ted Hobson 164
Paul Humann 13, 159
Mark Kerr (Sea Wildlife) 7, 39, 58
Avi Klapfer 32, 75, 109

Alison Kuiter 44
Rudie Kuiter 4, 6, 9, 10, 12, 17, 18, 21, 42, 43, 45, 48, 65, 73, 92, 96, 97, 98, 99, 121, 131, 133, 143, 145, 146, 150, 151, 152, 153
Dr. Peter Last 15
Doug Perrine 67, 78, 79, 87, 90, 93, 158, 163
Post (IKAN) 84
Andy Purcell (Planet Earth Pictures) 51, 105, 130
Richard Pyle 122
Dr. John Randall 25, 85, 115, 127, 142
Schmidt (IKAN) 38
Dr. Malcolm Smale 62, 63
Marty Snyderman 40, 41, 88, 89, 95, 112, 118, 126, 128, 154, 165
Jeremy Stafford-Deitsch 29
Roger Steene 101
Mark Strickland 34, 138, 142 (inset)
Wesley Strong 86
Rudy Van Der Elst 54, 129, 155
Gilbert Van Ryckevorse (Planet Earth Pictures) 110
Don Watson 135
Woodman (IKAN) 113
David Wrobel 20, 59
All other photographs by Scott W. Michael
All shark and ray drawings by Laura C. Williams

DEDICATION

To
Dr. Thomas B. Thorson
my friend and teacher.

INTRODUCTION

With sport diving on the increase, more and more people are encountering sharks and rays (collectively called elasmobranchs). With this increase in contact, divers are interested in identifying the species that they see and want to better understand their behavior. Although there are numerous identification guides to the sharks and rays of specific geographical areas, there is none that is worldwide in its coverage and limited to those species likely to be encountered by divers. This book describes 120 species of sharks and 112 species of rays, from around the world, that could be encountered near rocky reefs and coral reefs. I have attempted to include underwater or aquarium photographs of the majority of these species; in some cases the photographs of live specimens have never been published before. Information is also presented on the behavior and ecology of reef sharks and rays. This includes notes on depth range, food habits, social behavior, behavior toward divers, and aquarium care. These data were collected from the literature, interviews with divers, aquarists, and biologists, and from personal observations. Hopefully, these details will help the underwater observer to decipher the behavior of these creatures that has often been labeled "mysterious" and "unpredictable."

USING THIS GUIDE

If you are diving and see a shark or ray that you cannot identify, make notes on a slate or remember some of the key characteristics of the species in question. These would include: the body or disc shape, what fins are present (e.g. does it have an anal or second dorsal fin?), where the fins are in relation to one another (e.g. does the second dorsal fin originate before or after the origin of the anal fin?), any markings on the fins, the color pattern, and the tail morphology and length (e.g. in whiptail stingrays look to see if a dorsal finfold or dorsal keel is present). It is best to make your identification immediately after leaving the water while the mental image of the shark or ray is still fresh. Open the guide to the line drawings in the "Pictorial Key to Families" and find the sketch or sketches that look most like the animal in question. Under each family representative you will find page numbers to locate the family and species accounts. After reading the family account, examine the color plates and read the associated species accounts. Although I have attempted to be exhaustive in the guide's coverage, it is possible you may encounter a shark or ray not included in this book. I have given an extensive list of references at the end of this guide that can be used to assist in identifying species that have been omitted. The scientific nomenclature, classification scheme, and common names used are based mainly on the works of Compagno (1973, 1984), Randall (1986), and Compagno et al. (1989). Good luck with your elasmobranch watching ventures!

FOOD HABITS

All elasmobranchs are carnivorous (some ingest plant material incidentally) and, although many are opportunistic as far as what and when they eat, there are a number of species that show dietary preferences and many seek prey more actively at certain times during the diel and tidal cycles. A good example of a species with a more specialized diet is the sicklefin weasel shark *(Hypogaleus microstoma)*, which feeds almost exclusively on cephalopods. Other examples of elasmobranchs that show some degree of food preference are the crested bullhead shark (adults feed heavily on sea urchins), the bonnethead (feeds primarily on crabs and shrimp), the great hammerhead (favors stingrays), the cownose rays (they feed on bivalve molluscs) and the bentfin devil ray (feeds on planktonic crustaceans).

Trends in prey preference often reflect morphological features found between species. Tooth shape, jaw morphology, and mouth size are all characteristics that will have some bearing on what types of prey are eaten. For example, members of the smoothhound shark family have teeth that are well suited for clutching and crushing the carapaces of the crabs on which they feed, while the needle-like teeth of the sandtiger shark are adapted to grasping small, slippery fishes. The shape of the jaws and how they are suspended from the skull also has a bearing on what sharks and rays eat. Some elasmobranchs have heavy jaws, tightly buttressed against the skull, with large muscles that enable them to masticate heavy shelled invertebrates. Others have short upper jaws loosely suspended from the cranium that can be protruded forward to nimbly pluck a small crab off the ocean floor or to excise a hunk of flesh from a bloated whale carcass.

In general, larger sharks take the largest prey. This becomes apparent when examining the diet of different size classes within a species of elasmobranch. Take, for instance, the white shark: at smaller sizes ($\setminus$3 m, 10 ft), white sharks feed heavily on elasmobranchs and bony fishes, especially bottom dwelling forms. Case in point: of 29 juvenile white sharks examined from the New York Bight, 49 % of the stomachs examined contained sea robins and 24 % contained menhaden. Other food items included hake, skates, flounders, bluefish, crabs, a smoothhound shark, and even a starfish. These smaller sharks have teeth that are more slender, resembling those of mako sharks, and more finely serrated; this tooth shape is better for grasping than cutting. Larger white sharks ($\setminus$3 m, 10 ft) feed predominantly on seals, sea lions, and cetaceans. Their teeth are more triangular, heavily serrated, and thus are more effective for gouging hunks of flesh from large prey or for cutting prey into smaller pieces. Tiger sharks also show ontogenetic changes in diet. Smaller tiger sharks feed more on sea snakes, while larger specimens eat a greater number of turtles. This change is probably a function of prey handling capability; smaller tiger sharks would have a hard time capturing, cutting, and ingesting adult sea turtles. Among the batoids, adult cownose rays feed more on deep burrowing molluscs than the juveniles, which dig up clams that occur just under the sediment (the adults are apparently better equipped to dig deeper holes), and juvenile bentfin devil rays feed on krill and mysid shrimp, while the adults feed only on krill. In the case of the bentfin devil ray, the differences in diet between size classes may be a reflection of prey availability (a result of a difference in distribution between the adults and the juveniles) rather than any disparity in prey selection.

Sharks and rays usually increase their foraging activity at discrete times of the day or night or during certain phases of the tidal cycle. Some are more active at dusk and dawn (e.g. lemon shark), others are diurnal (e.g. bonnethead shark), but most of the shark species that have been studied are nocturnal (e.g. angel shark, blue shark, whitetip reef shark, scalloped hammerhead).

Some sharks and rays move into intertidal waters to feed at flood tide. For example, on coral cays of the Great Barrier Reef, blacktip reef sharks, sicklefin lemon sharks, whitespotted shovelnose rays, roundnose stingrays, bluespotted ribbontail rays, and eagle rays move onto the reef flat and sandy intertidal areas to feed at high tide. Sandbar sharks and cownose rays also move with tidal currents, infiltrating intertidal areas at flood tide. Although sharks and rays often show diel and tidal rhythmicity with respect to feeding activity, many will eat when ever the opportunity presents itself.

SCAVENGERS

Sharks are often thought of by the layperson as ocean dwelling garbage disposals. But while it is true that some sharks will devour dead animal matter, most only occasionally scavenge dead food items. There are, however, several shark species that regularly employ this foraging strategy. For example, along the eastern coast of the United States it has been suggested that large white sharks depend on whale carcasses as an important source of food. In this area dead whales are often accompanied by one to nine white sharks (they do not all feed on the carcass at once), which satiate themselves on the cetacean blubber. A telemetry study conducted on one shark that was accompanying a whale carcass, showed that over the 3.5 days the shark was tracked, it swam in the thermocline and made repeated deep dives, possibly in an attempt to locate marine mammal carcasses that had sunk to the ocean bottom. It is also possible that some carcasses get held up on the denser, colder water below the thermocline and so the shark swims along this gradient in an attempt to locate these food sources. Cetacean carcasses are not uncommon along the north eastern seaboard and the large slick created by a dead whale would send out an expansive olfactory signal to sharks in the area. White sharks could go for a long time between meals; it has been estimated that a white shark could exist for 1.5 months on 30 kg (66 lb) of whale blubber (the amount taken from the stomach of a 4.5 m, 14.9 ft, white shark). When feeding on a dead whale at the water's surface, white sharks will roll over on their backs just before biting the corpse. After the teeth have been thrust into the floating whale, the shark will upright itself with lateral sweeps of the tail; this twisting action neatly excises a mouthful of flesh. Other sharks commonly feed on dead whales (e.g. blue shark, oceanic whitetip shark); in fact, the sharks of the family Carcharhinidae are commonly called whaler sharks because of their habit of feeding on harpooned whales, in days of old.

Other sharks take advantage of natural catastrophes to scavenge on dying or dead prey. California angel sharks will feed on blacksmith (Chromis punctipinnis) killed by disease outbreaks, and these angel sharks and horn sharks eat dying squid and their egg capsules that sink to the bottom during squid mass spawnings.

HUNTING STRATEGIES

Although reef habitats often appear to teem with prey items, many of these organisms are equipped with defenses that make them unavailable as food to all predators. In response to prey adaptations, certain predators have evolved behavioral and anatomical features that enable them to thwart the different defense mechanisms of their prey. Elasmobranchs employ a variety of strategies to find, capture, and ingest the animals on which they feed. Below I will discuss these hunting tactics.

Predators on Large Invertebrates

A number of sharks and rays feed on large, armored invertebrates, like snails, bivalves, crabs, and urchins. Members of the bullhead shark, smoothhound shark, sharkfin guitarfish, guitarfish, whiptail stingray, cownose ray, and eagle ray families have specialized dentition to crush or grind up the exoskeletons of hard shelled invertebrates. However, the techniques used when handling these prey items can differ between the species. For example, eagle rays ingest the whole prey item, masticate it, spit it out, and then reingest only the soft body parts, while the bullhead sharks grind up, swallow the entire mouthful, and regurgitate hard parts later.

Not only do some invertebrates sport armor, some also have defensive armaments like spines and claws. The claws of larger crabs are effective for dissuading some predators, but the brown smoothhound has been observed to "disarm" cancrid crabs (a favorite food of this shark) by grasping a claw and shaking it free from the body. Even the long sharp spines of sea urchins are no match for certain elasmobranchs. The molariform dentition, powerful jaws, and thick skin of the bullhead sharks enable them to thwart the defenses of these spiny invertebrates. The eyes of the bullhead sharks are high on the head, far from the mouth, and out of the way of the urchin's spines.

Some elasmobranchs do not chew up large invertebrates, but instead swallow them whole. Tiger sharks are known to feed heavily on conchs in some areas, with dozens of these large snails having been taken from the stomach of a single shark. Although the conch opercula, soft parts, and occasionally intact shells are present, partially digested shells are never found in the tiger shark's alimentary tract. How the sharks succeed in getting rid of the shell while retaining the meat is a mystery. Similarly, in the stomach contents of draughtsboard sharks, I frequently found hermit crab remains without the snail shells that the crabs live in. In this case it may be that the sharks eat the crabs when they are engaged in changing shells, or that the crab may climb out of its shell when it contacts the strong acidic stomach juices and the shark than regurgitates the lot and reingests the crab. It may also be that this shark uses the same elaborate handling method employed by the related small-spotted catshark. This shark has been observed to knock snails and hermit crabs over with its snout. As the upended invertebrate retracts into its shell, the shark grasps the animal's body in its jaws and rips it out of its protective home by shaking its head vigorously from side to side. After knocking them over with their snouts, nurse sharks utilize suction, generated by increasing the size of their buccal and branchial cavities, to extract conchs out of their shells. The tawny nurse shark has been reported to use a similar technique to feed on small giant clams!

Some sharks mutilate invertebrate prey, only ingesting a part the animal. For example, leopard sharks will seize the extended siphons of buried clams and rip them off with violent head shaking and horn sharks will pounce on open sea anemones and bite off a mouthful of tentacles before the invertebrate can retract them. Round stingrays will also nip off clam siphons protruding from the sand or mud.

Ambush Predators

Ambush, or sit-and-wait, predators are those that remain motionless and let their prey amble into striking range. These animals rely on a quick strike, cryptic color, form, and behavior to catch their quarry unaware. The best example of ambush predators in the elasmobranch clan would have to be the wobbegongs. Wobbegongs are adorned with spots, bands, or reticulations that help them to disappear among coral, coralline algae, and larger macroalgae. To enhance this resemblance of reef substrate even further, these sharks possess flaps of skin around the mouth, which help break up the anterior body outline. Another way to avoid detection by potential prey is to hide under the substrate. Both the angel sharks and the torpedo rays will bury themselves in the sand or mud, from which they explode to capture passing fishes and crustaceans by surprise. In the case of the California angel shark, the prey must pass within a strike zone 4-15 cm (1.5-6 inches) from the shark's head to elicit an attack. If the prey is within this zone and of small size, the angel shark almost always succeeds in capturing it.

The swell shark is a sit-and-wait predator that takes up a nocturnal ambush site on the sandy bottom, adjacent to the reef, where blacksmith aggregate. The swell shark has been reported to use two feeding techniques to capture these refuging fish. One is the "gulp"; this is when the inactive swell shark rapidly opens its mouth and expands its gill and mouth cavities to suck in a blacksmith that has come too close. The second technique is the "yawn"; when a drifting blacksmith moves toward the swell shark it will slowly open its mouth and wait until the prey fish recklessly swims into its gaping jaws!

Luring Predators

Some ambush predators go one step further and use anatomical features or specialized behaviors to "bait" prey into the strike zone. The dermal flaps, and even the skin, of the wobbegong bears a resemblance to certain calcareous algae and encrusting invertebrates. Numerous bony fishes and some crustaceans feed on these marine plants and animals and may mistake the inactive wobbegong for food ridden substrate! Protective resemblance is another way sharks like the wobbegong could attract food. This is where a predator looks like a potential place to hide (e.g. a rock). In reef environments, space can be a limited resource and thus a quiescent wobbegong may attract a fish, octopus, or crab looking for a shelter site. The nurse shark and the yellow stingray apparently employ specific behaviors to mimic a hiding place. Juvenile nurse sharks have been observed to rest on their pectoral fins, which are rolled underneath their bodies, and remain motionless and the yellow stingray reportedly assumes a stationary position and lifts the front edge of the disc. In both cases it has been suggested the space under the bodies of these predators may be mistaken for a home by a shelter-seeking shrimp or fish.

Other non-reef sharks may rely on bioluminescent body parts to attract their prey. For example cigar sharks (*Isistius* spp.) and some other deepwater dogfishes have bioluminescent photophores that might mimic similar organs in krill, squid, and bony fishes. When a hunting elephant seal, cetacean, or billfish approaches one of these glowing sharks, the shark shoots forward and excises a plug of flesh from the squid-eater's body. The bioluminescent lining of the mouth of megamouth *(Megachasma pelagicos)* may attract krill right into its open jaws!

Stalking Predators

Stalking predators use stealth to approach their prey before an attack. Like the ambusher, the stalking predator relies on going unnoticed by their quarry. At night or in turbid waters, sharks are very effective at locating and sneaking up on their prey. Sharks have acute sense organs that can detect prey from great distances, and yet they themselves make little "hydrodynamic noise"; therefore, potential prey have difficulty detecting their approach.

An example of an elasmobranch that uses this hunting technique is the white shark, which is reported to sneak up on seals, sea lions, and sea otters basking on the water's surface. It is thought that white sharks would have difficulty capturing a healthy pinniped if the mammal were aware of the shark's presence; therefore, they rely on surprise to approach within striking range. A study conducted on white shark/pinniped interactions off the northern California coast demonstrated that elephant seals are more vulnerable to attack than sea lions and that subadults are attacked more often than adults. Young pinnipeds may be the targets of white shark attacks more frequently because they are less vigilant and have less experience with sharks than their elders. Behavioral differences also may explain why seals are eaten more than sea lions. First, these two types of pinnipeds swim differently. Sea lions swim by flapping the front flippers, while the seals propel themselves with the posterior part of the body and the hind flippers. Four detailed observations of white shark attacks on elephant seals followed a general pattern; the shark approached the seal from below and behind and usually bit the rear portion of the body. The seal did not flee, possibly because of injury or shock, and the shark returned within 1 to 5 minutes to consume the wounded mammal. In the case of the elephant seal, this initial bite to the posterior part of the body would incapacitate the animal because this is the region responsible for locomotion. A bite to the same area of a sea lion would not prevent normal movement and thus it could possibly still swim. Another behavioral difference that may influence differential pinniped predation is that elephant seals are often solitary when away from shore, while sea lions usually occur in herds. A group of sea lions would more likely detect an approaching shark and thus to take evasive actions than would a solitary individual (a lesson divers that spend time in areas frequented by white shark should take note of, i.e., never dive alone). The sleeping behavior of seals also makes them more vulnerable to attack than sea lions. When resting or sleeping in the water, seals usually hang vertically with their noses above the water's surface while sea lions, except when they are breathing, keep their heads under the water and group members often maintain body contact with one another.

The white shark is not the only shark known to stalk its prey. The broadnose sevengill, wobbegong, nurse, sandtiger, and some cat sharks also employ this hunting technique. Torpedo rays also stalk their prey. For example, the Pacific torpedo stalks fishes that hang in the water column above the reef at night. The torpedo ray will drift over the bottom until it comes near a fish, then it lunges forward, folds its disc margins over the fish, and shocks it with its electric organs. Oftentimes, the ray will somersault or barrel roll in the water column while moving the fish towards its mouth.

Pursuit Predators

Certain sharks and rays rely on speed and agility to capture their prey. The broadnose sevengill, the mako sharks, certain smoothhounds and requiem sharks, and hammerheads have all been observed to chase down their prey. Sharks will pick an individual from a group of potential prey animals and attempt to catch it. For example, a blacktip reef shark was reported to select one surgeonfish from a feeding school and pursue it until it succeeded in capturing it. Some sharks use surprise tactics to gain a competitive edge when chasing their quarry; for example, the gray reef shark has been observed to rush from deep water, moving just over the coral, in an attempt to catch fish before they retreat to shelter. In captivity, requiem sharks have been observed chasing bonyfish tankmates and incapacitating them by biting off their tails. The sharks then circle back to consume the rest of their catch.

The smooth and great hammerhead sharks are well known for their habit of chasing rays, often into very shallow water. In one incident, a great hammerhead beached itself when attempting to capture a spotted eagle ray. In another episode near the island of Bimini, biologists witnessed an amazing predation event involving a great hammerhead and an adult southern stingray. The shark was observed chasing the ray; when it had closed the distance, it knocked the batoid to the sea floor by hitting it with the front edge of its head. The ray bounced from the substrate and the shark immediately hit it again and pinned the ray to the bottom. The shark pivoted atop the ray, bit a large chunk from the left pectoral fin and began circling the wounded batoid. The ray attempted to swim for the shelter of a nearby ship wreck, but before it could reach refuge the hammerhead pushed it to the sea floor and took a bite from the right pectoral fin. The shark swam around the incapacitated ray for 24 minutes before it grasped the wounded animal by the head, bit off a piece of the ray, dropped it to the sea floor, and began circling again. The shark repeated this behavior four times before the rest of the remains were swallowed.

Recently, I watched a shortfin mako (1.5 m long, 5 ft) pursue a juvenile blue shark (approximately 80 cm long, 31 inches) up a chum slick. The mako easily caught up with the smaller shark and preceeded to "mouth" it several times before rejecting it. It is impossible to say for sure why the mako didn't eat the juvenile blue (makos are known shark eaters), but it may have been because the initial olfactory cues did not match the gustatory stimuli the mako shark received when it "tasted" the young shark.

Although fewer rays are known to pursue their prey, some of the more agile species (e.g. butterfly rays - Family Gymnuridae, eagle rays, bat rays) actively chase fishes and invertebrates on which they feed.

Crevice Hunters and Grubbers

Many prey hide in the reef or in the adjacent sand to avoid predators. Certain reef sharks and rays have evolved behavioral techniques and anatomical features that enable them to locate and capture these concealed species. The epaulette sharks have long, thin bodies and muscular pectoral fins that enable them to enter branching coral colonies and reef crevices to find cryptic prey. I observed one epaulette shark wedge the anterior part of its body into a crevice, turn itself over and suck a small shrimp from the roof of the crevice. These sharks apparently occupy a niche more similar to moray eels than most other sharks.

Like the epaulette sharks, the larger whitetip reef shark is a master at extracting prey from reef crevices. Although not nearly as eel-like as the epaulette sharks, this shark is more sinuous than most other members of the family Carcharhinidae. I had the opportunity to observe the nocturnal feeding behavior of the whitetip reef shark at Cocos Island, Costa Rica. After dark, the diurnally quiescent whitetips actively move over the reef, plunging their heads into cracks and crevices searching for sleeping fishes and octopuses. The hungry whitetips violently twist and turn in their attempt to penetrate deeper into crevices, with some sharks squirming into a hole in one side of a coral head only to exit through an opening on the other side. They were also observed to break off pieces of coral during these zealous forays and sometimes tear their skin and fins. The whitetips chased and caught Panamic soldierfish *(Myripristis leiognathos)* that were feeding over the reef and snapped at trumpetfish *(Aulostomus chinensis)* and Pacific creole fish *(Paranthias colonus)* that had been stirred from slumber by their frenetic activity. Although most hunting activity appeared to occur at this time, whitetips were observed to take advantage of unusual feeding opportunities during the day as well.

Not all sharks depend on flexibility to capture refuging prey; some species use brute force. For example, a 3-m (9.6-ft) tawny nurse shark was observed extracting a speared fish from under a coral head by wedging its body under the small bommie and lifting its head and body to raise the entire coral structure! By continuing to lift and squirm forward the shark was able to get close enough to suck the fish from underneath the coral head. The filmmaker who witnessed this behavior estimated the coral head to weigh in excess of 454 kg (1000 lb)! Although this was an artificially induced episode, there is little doubt this shark could use such herculean tactics to capture octopuses and reef fishes.

Sand dwelling crustaceans, molluscs, and fishes are also eaten by sharks and rays. Some rays are equipped with anatomical structures that aid them in locating hidden prey. The spotted eagle ray will root through the substrate with its elongated snout to find and uncover food and the sawfish will use its exaggerated rostrum to dig for clams and crabs. Others use special behaviors to excavate buried prey. For example, the southern bat ray pulls water in through its spiracles and jets it from its mouth and gills toward the sea floor. The ray will use this hydraulic jetting to blow depressions in the sand up to 20 cm (7.9 inches) in depth. Many stingray species dig holes in the substrate by undulating the disc margin, thus generating water currents that blow the substrate from underneath them. In areas where these fish are common, you can find numerous large depressions on the bottom as a result of this behavior. Port Jackson sharks pump water and bottom sediment through their mouths and out their gill slits to excavate buried molluscs and crustaceans, while leopard sharks suck innkeeper worms from their U-shaped burrows in the mud. These soft bodied worms are commonly consumed by adult leopard sharks and are usually found completely intact in their stomachs. The epaulette shark will force its head into the sand and locate buried prey with chemoreceptive nasal barbels. This shark also flips coral debris with its snout to expose hidden worms and crustaceans. Scalloped hammerhead sharks use a different technique to capture buried prey, as indicated by observations on captive specimens. At night these sharks hunt and capture wrasses that hide under the sand. They cruise slowly over the bottom and turn in tight circles or swim in figure eights when they detect a buried wrasse. The sharks swim over the sand and as they approach their targets, they drop their lower jaws and scoop the concealed fish from the substrate.

Predators on Small Schooling Prey

Many prey species school or aggregate for protection or reproduction. Certain elasmobranchs take advantage of grouped prey, having evolved anatomical characteristics or behavior patterns to feed on such assemblages. The thresher sharks, sawsharks (Family Pristiophoridae), and sawfishes are examples of such elasmobranchs. The tooth-studded rostrum of the saw sharks and sawfishes is flailed from side-to-side amid a school of fish, which impales or incapacitates the prey, while the tail of the thresher shark is used to herd, whip, and stun schooling fish.

Sharks like the blue shark use specialized behaviors when feeding on aggregated prey. When market squid form reproductive aggregations off the California coast, they are fed upon by blue sharks. Blue sharks swim through the mating squid with their mouths wide open, indiscriminately ingesting squid that inadvertently run into their jaws. Another technique used by blue sharks is to throw their heads from one side to the other as they swim through the school to catch squid in the corners of their mouths. Finally, blue sharks orient in a tail-stand posture under squid groups and propel themselves up through the bottom of the school, capturing squid as they ascend, then sink slowly back down below the school when they get a mouthful! The blue sharks have elongated gill rakers that prevent the slippery squid, and other small prey items, from simply sliding out of their gill slits. Oceanic whitetips use a technique similar to blue sharks. They swim, with jaws agape, through schools of baitfish that are being fed on by tuna. It was observed that unattentive tuna would swim into the jaws of the feeding oceanic whitetips. Likewise, spiny dogfish and leopard sharks swim into oncoming schools of small fish with their mouths opened wide. Spinner sharks *(Carcharhinus brevipinna)* and blacktip sharks will dash, with open mouths, through schools of baitfish. When the baitfish are near the surface, these feeding dashes often result in the sharks catapulting from the water. As these shark fall back into the sea they will often spin around their longitudinal body axis.

Sharks will also take bites from tightly massed schools of prey. Oceanic whitetips have been reported to use this technique to feed on small schooling fish and blue sharks have been documented to do the same to schools of krill. Numerous smoothhound sharks (e.g. gray smoothhound, brown smoothhound) I examined had stomachs full of small krill that were likely consumed in a similar manner.

Filter feeders
Like the great baleen whales, some of the largest elasmobranchs feed on small prey by straining it from the water. Whale sharks, basking sharks, megamouth sharks, and manta and devil rays all feed on zooplankton. The small fishes, fish eggs, crustaceans, and larvae these fish ingest are trapped in modified branchial structures just before the sea water passes through the gill slits. The filtering structures are enlarged gill rakers (basking sharks and manta rays) or net-like connective tissue (whale shark). These sharks and rays employ several different modes of filter feeding. Basking sharks and manta rays push the water through the gill rakers (ram-jet filter feeding) as they swim, while whale sharks suck in a mouthful of water (suction filter feeding) and purge it through their gill slits. The feeding mode employed by the whale sharks enables them to eat a broader range of prey species, including larger fishes, than the other filter feeders. Basking sharks can filter over 2,000 tons of water per hour when swimming at a normal speed. Since it requires much energy to feed in this manner, it has been suggested that basking sharks shed their gill rakers and lie torpid on the ocean floor, taking advantage of the huge oil reserve deposited in their livers, when prey densities drop. Devil rays have projections on each side of the mouth, called cephalic fins, that are rolled out and direct water and plankton into the mouth of the animal as it swims forward. These rays are known for their habit of leaping from the water. Although the purpose of this behavior has been attributed to parasite and shark sucker removal, it may be that breaching near small schooling fish and invertebrates causes the prey to form a tight, ball-like mass, a typical defensive response of many zooplankton species. This concentrated mass of plankton would be a more productive target for a filter feeding ray than a dispersed school. When they locate a cloud of zooplankton, devil rays feed by somersaulting within the plankton with their cephalic fins unfurled and their mouths open wide.

Hunting Prey on Land
Several sharks have been observed to employ unusual techniques for capturing prey animals that live near the water's edge. As noted earlier, tiger sharks feed heavily on sea turtles and are reported to congregate in areas where these reptiles go on shore to nest. Sharks intent on eating a turtle have been observed to swim out of the water and onto the sand in order to capture it. Similarly, there is a report of a tiger shark chasing a dolphin out of the water. The shark slunk back into the sea, leaving the wounded mammal stranded on the beach. Tiger

sharks also feed on sea birds. Frigate birds, shearwaters, cormorants, pelicans, and albatross have all been found in tiger shark stomachs. In the leeward Hawaiian Islands, tiger sharks annually aggregate in areas where fledgling albatross chicks learn to fly. The chicks are captured when they fall to the water on their first flights and are resting on the water's surface.

White sharks are reported to swim part way up and out of the water to pick resting pinnipeds off rocks. White sharks baited to dive boats will often lift their heads up above the water, similar to orca spy-hopping, and bite baits suspended well above the water's surface. This behavior, which is unique to the white shark, may allow the shark to visually locate seals basking on the shore.

Even more incredible is the acrobatic behavior of the smoothhound shark, which feeds upon semiterrestrial crabs that live on muddy banks of estuaries and bays. These sharks have been observed launching themselves out of the water and onto the mud flats in pursuit of their quarry and then wiggling back into the water.

Cooperative Hunting Behavior

Cooperative hunting behavior is two or more animals, of the same or different species, interacting to locate and capture food. These relationships are apparently mutualistic in nature, with all participants equally likely to benefit from the association. Several shark species cooperatively hunt their prey, although most observations are anecdotal in nature. For example, aggregations of sandtiger sharks have been observed to "herd" schooling fish into shallow water before attacking them. Groups of gray and blacktip reef sharks drive and trap schools of mullet inshore before commencing their feeding assault. There is even one report of blacktip reef sharks chasing schooling fish onto shore and sliding up onto the beach to capture them! Broadnose sevengill sharks are also reported to hunt sea lions in packs. A popular account of white sharks hunting jointly suggested that one shark approached a fur seal from one direction while another launched an attack from the opposite side. Whether these apparently coordinated attacks are made intentionally or are just a matter of chance is impossible to determine.

INTERSPECIFIC INTERACTIONS

Cleaner Hosts

A number of reef fishes acquire nutrients by picking parasites, necrotic tissue, and mucous from the body of other fishes. Divers usually observe these fishes picking at other bony fishes, but in recent years more and more reports of elasmobranch-cleaner fish interaction have been documented. Members of the wrasse, butterflyfish, angelfish, goby, and discfish (i.e. the remoras and shark suckers) families have all been observed picking parasites off elasmobranchs. These species vary in the degree to which they depend on nutrients acquired by cleaning. Some, like the cleaner wrasses *(Labroides* spp.*)*, depend solely on this feeding mode for nourishment (obligatory cleaners), while others, like the king angelfish *(Holocanthus passer)*, only consume parasites on occasion (facultative cleaners). Some species clean throughout their lives while others clean only as juveniles. Cleaner fishes enjoy almost total immunity from predation, but I have seen captive wobbegongs eat cleaner wrasses and the sandtiger shark has been reported to ingest sharksuckers *(Echeneis naucrates)*.

Parasites consumed by cleanerfishes include isopods, copepods, and flatworms. All of these are found on the body surfaces, in the gills, and in the mouths of sharks. The occurrence of parasites on rays varies greatly from one species to the next. For example, southern stingrays in one study were free of crustacean parasites, but monogenetic flatworms were present on the body. Devil rays, on the other hand, are often infested by parasitic copepods and isopods that reside on the dorsal body surface and in the gills, mouth, and nostrils. In some cases, cleaners may feed more on the mucus produced by the ray's skin than on parasites. In these incidences, the relationship between the batoids and the cleanerfish may best be described as commensal (i.e. where only one member of the association benefits), or possibly even parasitic (i.e. where one member benefits at the expense of the other). However, most of the shark-cleaner associations described are mutualistic, where both species involved in the relationship benefit.

Two types of cleaning strategies are recognized. Firstly, cleaners may have stations, often on conspicuous reef pinnacles or in caves or crevices, that their "clients" visit when in need of cleaning. A fish wanting to be groomed (host fish) will often adopt a specific posture that communicates its desire and enables the cleaner to better inspect for ectoparasites. Sharks and rays expand their gill slits, distend their jaws, slow their swimming rates, and adopt specific postures to help the parasite-feeding fish accomplish its work. For example, I observed a bluespotted ribbontail ray arch its back and pelvic area, allowing blue streak cleaner wrasses to pick at the cloaca and ventrum, while mantas will slow their swimming rate as they are being cleaned by wrasses.

Scientific studies of cleaner fishes indicate that the host fish apparently visit cleaning stations because they "enjoy" the tactile stimulation they receive from the cleaner. For example, cleaner wrasses will run their pelvic fins over the host's body before and during the cleaning bout. This may serve as positive reinforcement, encouraging the host to pose for cleaning. The desirability of tactile stimulation may explain why some manta rays will swim up to and seemingly solicit the diver to pet and even ride them.

Of the species that establish cleaning stations, those most often observed cleaning sharks and rays are the wrasses, Family Labridae. The genus *Labroides* consists of five species, all of which are obligatory cleaners. In the wild, members of this genus have been observed cleaning epaulette, tasselled wobbegongs, zebra, whitetip reef, gray reef sharks, and bowmouth guitarfish, feathertail stingrays, bluespotted ribbontail rays, marbled ribbontail rays, and manta rays. In captivity, one member of this genus has been reported to clean nurse, bull, lemon, and sicklefin lemon sharks. In most cases, the cleaner involved in these symbiotic bouts was the bluestreak cleaner wrasse *(Labroides dimidiatus)*, the most common member of the genus. I witnessed this species cleaning a tasselled wobbegong on the Great Barrier Reef near Heron Island. As the wobbegong swam along a reef channel, it was met and inspected by a cleaner wrasse. The shark settled to the bottom and the wrasse probed and disappeared into the first gill slit. After several seconds of inspecting this branchial cavity, the wrasse emerged head first and began to inspect other gill openings; the shark facilitated the wrasse's efforts by expanding the gill slits. The wrasse entered the first, third, and fifth slits a total of 10 times before moving down the body to the left pectoral fin, the edge of which was torn. It inspected the torn fin, moved to the right gill slits, then began cleaning them. After cleaning the gills, the wrasse moved down the shark's body and abandoned the shark to pursue a school of jacks (the entire cleaning bout lasted 8 minutes). I also observed a bluestreak cleaner wrasse cleaning an epaulette shark in a nearby cave. In this bout, the shark opened its mouth and distended the gill slits, allowing the wrasse to stick its head in and pick at the gill arches, roof of the mouth, and one of the nasal barbels. This incident also lasted about 8 minutes and, like the previous bout, the wrasse spent most of its time picking at the gills. Other *Labroides* spp. also clean sharks and rays, such as the bicolor cleaner wrasse *(Labroides bicolor)* which has been observed to clean gray and white-tip reef sharks. Although one wrasse usually attends to each host shark, groups of cleaner wrasses have been observed to clean elasmobranch clients, especially large rays. For example, in Rangiroa, French Polynesia, groups of bluestreak cleaner wrasses and a unidentified hogfish were observed picking at the ventrum of a large manta ray as it swam in circles above a coral head, and in the Coral Sea a group of approximately 13 bluestreak cleaner wrasses were documented cleaning a large bowmouth guitarfish (see photo species account 94).

Other wrasses are also known to clean elasmobranchs. For example, the bluehead wrasse *(Thalassoma bifasciatum)*, common in the Caribbean, cleans batoids. The interactions of these wrasses and southern stingrays have been studied in detail near Bimini. Rays would swim slowly over a cleaning station or settle to the bottom to "stand" on their pectoral and pelvic fins with their tails lifted. This posture lifted their ventral surfaces off the substrate, an action pattern only observed in the context of cleaning. Bouts lasted from less than 1 minute to 26 minutes, with the wrasses spending most of their time picking at the tail, head, and the dorsum of the ray. In contrast to the *Labroides* spp., these fish were never observed cleaning the ventral surface of the rays. Groups of bluehead wrasses have also been observed cleaning manta rays that had aggregated around a cleaning station.

Several wrasses of the genus *Bodianus*, commonly known as hogfishes, also clean elasmobranchs. At Cocos Island, Costa Rica, I observed groups of juvenile Mexican hogfish *(Bodianus diplotaenia)* picking at the first dorsal fin and head, and probing the gills of resting whitetip reef sharks. At the same location, adult Mexican hogfish were observed cleaning scalloped hammerheads. In the Bahamas, I observed a Spanish hogfish *(Bodianus rufus)* pick at the cloaca region of a southern stingray that was circling a bluehead wrasse cleaning station and an unidentified hogfish was observed cleaning the ventrum of a manta near Rangiroa, French Polynesia. And, finally, the senorita *(Oxyjulis californica)* has been observed grooming bat rays in California kelp beds.

Several angelfish species (Family Pomacanthidae) engage in cleaning as juveniles, but only one of these has been observed to clean sharks and it is the adult specimens that do the parasite picking. I observed the fascinating relationship between adult king angelfish and scalloped hammerheads off Cocos Island, Costa Rica. Small groups of hammerheads were observed to move along the reef-sand interface (water depth of about 20 m, 66 ft) where king angels grazed on sessile invertebrates. As the sharks approached, the angels would swim out to meet them. The sharks would slow their swimming rate while the angels picked at their flanks, gill slits, bellies, and under the extended head lobes (i.e. the hammer) of the sharks. Sharks were also observed to swim so slowly they began to sink! As if eventually irritated by the picking, some sharks were observed to suddenly shake their heads or perform torso thrusts as the angels nipped them. Clarion angelfish *(Holocanthus clarionensis)* have been reported to clean manta rays around Socorro Island.

There is at least one species of goby (Family Gobiidae) that is an elasmobranch cleaner. I observed redhead gobies *(Elacatinus puncticulatus)* inspecting the bodies of whitetip reef sharks on a number of occasions at Cocos Island, Costa Rica. Sometimes a number of gobies would clean a resting whitetip in concert with a group of juvenile Cortez hogfish. Whitetips disturbed by the observer while being cleaned would circle and settle in the same spot once the observer left. It may be that these resting areas (sand patches among large boulders) are cleaning stations visited by sharks for the primary purpose of being relieved of parasites.

The discfishes or remoras (Family Echeneidae) employ a different strategy to clean elasmobranchs and other marine animals. Rather than waiting on a shark or ray to visit a specific cleaning area, discfishes ride on the host fish, cleaning them at will. Remoras possess a suction-cup like dorsal fin that is used to attach to the body surface of their host. As juveniles, they will reside in the mouth, gill chambers, and spiracles of their host, possibly to avoid competition with larger remoras. Sometimes groups of these fish are found on a single shark or ray; for example, a whale shark may have dozens of sharksuckers hanging from its body. The discfishes not only eat parasites, they also scavenge on scraps of food resulting from shark meals and ingest zooplankton. For the discfish, its elasmobranch host not only serves to supply food, but it is also a form of transportation (i.e. to save energy) and protection; it may be that by associating with a large, predatory fish discfishes reduce the danger of being eaten by other fish eaters.

The discfish family consists of seven species; three are commonly observed associating with elasmobranchs, and their dependency on a host varies from one species to the next. Some of the discfish are full-time cleaners; for others, zooplankton and fishes make up the bulk of their diets. Remoras *(Remora remora)* commonly associate with sharks and devil rays. They feed almost exclusively on parasitic copepods, which they scoop from their host with their elongate lower jaw. One study demonstrated that remoras rarely clean parasites from the fins, but concentrate their efforts on the head, body, and gill chambers of their hosts. The white suckerfish *(Remora albescens)* is a circumtropical species that most frequently associates with devil rays, although it occasionally is observed on large sharks. Unlike remoras, parasitic copepods are only a minor food for white suckerfish; instead, their main foods are fishes and zooplankton. Shark suckers *(Echeneis neucratoides)* are common discfish not nearly as dependent on a host as the aforementioned species. They are often free-swimming, but also attach to a wide range of hosts, including a number of elasmobranch species. Parasitic copepods and isopods are its major food, but it also eats scraps, resulting from shark feeding episodes, and small fishes.

Bonyfishes are not the only shark cleaners. Certain shrimp also pick at the body surface of sharks. Cleaner shrimp often clean at night and in reef caves and crevices, where they might clean sheltering elasmobranchs. Examples of cleaner shrimp-shark interactions include observations of banded coral shrimp *(Stenopus hispidus)* picking at wobbegongs with their claws and documentation of a species of *Periclimenes* shrimp climbing over the head and body of the tasselled wobbegong. The cleaner shrimp commonly cleans reef fishes and may remove ectoparasites and tissue from sedentary shark species like the wobbegong. I kept a coral banded shrimp in an aquarium with a juvenile ornate wobbegong. Most of the time the shrimp hung upside down, over the wobbegong, as the shark rested in a small cave, but the shrimp occasionally picked at the shark's skin. With more and more observations of sharks and rays, more associations of this type are bound to be described!

Feeding Associations

A number of bony fish species use sharks and rays to help them locate and capture their prey. Usually this consists of following an elasmobranch as it swims or feeds. For example, schools of cownose rays are often accompanied by drum and jacks that benefit from the ray's disruption of the ocean floor and subsequent exposure of prey items. These huge schools of rays dig out and expose concealed invertebrates that the associating bony fishes can then exploit. The most frequently observed example of this type of association on or near coral reefs involves wrasses and whiptail stingrays. Often several of these opportunistic fishes follow a ray as it digs deep depressions in the sand in search of burrowing prey. Studies carried out on a species of wrasse in the Caribbean demonstrated that these fish enjoy greater hunting success when they follow a substrate-disturbing fish than when they forage alone. Wrasses are not the only reef fishes taking advantage of stingray activities to locate food; goatfishes, snappers, lizardfishes, jacks, emperors, and triggerfishes have been observed following bluespotted ribbontail rays.

This association between rays and bony fishes is not limited to the coral reef community. A study carried out along the California coast documented that sand dabs *(Citharichthys stigmaeus)*, which are small flatfish, are attracted to foraging bat rays and round stingrays and consume invertebrates that are flushed from the sand as these rays feed. Sea stars move into pits made by these rays to feed on exposed infauna. In another study, it was documented that juvenile horn sharks are often found in bat ray feeding depressions. These sharks may feed on polychaete worms exposed and not eaten by the bat rays.

The cobia *(Rachycentron canadum)* belongs to the Family Rachycentridae and has been observed associating with whale sharks, tiger sharks, bull sharks, cownose rays, eagle rays, whiptail stingrays, and mantas. In the case of the cownose ray, the cobia will maintain a position just above the ray and seemingly benefits by feeding on food the ray rejects. I observed a small group of five cobia swimming above a large marbled ribbontail ray as it glided over the reef. When the ray settled to the bottom, the cobia circled continuously over the ray until it eventually lifted off the sea floor and the group swam from my view. Jacks (Family Carangidae) are voracious, midwater predators that are frequently observed interacting with elasmobranchs and may benefit from the association in a number of ways. Some jacks hide behind moving rays or sharks to get near their prey, or they may take advantage of the momentary confusion of prey species caused by the hunting behavior of a shark. I observed a bluefin jack *(Caranx melampygus)* swimming just beneath a scalloped hammerhead and on another occasion beneath a marbled ribbontail ray as it cruised over a reef. This jack has also been reported to associate with the blacktip reef shark.

Jacks also follow sharks to scavenge on leftovers from shark feeding bouts. For example, in a feeding event involving a great hammerhead and a southern stingray, two species of jack, a snapper, and a shark sucker were observed ingesting small pieces of flesh from the wounds of the ray after the shark had bitten off its pectoral fins.

In the Caribbean, bar jacks *(Caranx ruber)* are frequently observed swimming over the discs of the southern stingray. I have seen bar jacks dash forward to ingest prey disturbed by the stingray as it moved just over the bottom. The importance of this relationship to the jack is exemplified by their aggressive defense of "their" ray! On a number of occasions, I have observed bar jacks that were associated with a ray, chase off members of their own species that apparently came too close.

Near Cocos Island, I observed a complex feeding interaction between bluefin jacks and whitetip reef sharks. Groups of these jacks patrolled the reef-sand interface where schools of Pacific creole *(Paranthias colonus)* fish feed in the water column on zooplankton. Suddenly, one of the jacks would rush at a creole fish, causing the entire school to flee toward the reef below. The sudden attack apparently sent auditory signals to nearby whitetips laying on the sand as the group of jacks, which numbered up to 13, began to vigorously circle the coral head in which the intended prey fish disappeared. The sharks accelerated on a straight path to the source of the commotion, with up to eight sharks being attracted to the area. Upon arriving, the sharks began to probe and enter the crevices of the coral head while the jacks vigilantly circled. On one occasion I observed a fish flushed from a reef crevice that was immediately ingested by one of the circling jacks. Whitetips were occasionally observed to follow groups of jacks, possibly waiting for them to launch an assault. This feeding interaction between jacks and whitetips is apparently not uncommon at this location; I observed it on five occasions during 8 days of diving. This association appears to be mutualistic in nature; the jack benefits from the shark's ability to ferret prey from reef nooks and crannies and the jacks, in turn, put the creole fish into a situation where they are vulnerable to the sharks and signal the sharks to their location on the reef.

In the Sea of Cortez, I have observed a feeding association of a different kind between scalloped hammerheads and yellowfin surgeonfish *(Acanthurus xanthopterus)*. When the hammerheads defecated, the surgeonfish would swim up into the water column to feed on the feces. This feeding strategy, known as coprophagy, is common in coral reef fish communities and is practiced by a number of surgeonfish species. The fecal material of carnivorous fishes contains many nutrients and may provide significant nitrogenous reserves to a nitrogen-poor diet of the herbivore.

Pilotfish

Another jack that commonly associates with open water sharks is the pilotfish *(Naucrates ductor)*. These fish are often observed swimming close to the shark's body and fins and even in front of the shark's snout. They were originally given their name because it was thought they led, or "piloted," their shark host to food; this suggestion has since been rejected. Instead, it is now believed that pilotfish derive energy savings by moving in the pressure wave created by their host as it swims, and protection from open ocean predators reluctant to approach a large shark. Also, pilotfish eat scraps resulting from shark meals and may eat shark feces (this has yet to be confirmed). Whether this association benefits the shark is not known; it has been suggested that pilotfish clean ectoparasites from its host. Juvenile golden jacks *(Gnathanodon speciosus)* are reef dwellers that also "pilot" sharks, devil rays, large groupers, and dugongs. Unlike the pilotfish, which typically is observed with active, oceanic species, these fish associate with both inactive and active shark species, having been observed near a host reef white-tip or tawny nurse shark even when the sharks were lying in a cave or crevice. They apparently benefit in a similar way to the pilotfish. The benefit to the host shark may include being "cleaned" by the jack (e.g. they have been observed to occasionally pick at the skin of resting reef whitetips).

Chaffing of Sharks by Bony Fishes.
In 1960, in his book *Galapagos*, Dr. Eibl-Eibesfeldt described how schools of rainbow runners *(Elegatis bipinnulata)* converge on requiem sharks and begin chaffing against their bodies. He suggested that the runners use the abrasive skin of sharks to rid themselves of irritating parasites and added that "the sharks certainly found this disagreeable since they disappeared into the abyss." Since then, I have seen several fish species chaff against a number of different types of shark.

Since Eibl-Eibesfelt's observations, questions have been raised as to the function of this unusual behavior. It appears that rainbow runners put themselves at considerable risk chaffing against a known bonyfish predator. Why not rub against a piece of rock or coral? In the case of oceanic fishes, the shark may be the only substrate available to relieve parasite irritation. For example, the dolphinfish *(Coryphaena hippurus)* scrapes against the body and tail of oceanic whitetips, a shark that is a known dolphinfish predator. But this behavior is not limited to the open ocean habitat where suitable scratching surfaces are in short supply. At Cocos Island, Costa Rica, I observed rainbow runners chaffing against the reef, visiting Mexican hogfish cleaning stations, and yet they were frequently seen rubbing against the sides of whitetip reef sharks and silky sharks (a species known to include the rainbow runner in its diet).

Another possible explanation for this risky behavior is that the bonyfishes are trying to drive the sharks from the area. It may be this behavior is analogous to "mobbing," a phenomenon originally described in birds and latter documented in reef fish species. For example, it has been reported that and butterflyfishes "mob" moray eels and drive them from their territories. As far as "mobbing" elasmobranchs is concerned, there is one study describing how groups of blacksmith assault diurnally active swell sharks, a major predator of these fish, apparently trying to rid their nighttime refuge of this potential threat. A more extreme example was given by Palauan spearfisherman who report that jacks rammed sharks with their bony foreheads until the sharks were mortally wounded! I observed a scalloped hammerhead shark and a silky shark behave in a seemingly irritated fashion (similar to that suggested by Eibl-Eibesfeldt) when scraped by groups of green jacks *(Caranx caballus)*. The silky shark turned on its side and performed exaggerated tail strokes, propelling itself forward at an increased rate of speed, and the hammerhead spun in a tight circle, its nose and tail almost touching. In one case, it was reported that a rainbow runner bumped a small Galapagos shark causing it to regurgitate a meal, which the bony fish promptly ate!

The shark recipient of the bonyfish contact does not appear to be disturbed in all cases. I have seen whitetip reef, silky, silvertip, and gray reef sharks enveloped in clouds of rainbow runners, which ricocheted off the flanks of the sharks like bullets off tank armor. The sharks seemed indifferent to their activities. Although only speculation, it may be that a mutualistic relationship exists between the sharks and jacks. It may be that the wall of fish acts as a moving blind for the shark, allowing it to get within striking range of potential prey. A similar stalking behavior (known as "hunting by riding") has been described in trumpetfishes, where they lay along the back or side of a larger fish or position themselves in a school of algae-eating fish in order to close the distance between themselves and their prey. Some jacks may also pick crustacean parasites off the sharks they associate with. The jacks benefit by using the shark as an abrasive surface to rub off ectoparasites and as a "body guard."

REPRODUCTIVE BEHAVIOR

Although we know little about the reproductive behavior of sharks and rays, the popularization of scuba diving, underwater photography, and advances in aquarium care techniques have revealed more about this secret aspect of elasmobranch life. All sharks and rays practice internal fertilization. The medial edge of the male's pelvic fins are modified to form organs known as claspers. These organs are tube-like in form and some species possess terminal hooks and spines which help secure the clasper in the female's cloaca during copulation. Before mating, the clasper is rotated into position (its direction varies depending on the mating posture of the species) and inserted into the female's cloaca. In most sharks and rays only one clasper is inserted at a time; however, there are a few reports of two claspers being inserted simultaneously.

In sharks, a pair of siphon sacs, located on the abdomen just under the skin, are connected to the claspers by way of small openings. These sacs are filled with sea water prior to copulation, possibly by repeated flexing of the clasper or by swimming forward with it flexed. Water, secretions from the sac (e.g. serotonin—a smooth muscle contractant), and semen are injected into the female's reproductive tract during mating. Instead of the siphon sacs, rays have smaller structures known as clasper glands, located at the base of each clasper. These solid structures are glandular tissue that secretes a fluid that may serve to transport sperm, lubricate the clasper, seal the clasper groove, or plug the female's oviduct to prevent her from being fertilized by other mates.

Courtship and mating in elasmobranchs is often behaviorally complex and is anything but tender (see Appendix). Although the behavior patterns of courtship vary somewhat between species, many similarities exist. In most sharks and rays, courtship begins with the male following close to the female, often with his nose near her cloaca (blacktip reef sharks, gray reef sharks, round stingrays, eagle rays, bat rays). The male may assess the female's reproductive condition by sampling chemical signals.

Another universal trend in elasmobranch premating behavior is biting. In the majority of cases, the male bites the female prior to, and often during, copulation. In fact, many male sharks and rays have teeth with more elongate, slender cusps than members of the opposite sex. This is possibly an adaptation for grasping females during mating. The functions ascribed to this behavior include: to release an appropriate behavioral response in the female (i.e. to induce her cooperation) and to hold the female to ensure successful mating. Two species (i.e. nurse and blacktip reef sharks) are also known to nudge and push their potential mates with their snouts to manipulate them (usually to flip them over) into mating position.

In some shark species (e.g. sandtiger shark, whitetip reef shark, gray reef shark, silvertip shark) males bite the female's back, flanks, or fins to induce her cooperation. Infliction of such bites has been observed in the gray reef sharks in the Red Sea. A female was observed to swim away from a milling group of individuals and was pursued by a male. As they swam the male nipped and slashed at her side and fins. These "love bites" result in torn fins, deep puncture wounds, gashes, and semi-circular skin lacerations, but although they look severe, they heal quickly. In one species (i.e. the blue shark) females have skin more than twice as thick as males, an apparent adaptation to prevent the male's teeth from damaging deep muscles and vital organs. It may be that females of other shark species are thick skinned as well. In batoids, where males are known to bite prospective mates, the back, pelvic, and the pectoral fin margins are the areas most often bit. For example, male spotted eagle rays gouge the back of females with their upper dental plates.

When holding a female before and during copulation, male sharks bite and grasp the female's pectoral fin or gill area. Male Japanese wobbegongs bite and grasp the gill region, while male epaulette sharks grip the female's pectoral fin. In some rays, males hold the female's pectoral fin margin, or disc edge, during mating.

Some elasmobranch males expend considerable energy attempting to mate with reluctant females. I once watched a female epaulette shark pull a male latched onto her pectoral fin for almost 19 minutes before he finally succeeded in mating with her. During this period the female pulled the male over and through beds of staghorn coral and once succeeded in temporarily dislodging him. Unreceptive behavior has also been observed in round stingray courtship. Unreceptive females will stab males, who have grasped their fin margin, with their tail sting. On one occasion I observed a female sting a male 27 times before he released his grip and swam away! Persistence is apparently a necessary attribute for a male shark or ray to successfully reproduce.

Nurse sharks form assemblages in shallow water during the mating period. In these breeding areas observers have reported as many as five pairs courting at the same time. Courtship in the nurse shark begins with a male and female swimming side by side ("parallel swimming"). When next to and slightly behind the female, the male will bite the posterior edge of a pectoral fin ("pectoral biting"). The female pivots in front of the male, so the axis of her body is perpendicular to his, and at the same time she rolls onto her back ("pivot and roll"). The male then lifts and pushes the female with his rostrum ("nudging") so that the bodies of the two sharks are oriented parallel to each other. Oftentimes during this sequence, the caudal fins of the courting sharks are flailed into the air and slap the water's surface. At this time the male moves on top of the female, inserts a clasper, rolls onto his back (maintaining sexual contact), and lays there for about 2 minutes. Both sharks then right themselves and swim away.

When a female round stingray is receptive to a male's advances, the pair will swim parallel to one another. As the male holds the female's fin margin in his mouth, he will lift her disc, pivot under her, and insert a single clasper. Sometimes one or more other males will appear on the scene and try to dislodge the male. In the round stingray, a female will occasionally have one male grasping each pectoral fin and simultaneously trying to flip under her into copulatory position. Male Arabian bamboo sharks have been observed to bite the clasper of another male that was attempting to mate with a female and groups of male yellow stingrays and small-spotted catsharks have been reported to bite copulating conspecifics.

When mating, sharks employ several different postures. Most lie or swim alongside one another, the male's posterior body region under that of the female (e.g. reef whitetip shark, epaulette shark, Arabian bamboo shark, Japanese wobbegong, lemon shark), while a few species mate with the ventral surfaces apposed (e.g. blacktip reef shark). In the more supple bodied catsharks (e.g. cloudy catshark, small-spotted catshark), the male coils around the female while they lay on the sea floor. In rays, most species adopt a ventrum-to-ventrum (belly-to-belly) posture (e.g. round stingray, shorttail stingray, spotted eagle ray, flapnose cownose ray), but bat ray males swim under a female (so the male's back is in contact with the female's belly) and rotate a clasper up and to the side in order to insert it into her cloaca. In some species in the family Myliobatidae (e.g. the bull ray), males have enlarged spines, or tubercles, above each eye that may jab into the females ventrum and help the male maintain his position under her during mating. In the sepia stingaree, the male lies partially on top of and to one side of the female and curls the pelvic region toward the female's cloaca. Some species rest on the bottom while copulating (e.g. round stingray) while others continue to swim (e.g. shorttail stingray, bat ray).

Duration of copulation varies greatly between shark and ray species. For example, in the epaulette shark copulation lasts about 1.5 minutes while in the clearnose skate *(Raja eglantaria)* it can take hours! It is speculated that mating has been described in so few species because most copulate under the cover of darkness. This may be true for some species, but I have observed that frequency of round stingray reproductive behavior is greatest in the morning, just after sunrise. Nurse sharks have also been reported to mate frequently during daylight hours.

Many elasmobranchs form large aggregations during the breeding period, but little information exists on the details of shark and ray mating systems. Studies carried out by myself on the reproductive behavior of round stingrays gives insight into the complexity of batoid mating systems. Most of the year round stingrays, like many elasmobranchs, segregate by sex, with females occupying deeper water than males. In late winter and spring, the females move into shallow bays to mate and several months later they return to inshore waters to give birth. During the mating phase, females spend the morning buried in the shallows (often in groups), or lie side by side and on top of one another and form large aggregations on the substrate (dubbed "piles"). Buried females are apparently trying to avoid amorous males, possibly because they have already mated or because they are not yet in reproductive condition. Females in the piles are receptive individuals that are often observed to mate. At this time, males patrol along the beach in search of females. In the afternoon, a behavioral shift occurs. The males bury in the sand or mud while many of the females emerge to feed in nearby sea grass beds. The cycle begins again the next morning, with the whole reproductive phase probably lasting several weeks.

In captivity, females of two ray species are known to mate with multiple males during the breeding period. For example, a female flapnose ray mated with three males in a time period of about 1.5 hours and a spotted eagle ray mated with three or four males in a 1-hr period. In the case of the flapnose rays, only one female at a time was sexually receptive and this individual was harassed by many males. Several female flapnose rays died as a result of the wounds and fatigue that resulted from courtship and mating. That these mating-related deaths may occasionally occur in wild populations is supported by the fact I once found three dead female round stingrays, with numerous mate inflicted bite marks, near a breeding aggregation in the wild.

DEVELOPMENT OF YOUNG

Following mating and the fertilization of the eggs, the young develop in one of three distinctly different ways:

Oviparity. Some sharks lay eggs that are protected by a leathery eggcase. The developing embryo relies solely on the egg yolk for nourishment. The eggs hatch in 2 to 15 months, depending on the species and the water temperature. Two types of oviparity are recognized: extended oviparity (where the eggs are encased in a keratin capsule and soon after are deposited on the sea floor) and retained oviparity (where the eggcases are held in the uteri until the embryos are in latter stages of development and are then expelled). Elasmobranchs that exhibit oviparity are the bullhead, collared carpet, bamboo, cat, and finback catsharks (Family Proscyllidae), and the skates. Forty-three percent of all cartilaginous fishes are thought to be oviparous; this includes over 220 species of skates and 31 species of chimeras. If these two groups are omitted, then approximately 18 % of the remaining species are oviparous.

Ovoviviparity (aplacental viviparity). In ovoviviparous elasmobranchs, the eggs are retained in the oviducts where they hatch, usually from a thin membranous eggcase, and remain until the young are fully developed. In some species (nurse sharks, possibly whale sharks), the eggs are enclosed in heavy eggcases, more like the oviparous species, that hatch just before birth. Developing embryos are nourished in several different ways depending on the shark or ray species. Most commonly, the embryos absorb yolk from a yolk-sac attached to their digestive system *(yolk sac viviparity)*. In some species (e.g. mackerel sharks, thresher sharks, sandtiger sharks), the embryos consume infertile eggs that continually migrate from the ovaries to the oviducts *(oophagy)*, and, in at least one species (e.g. sandtiger shark), eggs and siblings are eaten *(embryophagy)*! Other species display ovoviviparity known as uterine viviparity. In these species (e.g. torpedos, electric rays, whiptail stingrays, round stingrays, eagle rays, cownose rays, devil rays), the embryo absorbs the yolk early in development and then relies on nutrient rich secretions from the uterine lining. This "uterine milk" enters the embryo's stomach via the spiracles and mouth. In several species, finger-like extensions from the uterus migrate into these openings and secrete the uterine milk directly into the digestive tract. Of all the chondrichthyians, 48% are ovoviviparous (yolksac viviparity 27%; oophagy and embryophagy 2%; uterine viviparity 19%).

Viviparity (placental viviparity). In viviparous development, the embryo initially uses nutrients from the yolk sac and "uterine milk" secreted by the uterus. The yolk sac begins to form a placental attachment to the oviduct wall and, during the latter part of development, nutrients and waste products are exchanged through this placental structure. In some species (e.g. sharpnose sharks, hammerheads), the yolk stalk (or umbilical cord) is covered with hair-like filaments that may serve to absorb "uterine milk." Viviparous species produce relatively few, large young, after a gestation period of 8 to 12 months. Only 9% of all living chondrichthyians display this mode of reproduction; all of these are more "advanced" requiem sharks and hammerheads.

Oviposition and Parturition

Although protected by a leathery case, the eggs of oviparous sharks and skates often fall prey to invertebrates, bony fishes, and elasmobranchs. Certain snails, for example, are known to bore holes through the protective eggcase with their radula and to ingest the capsule's contents. Captive horn, Port Jackson, and epaulette sharks have been observed to eat their own eggs and food habit studies have shown that the broadnose sevengill, angel, shortfin mako, white, Japanese wobbegong, and blotchy swell sharks will eat elasmobranch eggcases. The eggcases are at the mercy of ocean currents as well, which may take them into unfavorable environments; therefore, they are often anchored to corals or algae by thread-like tendrils (e.g. certain bullhead, collared carpet, catsharks) or adhesive filaments (e.g. bamboo, epaulette, zebra sharks). Certain catsharks deposit their eggcases by swimming around the reef structure and dragging the tendrils, the first part of the eggcase to extrude from the cloaca, across a potential anchoring site. When the tendrils attach to the bottom the female circles rapidly and wraps the filaments around the structure which jerks the eggcase from the oviduct. Bullhead sharks have a cone-shaped eggcase, with a spiral flange encircling it, and in some species there are tendrils on the smaller end. In these sharks, the eggcase, which is soft and slimy during deposition, slowly (over several hours) rotates out of the cloaca. In the Port Jackson shark, the eggcases are usually found in reef crevices (they have also been observed under pipelines and in empty cans) with the broad end always sticking out. The female will take the newly laid eggcase in her mouth and insert it under or in a benthic structure. One female was also observed to slap an eggcase in an interstice with her tail. When the eggcase hardens, it is difficult to extract due to the auger-like flanges. Several of the bullhead shark species use communal oviposition sites, or "nests," which they return to year after year.

Although many sharks and rays abort their young when captured, the natural birthing process has been observed in a few elasmobranchs. From the few accounts that do exist, it appears that females utilize sudden movements and/or sharp contact with the water's surface or inanimate objects to help them to expel their young. In the islands of Micronesia, natives report having observed blacktip reef sharks and gray reef sharks rubbing their abdomens against submerged logs and mangrove tree branches to help in parturition. Similarly, a pregnant whitetip reef shark was observed rubbing its abdomen against the ocean bottom in what may have been an attempt to give birth. Gravid sandbar sharks make abrupt, sharp turns, releasing a pup at the pivot point, while spotted eagle and manta rays have been observed to leap from the water and give birth when they impact its surface. It was reported to me that captive male shortail stingrays will nudge the female's abdomen with their rostrums just before and during parturition. Depending on the species, young are born head first (e.g. sandtiger shark), tail first (e.g. whitetip reef shark, sandbar shark), or both ways (e.g. spotted eagle ray).

ELASMOBRANCH EGGCASE TYPES:

A number of shark species are oviparous, depositing leathery eggcases, composed of proteinaceous keratin, on the sea floor. At least one group of batoids, the skates, also lay eggs. In general form, their eggcases are rectangular with horns (not tendrils) projecting from all four corners. The related chimeras (subclass Holocephalii) are also oviparous. Their eggcases are elongate and spindle shaped and, in some species, there is a ribbed fin running down each side (e.g. elephantfish, *Callorhynchus milii*).

Below you will find descriptions, with photographic examples, of the different eggcase types found in oviparous sharks:

Auger Type (e.g. bullhead sharks)

This type of eggcase is conical with a flange that spirals around it. Apparently the female shark wedges the case in a crevice or hole (possibly orally or by slapping it with her tail) when it is still soft and as the flanges become more rigid the egg becomes difficult to extract. In some bullhead shark species the eggcases possess tendrils that extend from the narrower end and can exceed 2 m (6.6 ft) in length (e.g., crested bullhead shark). As the embryo develops, the larger end of the case erodes and splits to provide an escape path for the fully developed "pup." These cases are usually brown, greenish brown, or black.

Tendril (e.g. collared carpet, cat sharks)

This eggcase is a flattened pillow with tendrils extending from two or all four corners. These tendrils are usually well developed and may form spirals which wrap around calcareous tube worms, gorgonians, macroalgae, and even man-made objects deposited on the ocean floor (e.g. telephone cables). Fibrous adhesive "hairs" may also occur on one end or on the sides of the eggcase and these also help secure the egg to a holdfast. In most

species, the sides of the cases are smooth, but in others the cases have transverse ridges (e.g. Tasmanian carpet shark, Australian swell shark). An end splits open to aid in oxygenation and to provide a way of escape for the embryo. These cases can be yellow, cream, dark brown, greenish brown, or golden brown.

Atendril Adhesive
(e.g. bamboo, epaulette, zebra sharks)

This is an oblong eggcase, the terminal ends of which are irregularly folded. There are no tendrils, but instead the edges and sometimes the sides of the eggcase have numerous sticky fibers which attach the egg to the substrate. As the embryo develops, slits appear at the end of the case to allow fresh sea water to irrigate the inside chamber. These slits later provide an exit point for the fully developed shark. In the case of the bamboo and epaulette sharks, these eggcases are usually dark or golden brown; the zebra shark eggcase is deep purple.

SOCIAL BEHAVIOR

Social mechanisms

Social behaviors are those that structure animal societies. Aggression is one mechanism that disperses populations, is important in reproduction, and is an efficient antipredator defense. Interestingly enough, overt aggression is a relatively rare feature of the few elasmobranch social groups studied. It may be that aggression is more common in specific social contexts that have not yet been investigated. Most studies on shark and ray social behavior have been on captive animals, with few observations made during the reproductive season. In many bony fishes, males are more aggressive during the mating period. That this also occurs in sharks and rays is supported by anecdotal accounts of male wobbegongs and sawfish fighting for mates. Furthermore, I have observed that male round stingrays often charged, struck, and nipped one another during the breeding season. These interactions could have resulted from males initially misidentifying other males as females or aggressive behavior toward members of the same sex competing for mates. The distribution of bite marks on males and females (from underwater photographs and field notes) indicated a significant difference in their distribution between the sexes, suggesting that more than misidentification was prompting the male-male aggressive behavior. Another unusual observation I have made involved a male bluespotted ribbontail ray and a male bluespotted stingray. The larger male ribbontail ray was grasping the left pectoral fin of the stingray in his mouth. It held the stingray, which was trying frantically to escape, for over 7 minutes until I moved too close and caused the assaulting ray to release its grip. Was this a case of an amorous male ribbontail ray mistaking a male heterospecific for a mate or was the ribbontailed ray trying to drive potential competitors from its territory?

Although mature females often have bite wounds resulting from mating activities, males of several species (e.g. broadnose sevengill, white, and shortfin mako sharks) occasionally exhibit similar injuries. Observers sometimes see unusual wounds on the fins of certain sharks that may be the result of ritualistic combat. For example, I have seen smooth hammerheads with the distal part of the upper caudal lobe missing, and this has also been reported in scalloped hammerheads. During competition for females, some males also "bite below the belt." For example, Arabian bamboo sharks have been observed to bite the clasper of a courting individual and shortfin mako sharks and bull sharks have been collected with all or part of a clasper missing!

Aggression between individual sharks of the same (intraspecific) and different species (interspecific) results in dominance hierarchies. The existence of dominance hierarchies, where subordinate animals avoid dominant ones, in elasmobranch social groups could explain why overt aggression is rarely observed between individuals. An individual's size usually determines its position in the social order. For example, in white shark aggregations near a whale carcass, larger individuals will aggressively bite smaller sharks that attempt to feed. In captive dusky smoothhound sharks, smaller sharks "gave way" (i.e. abruptly maneuvered to avoid another shark) to larger individuals when the difference in size was greater than 7.4 % of the total body length. Sex also plays a role in determining an individual's status in the hierarchy. In a study conducted on bonnethead sharks, females were observed to "give way" to males of similar or slightly smaller sizes. This apparent avoidance of males by females is probably because males occasionally bite and "hit" females.

Some field observations suggest dominance hierarchies exist between different species of sharks as well. In most cases, the larger the shark, no matter what species, the more dominant it is. For example, oceanic whitetip sharks are avoided by silky sharks when their paths overlap. Dominance relationships among individuals of similar size suggest that certain species are avoided by others. For example, near the Clipperton Islands, silvertip sharks were reported to dominate Galapagos sharks of similar size, and the blacktip shark was subordinate to both species. In captivity, and possibly in the wild, at least one species of sawfish has particular disdain for sharks. In aquarium confines, the smalltooth sawfish will swing its tooth-studded rostrum at sharks that come near and even attack sharks that are resting on the bottom. In one report, a 2.4-m (8-ft) sawfish approached a resting 1.8-m (6-ft) nurse shark and delivered three swift blows with its saw to the shark's dorsum. The nurse shark did not respond, and immediately the sawfish hit the fish three more times! After this final assault, the nurse shark swam away and the sawfish came to rest on the tank bottom. Sharks and sawfish have been captured with sawfish inflicted rake marks, indicating that aggressive interactions involving sawfish and sharks and between individual sawfish occur in the wild.

Territoriality (i.e. the defense of a specific area) has not been demonstrated in elasmobranchs. In part this may be because few behavioral studies have been carried out on sharks and rays in their natural environment. Some of the bottom dwelling reef sharks (e.g. the tasselled wobbegong) have limited home ranges; that is, they return to the same daytime resting site regularly, sometimes for months or years. More detailed behavioral observations may show that they guard an ambush or resting site from competitors. Studies do exist that indicate certain species defend a "personal field," that is a specific area surrounding the individual. The "exaggerated swimming display" of the gray reef shark may be elicited because a diver or another shark enters this personal space.

Sharks may also guard food from competitors. For example, a shortfin mako shark was observed to "jaw gape" and chase away a rival that was nearing a bait. A great hammerhead chased a blacktip shark away from the carcass of a southern stingray as the blacktip prepared to take a second bite and, near Cocos Island, Costa Rica, large silky sharks were observed chasing scalloped hammerheads away from food.

Aggressive behavior patterns

Several threat displays have been described in sharks and rays. The best known example is the "exaggerated swimming display" which was studied in the gray reef shark at Enewetak Atoll in the central Pacific. When confronted and pressed by a small submarine or a diver, the gray reef sharks lower their pectoral fins, raise their snouts, arch their backs, bend their bodies to the side, and move in an exaggerated swimming mode. The swimming trajectory of the shark may follow an S-shaped path when the display is less intense, or a figure-eight pattern when it is most intense. For example, cornering or charging an approaching gray reef shark releases the most intense posturing. If the source of threat continues, a lightning fast attack might ensue. The shark will charge, slash with its upper teeth or bite, and flee at high speed.

Other elasmobranchs are also known to engage in threat posturing. Galapagos sharks will perform head swinging and exaggerated lateral swimming when followed by a diver. Bonnethead, silky, and blacknose sharks "hunch" (i.e. arch the back, raise the snout, and lower the tail) when confronted by divers or conspecifics. The apparent agonistic displays of shortfin makos and lemon sharks consist of swimming in figure-eights and "jaw gaping." In the Sea of Cortez, I and others noted that blacktip sharks swam in an exaggerated fashion when approached. Scalloped hammerheads "head snap" (i.e. throw the head to one side and the other in a wide arc) in the presence of divers, and direct seven different action patterns, that are apparently aggressive in nature, toward other hammerheads. These include the "head-shake" (the individual shakes its head from side to side while accelerating forward), "torso-thrust" (the shark accelerates forward, throws its torso to one side, and tilts its body to the side), "hit" (one shark rams another on the back with the underside of its head), and "corkscrew" (the shark accelerates forward and does a 360 degree turn on its longitudinal axis). Bonnetheads also "hit" conspecifics. In a captive study, a newly introduced female was "hit" by resident males. In hammerhead species, a "hit" often results in dermal abrasions on the individual that is struck. Near seamounts in the Sea of Cortez, adolescent silky sharks associating with large schools of scalloped hammerheads were observed with abrasions similar to those seen on hammerheads. Apparently, hammerheads may "hit" silky sharks as well as members of their own species.

Sharks are not the only elasmobranchs to execute aggressive displays. Torpedo and electric rays engage in threat posturing. Pacific torpedo rays have been reported to swim at divers with their mouths agape and Fairchild's torpedo rays will arch and twist their bodies when approached. Cortez electric rays will arch their backs when prodded and somersault in the water column if harassment continues. In one incident reported to me, the electric ray landed on and shocked a diver after performing this acrobatic display! I also observed looping in a shorttailed electric ray that I annoyed. Finally, certain round stingrays (e.g. crossback stingaree) and whiptail stingrays (e.g. southern stingray) raise their tails and stings above their heads, in a scorpion-like fashion, when approached by a potential predator.

Other social behaviors

The behavioral repertoire of sharks and rays includes other social behaviors, the function of which is not fully understood. For example, one common behavior in several shark and ray species is "circular swimming formation," in which a group of animals swims in a circle, in a head-to-tail formation. Leopard sharks, lemon sharks, bonnetheads, and sicklefin devil rays all engage in this behavior. Related to this behavior is "follow formation," when individuals form a line behind the lead individual and follow its movements. Oftentimes one shark or ray will follow behind another individual with its snout near the lead animal's pelvic region; this is often observed in a reproductive context.

Although it is generally considered a way to detach ectoparasites and discfishes, breaching may have a communicative function in elasmobranchs. Basking, shortfin mako, white, thresher, spinner, and blacktip sharks, and cownose, eagle, and devil rays are known to leap from the water. Some create loud claps as they fall into the sea, possibly sending a signal to rivals or potential mates. Another function breaching may serve is to aid the elasmobranch in capturing prey; the audible signal may cause small schooling prey to form a tighter mass, making them more vulnerable to sharks and rays. It has been suggested that breaching in some whale species serves to stun and alarm shoals of fish and krill.

SEGREGATION

Many shark and ray species segregate by sex and/or size. In Port Jackson sharks, most females are found in deeper water than the males, while blue shark females occupy a different geographical range than males during most the year. In the spiny dogfish, adult males are generally taken in inshore waters while adult females occur in a more pelagic habitat. In school shark populations, studied off the Pacific coast of the U.S.A., the adult females occur in more inshore waters than mature males. Scalloped hammerheads segregate by sex and size. Life for the newborn hammerhead usually begins in turbid inshore waters, often in coastal bays. As the sharks mature, adolescent females migrate to offshore islands and seamounts at a smaller size than the males. The females enjoy greater hunting success in this pelagic habitat and grow to maturity faster. Mature males join the females and they form large schools of both sexes. In these schools, females usually out number males about three to one. Mating occurs in these assemblages and, when near term, pregnant females move back inshore to give birth.

Segregation may serve a number of functions. Segregation may spread the population over a larger area and decrease competition for food. Females may move to areas where prey is more abundant, thus growing faster than males and reaching maturity at a similar age (in most species females mature at larger sizes). Furthermore, size segregation may prevent larger specimens from preying on smaller conspecifics and sexual segregation may prevent harassment of females by amorous males, a potential waste of energy if females are not in breeding condition.

In many species that segregate by sex, males and females converge in shallow, inshore waters to mate and females return to give birth. These nursery grounds are usually in areas like estuaries, where nutrients for the developing pups abound. When the females enter the nursery grounds to give birth, they often do not feed. This may be an adaptation to prevent the females from eating their young. Several shark species (e.g. the silky shark and Izak catshark, *Holohalaelurus regani)* are known to give birth in deeper water than that normally occupied by the adults.

SOCIAL UNITS

Sharks and rays may display different social units during the day or during various phases of their life cycles. For example, gray reef sharks are found singly, in loose aggregations, and in schools. Solitary individuals are usually observed around lagoon pinnacles and are often pregnant females. Loose aggregations occur near reef drop-offs and are apparently brought together by an attractive stimulus (e.g. currents, diver activity). Polarized schools form over horizontal sand and coral bottoms. These schools are observed during the day when the sharks are less active. At night, school members disperse, often to shallower lagoon reefs. A discussion of the major social units observed in elasmobranchs follows:

Solitary. Many sharks and rays lead a solitary existence. For example, the tasselled wobbegong is usually found singly, in caves and under overhangs. Mating may occur when a male searches for and finds a sexually receptive female and the pair remains together for the short duration of the mating bout. Solitary animals may also form breeding assemblages at specific times of the year. The shorttail stingray and the round stingray aggregate in shallow inshore areas during the breeding season.

Pairs. Although some shark species are often seen in pairs (e.g. bull sharks), it has yet to be determined if elasmobranchs form longterm pair bonds. Advantages to pairing would be increased predatory efficiency and less time investment seeking a mate. Pairing is most frequently observed during courtship and mating.

Schools. A school is a group of fish brought together by an attraction to one another, not a commonly sought after resource (e.g. food, hiding places). Numerous sharks and some rays are known to school. In some instances (e.g. cownose rays), these groupings may consist of thousands of animals. Schools in which all individuals are oriented in the same direction, equidistant to one another, and change direction simultaneously are known as polarized schools. This type of schooling has been recorded in scalloped hammerhead sharks and some myliobatid rays. Schooling may aid in prey location and capture, serve as an antipredation tactic, increase hydrodynamic efficiency, or act as an arena for social interaction (e.g. mating).

By schooling, sharks and rays may increase their chances of locating prey by increasing the amount of senses available. This is particularly profitable for individual school members when the prey hunted also occurs in groups and are clumped in their distribution. A group of sharks may capture prey that would be difficult for a single individual to handle. For example, it is hypothesized that schools of green dogfish *(Etmopterus virens)* overwhelm the defenses of the large squid that they often feed upon.

In some shark and ray species, schooling may lower the risk of predation. This is particularly true of juveniles or small species that commonly fall prey to larger sharks. Some species, like the leopard shark, spiny dogfish, and smoothhound sharks, may even form mixed schools to reduce the chances that they will be eaten.

By schooling, some fish may increase the efficiency with which they swim. By moving in the slip stream of a fish in front and around them, individuals move through the water more easily due to reduction in drag.

Scalloped hammerheads form large polarized schools in a number of locations apparently to facilitate social interaction. In the Sea of Cortez, these schools are regularly encountered by divers near seamounts. During the day, these sharks swim around the seamounts and perform a number of social behaviors. At night they disperse into the surrounding mesopelagic zone, either as solitary individuals or possibly in small groups, to feed on squid and small fishes. Hammerheads may use the seamounts as landmarks to assist them in locating productive feeding sites. Also, they may gather around the seamounts to take advantage of the cleaner fishes, such as the king angelfish and Mexican hogfish.

Aggregations. An aggregation is a group of animals brought together by an environmental condition (e.g. food, current, preferred habitat). For example, white sharks aggregate around whale carcasses and groups of swell sharks take refuge in rocky reef crevices. Sometimes aggregations consist of more than one species of elasmobranch and can be quite large in size. For example, in the summer of 1977, a massive aggregation of sharks and rays was reported near Mustang and Padre islands off the coast of Texas. The assemblage of elasmobranchs was concentrated in a 24 km (15 mile) stretch of surf zone. Environmental conditions brought large concentrations of prey species into the shallows and this attracted at least 17 species of sharks and rays.

DIVER-SHARK INTERACTION

Whether by choice or by chance, more and more divers are encountering sharks on the shark's "turf." Usually these meetings consist of the diver observing a dark shape looming at the periphery of his or her visual field or spotting a bottom-dwelling species at rest under a ledge. There was a time when encountering a shark underwater was considered to be synonymous with death or dismemberment. But, as our understanding of shark behavior has increased, more divers are unafraid of confronting these fish and many seek to observe and photograph sharks in their own environment. That numerous resorts and live-aboard vessels now offer special dives where aquanauts get close to large sharks is testimony to this new view of these long misunderstood and misrepresented animals.

Although current attitudes about sharks reflect appreciation for the predatory role they serve in the oceans, it has also led many in the dive community to the other end of the continuum. Rather than respecting the predatory prowess of these amazing animals, they are viewed as domestic livestock. For example, I saw dive masters hit adult gray reef sharks (a species responsible for a number of attacks on divers) on the head with fists and dead fish to chastise them for prematurely approaching a bait bucket at a "shark feed!" I equate this behavior to offering a large, hungry dog a piece of meat and swatting it on the head for approaching the food! Not surprisingly, several provoked attacks have occurred in similar situations as a result of diver carelessness. Sharks are clearly not the oceanic assassins Hollywood would like to portray, but these predatory animals are certainly worthy of our respect.

Attack Factors

Shark attacks on divers are a rare phenomenon and many of those that do occur are usually the result of provocation. The term provocation is used in a broad sense to include attacks occurring during baiting and spearfishing. Below I have listed factors that may explain why sharks attack and precautions divers can take to avoid becoming a victim:

Species Specific Trends. Obviously, certain species are more aggressive than others. Some, like the smoothhounds, are so flighty that it is difficult for divers to get close enough to take photographs. Others, like the oceanic whitetip shark, will approach, persistently circle, nudge, and even attack a diver. It is important for the diver to know the behavior of sharks that he or she may potentially encounter, especially if they are purposefully trying to bait them in. Sharks to be wary of include the broadnose sevengill, white, mako, tiger, Galapagos, oceanic whitetip, gray reef shark, and any other larger (1.5 m) members of the requiem shark family. Disposition may vary within a species, and many factors can influence how an individual behaves from one context to the next. Also, the behavior of a species may vary from one geographical location to the next. For example, near Clipperton Island, the blacktip shark has been described as "afraid of its own shadow," while in the Sea of Cortez, I found this species to be bold and aggressive. Similarly, gray reef sharks from the Red Sea and Indian Ocean are reported to be less belligerent than their south Pacific counterparts.

Diver Carelessness. Many divers do not respect sharks and occasionally get bitten. Grabbing, spearing, hitting, or touching sharks, no matter how small or sluggish, can release a retaliatory response. For example, I watched a frustrated epaulette shark (normally a placid fish) bite and tenaciously hold to a diver's glove as it was lifted from the coral. Fortunately, epaulette sharks are not equipped with dental equipment that inflict serious damage, but this episode shows that even species considered docile will sometimes bite, if provoked. Species like the nurse, tawny nurse, and the wobbegong sharks look placid, but they can attack or defend themselves with incredible ferocity if harassed. Furthermore, the only time hitting a shark is warranted is if you are charged by an aggressive individual. In this situation, hitting the shark in its sensitive nose and eyes may be an effective way to parry an attack.

Another activity that has gained popularity with thrill seeking divers is feeding sharks by hand or from the mouth! It goes without saying that this is a risky practice. Several of those considered to be "experts" at this activity have been severely bitten, and some on more than one occasion!

Feeding Stimuli. Many shark attacks occur in the presence of feeding stimuli. Stimuli may be the attractive odor that comes from a bait brought to attract sharks or the smell and sounds emitted by the quarry of a successful spearfishermen. In this context, shark attack may be motivated by several different factors. On occasion, sharks have apparently mistaken divers as the source of the stimuli. Some sharks make bites to test if an object in an odor corridor is the source of a chemical signal. In other instances, the reason for attack may be the efforts of a shark to drive the diver (i.e. a potential food competitor) away from a food source. If you are spearfishing in areas where sharks are common, do not keep your catch on your person and remove speared fish from the water immediately. If a large shark approaches, give up your catch and leave the water.

When an attractant is not present, sharks generally show passing interest in divers. So indifferent are most sharks that photographers usually use bait to bring them into camera range. As mentioned previously, many dive operations offer "shark feeds" to get photographers closer to their subjects. Although the chances of being bitten during one of these sessions is slight, baiting sharks is not without risk. Even sharks "conditioned" to this type of food presentation will sometimes inflict an accidental bite. Precautions to avoid attack when baiting sharks include staying up current from the bait, close to the bottom or reef (but be careful not to break the coral), and close to the other divers, and restrict hand and feet movements (i.e., do not wave your hands to get someone's attention).

Never underestimate the swiftness at which a shark can attack. I have seen sharks moving at a leisurely cruising pace rocket into a strike that was so explosive a diver would not have a chance at self defense if he or she had been the target of the shark's assault. If a shark repeatedly makes close, quick passes, the dive should be aborted. If sharks become aggressive, it is best to move away from the shark along the bottom until you are near the boat and then make your ascent with another diver in a back-to-back position so that you can keep an eye on the sharks. A shark billy or camera strobe can be useful protection to deflect an attack (in some cases anyway).

Threat and Aggression. At least one shark is known to attack when threatened. The gray reef shark is responsible for a number of attacks on divers that are apparently motivated by threat. When threatened, gray reef sharks perform an exaggerated swimming display that, if the threat persists, is often followed by the shark charging and biting the source of agitation. If the shark is chased, charged, or cornered, threat posturing will often occur. When the shark performs this display, the diver should stop and let the shark move away before retreating. Do not photograph this display with a strobe as the flash has been known to trigger an attack. Other sharks perform threat displays as well. Blacktip sharks have been observed to swim in an agitated fashion when approached around seamounts in the Sea of Cortez. Aggression (possibly a result of competition between males for females) toward conspecifics and divers may also vary with the reproductive cycle. Sandtiger sharks and wobbegongs are reported to be more aggressive during the mating season.

Misidentification and Predation. Sharks that feed on large animals may mistake a diver as normal prey. It has been suggested that white sharks attack snorkelers, divers, and surf and boogie boards because they look like a pinniped (important sources of food for larger white sharks) basking at the ocean's surface. In many cases the victim is bitten and spit out. Thus, it has been hypothesized that when the shark bites a wet-suit clad human, and encounters an unfamiliar taste, it rejects it as prey. Another theory, the "bite-and-spit hypothesis," is that white sharks bite their large pinniped victims and let them bleed to death before eating them. This strategy decreases the shark's chances of being injured by the teeth or claws of a large pinniped, and may explain why divers or surfers are bitten and appear to be rejected as food. Snorkeling near seal or sea lion rookeries has inherent risks, especially where white sharks are known to be abundant. Scuba diving may be slightly less dangerous in these areas, but divers have also been attacked by white sharks.

GLOSSARY

Alar spines. Enlarged, hooked spines on the pectoral fins of skates.

Ampullae of Lorenzini. Skin pores that contain receptor cells that detect electric fields.

Anemones. Invertebrates that belong to the class Anthozoa that have a central gut cavity surrounded by stinging tentacles.

Anterior. Pertaining to the front of the body.

Ascidians (Sea Squirts). Sponge-like members of the subphylum Urochordata that are usually sessile, filter-feeders with a body covered by a fibrous tunic.

Atoll. A reef that is usually circular or oval with a central lagoon that rests on the top of a submerged volcano.

Barbel. A small tentacle-like protuberance, usually present near the nostrils, that serves a sensory function.

Barrier reef. A reef separated from the adjacent shoreline by a lagoon.

Benthic. Referring to flora and fauna of the sea bottom.

Bioluminescent. When live organisms convert chemical energy into light.

Bivalve. A class of mollusks that includes clams, oysters, and mussels.

Bony fishes. Members of the class Osteichthyes. A diverse group that contains most of the modern fish species.

Branchial. Pertaining to the gills.

Buccal. Pertaining to the mouth.

Caudal fin. The tail fin, which can be divided up into the lower and upper caudal lobe.

Cephalopods. A class of molluscs that includes octopuses, squid, cuttlefish, and nautilus.

Cephalic fins. The projections on either side of the mouth of devil rays used to direct food into the mouth.

Claspers. Modifications of the male elasmobranchs pelvic fins that are rod-like and are used to transfer sperm during mating.

Cloaca. Cavity into which the intestinal, urinary, and reproductive canals open.

Conspecific. Referring to a member of the same species.

Coralline algae. A red, calcareous algae of the family Corallinae. Usually encrusting and pink in color.

Crepuscular. Most active at dusk and dawn.

Crustacea. A subphylum of the phylum Arthopoda that includes the barnacles, copepods, mantis shrimp, mysids, crabs, shrimp, and krill. They all have chitinous exoskeletons.

Cryptic. Pertaining to concealment, usually in reference to color pattern or behavior (e.g. hiding in reef crevices.)

Demersal. Living on the sea bottom.

Diel. Pertaining to the day-night cycle.

Disc. Pertaining to the head, pectoral fins, and trunk of a ray.

Disc width. Refers to the widest portion of the disc.

Disc length. Refers to the longest portion of the disc (i.e. from the tip of the snout to the posterior edge of the pectoral fin).

Diurnal. Active during the day.

Dorsum. The back or upper part of the body.

Drop-offs. A reef face that plummets vertically into deep water.

Echinoderms. The phylum which is comprised of sea stars, serpent stars, sea cucumbers, and sea urchins. They are radially symmetrical and some have sharp spines.

Elasmobranch. A subclass of cartilaginous fishes which includes the sharks, rays, and skates.

Heterospecific. Referring to a member of a different species.

Falcate. Long, narrow, and curved (sickle-shaped).

Fringing reefs. Reefs that occur along the shore of islands and continental coastlines.

Infaunal. Living within the sediment of the sea floor.

Interdorsal ridge. A ridge of skin between the two dorsal fins.

Intertidal. A part of the shore or reef that is exposed to the air at low tide and covered by water at high tide.

Labial furrows. Fold of skin around the edge of the mouth.

Lagoon. Area enclosed by a barrier reef or reef flat.

Molariform. Flat, broad and round; molar-like in form.

Mollusca. A diverse phylum, many of which have an external shell, whose members include the chitons, snails, bivalves, octopuses, and squid.

Motor patterns. A stereotypical group of actions or behaviors.

Nasal flap. A skin flap just in front of the nostril.

Nasoral groove. A channel that connects the nostrils to the mouth and allows the shark or ray to irrigate the nostrils with fresh sea water by pulling water through the mouth.

Nictitating membrane. A moveable lower eyelid.

Nocturnal. Active at night.

Oceanic. Pertaining to the open ocean.

Ocelli. A pigment pattern that resembles an eye; also known as an eye spot.

Ontogenetic. Referring to a change that occurs with age.

Oviposition. The process of depositing eggs.

Papillae. A small fleshy projection.

Parturition. The process of giving birth.

Patch reef. Small reefs that are present in coral reef lagoons or along rocky coastlines.

Pelagic. Pertaining to organisms which live in the water column.

Pinnipeds. Marine mammals in the order Pinnipedia represented by the true seals, walrus, and eared seals (e.g. sea lions).

Piscivorous. Fish-eating.

Plankton. organisms that drift about in the ocean that are usually minute.

Posterior. Pertaining to area toward the back or tail.

Precaudal pit. An indentation located just in front of the tail fin.

Reef channels. Channels that run through the barrier reef and connect the lagoon with the open ocean.

Reef face. This is the section of the reef on the seaward side of the reef flat and lagoon.

Reef flat. The area behind the reef crest that ends at the shore on a fringing reef or at the lagoon on a barrier reef. It varies in width and often includes deeper channels, tidal pools, sea grass beds, or coral boulders.

Salp. A type of tunicate (subphylum Urochordata) that is pelagic and transparent.

Seamount. This is an isolated peak rising from the ocean floor that is submerged under the water's surface.

Sessile. Permanently attached or stationary.

Spiracle. A respiratory opening located behind the eyes.

Subrostral lobes. The fleshy ridges under the snout of eagle and cownose rays.

Substrate. Any solid surface or substance (e.g. rock, sand).

Supraorbital ridge. A ridge above the eye.

Terminal. At the end of the head.

Thermocline. A subsurface zone of rapid temperature and density change with depth.

Thorns. A flat denticle with a sharp crown.

Tubercles. Enlarged, thorn-like denticles.

Ventrum. The stomach or lower part of the body.

Worms. A general term used for the annelid, sipunculid (peanut) and echiuran (innkeeper) worms. Most of these live on the sea floor often within bottom sediments.

Zooplankton. Plankton composed of animal life.

SHARK AND RAY BODY PARTS

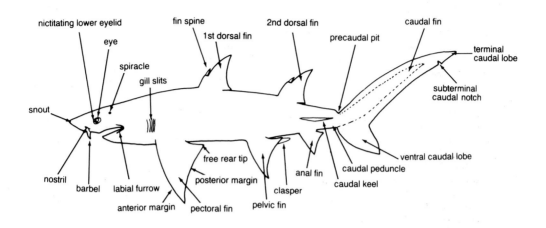

nictitating lower eyelid
fin spine
1st dorsal fin
2nd dorsal fin
precaudal pit
caudal fin
terminal caudal lobe
eye
spiracle
gill slits
subterminal caudal notch
snout
nostril
barbel
labial furrow
free rear tip
posterior margin
anterior margin
pectoral fin
pelvic fin
clasper
anal fin
caudal keel
caudal peduncle
ventral caudal lobe

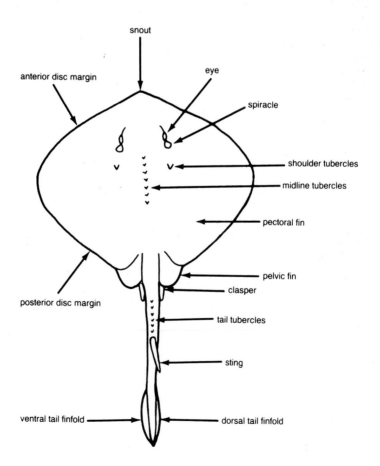

snout
anterior disc margin
eye
spiracle
shoulder tubercles
midline tubercles
pectoral fin
posterior disc margin
pelvic fin
clasper
tail tubercles
sting
ventral tail finfold
dorsal tail finfold

PICTORIAL KEY TO SHARK AND RAY FAMILIES

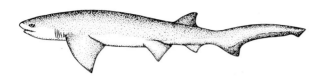

1. COWSHARKS (HEXANCHIDAE) p. 34

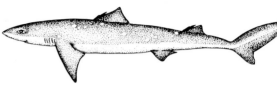

2. DOGFISH SHARKS (SQUALIDAE) p. 34

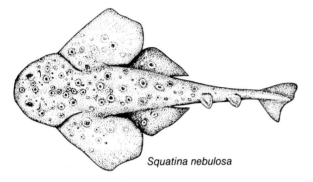

Squatina nebulosa

3. ANGEL SHARKS (SQUATINIDAE) p. 35

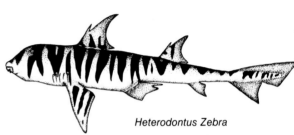

Heterodontus Zebra

4. HORN SHARKS (HETERODONTIDAE) p. 37

5. COLLARED CARPET SHARKS (PARASCYLLIDAE) p. 39

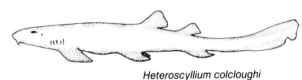

Heteroscyllium colcloughi

6. BLIND SHARKS (BRACHAELURIDAE) p. 40

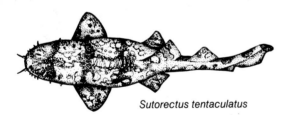

Sutorectus tentaculatus

7. WOBBEGONGS (ORECTOLOBIDAE) p. 41

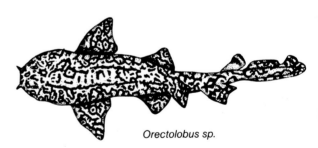

Orectolobus sp.

Hemiscyllium hallstromi

Chiloscyllium hassleti

8. BAMBOO AND EPAULETTE SHARKS (HEMISCYLLIDAE) p. 43

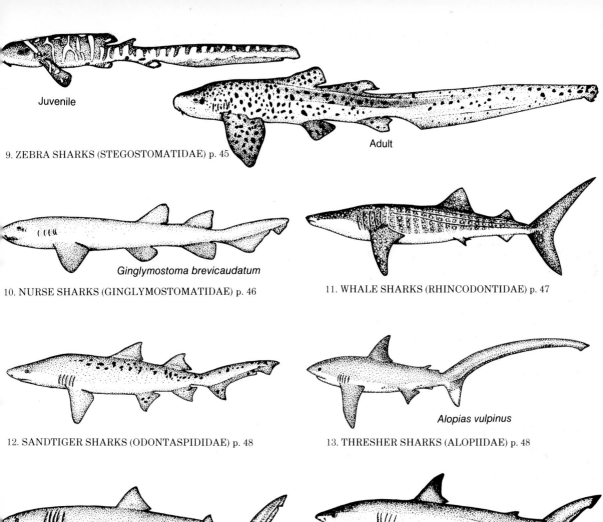

Juvenile

Adult

9. ZEBRA SHARKS (STEGOSTOMATIDAE) p. 45

Ginglymostoma brevicaudatum

10. NURSE SHARKS (GINGLYMOSTOMATIDAE) p. 46

11. WHALE SHARKS (RHINCODONTIDAE) p. 47

12. SANDTIGER SHARKS (ODONTASPIDIDAE) p. 48

Alopias vulpinus

13. THRESHER SHARKS (ALOPIIDAE) p. 48

14. BASKING SHARKS (CETORHINIDAE) p. 49

15. MACKEREL SHARKS (LAMNIDAE) p. 50

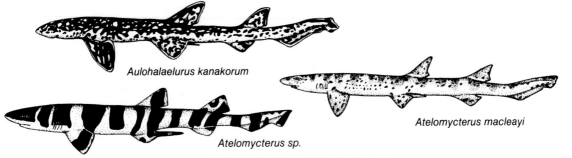

Aulohalaelurus kanakorum

Atelomycterus macleayi

Atelomycterus sp.

16. CATSHARKS (SCYLIORHINIDAE) p. 51

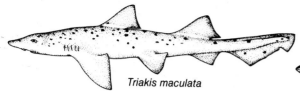

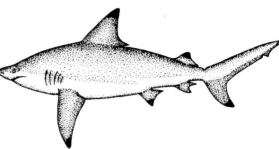

17. SMOOTHHOUND SHARKS (TRIAKIDAE) p. 56

Triakis maculata

18. REQUIEM SHARKS (CARCHARHINIDAE) p. 59

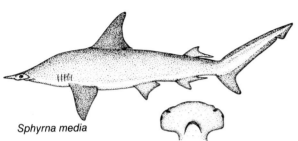

Sphyrna media

19. HAMMERHEAD SHARKS (SPHYRNIDAE) p. 68

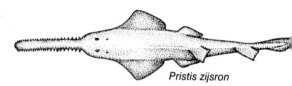

Pristis zijsron

20. SAWFISHES (PRISTIDAE) p. 70

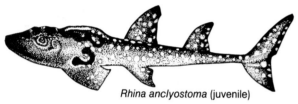

Rhina anclyostoma (juvenile)

21. SHARKFIN GUITARFISHES (RHINIDAE) p. 71

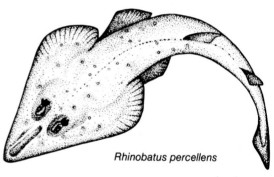

Rhinobatus percellens

22. GUITARFISHES (RHINOBATIDAE) p. 71

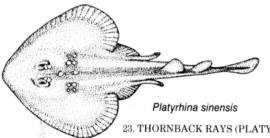

Platyrhina sinensis

23. THORNBACK RAYS (PLATYRHYNIDAE) p. 75

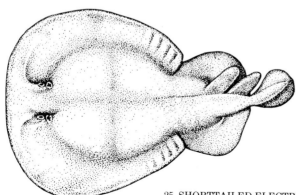

Torpedo fuscomaculata

24. TORPEDO RAYS (TORPEDINIDAE) p. 76

25. SHORTTAILED ELECTRIC RAYS (HYPNIDAE) p.79

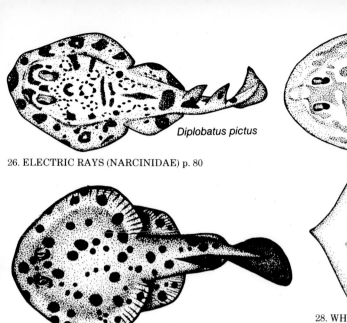

Diplobatus pictus

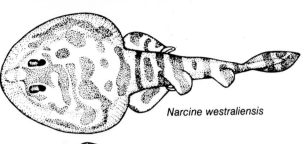

Narcine westraliensis

26. ELECTRIC RAYS (NARCINIDAE) p. 80

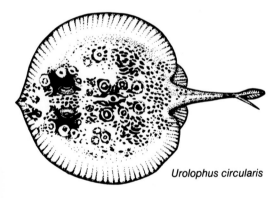

Dasyatis bennetti

28. WHIPTAIL STINGRAYS (DASYATIDAE) p. 82

27. SHORTNOSE ELECTRIC RAYS (NARKIDAE) p. 82

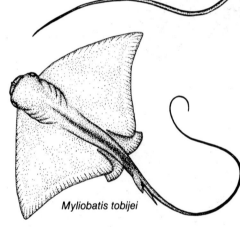

Urolophus circularis

Myliobatis tobijei

29. ROUND STINGRAYS AND STINGAREES (UROLOPHIDAE) p. 89

30. EAGLE RAYS (MYLIOBATIDAE) p. 93

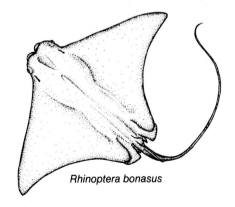

Rhinoptera bonasus

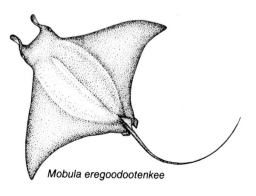

Mobula eregoodootenkee

31. COWNOSE RAYS (RHINOPTERIDAE) p. 95

32. DEVIL RAYS (MOBULIDAE) p. 96

FAMILY HEXANCHIDAE (COW SHARKS)

This family consists of four species, two of which are observed inshore around rocky reefs. The distinctive morphological characters of this family include a single dorsal fin, six or seven large gill slits, and broad based, cockscomb-like teeth in the lower jaw. All of the species in this family are deepwater inhabitants, except for the broadnose sevengill, which is most common in shallow, coastal habitats. In certain parts of its range, the bluntnose sixgill shark is regularly encountered by divers and is known to frequent shallow waters at night. These sharks are ovoviviparous (yolksac viviparity) and relatively fecund (the bluntnose sixgill is second only to the blue shark in size of its litters). Their large size and predilection for large prey makes them potentially dangerous to divers. The bluntnose sixgill shark is rarely housed in public aquariums, whereas the broadnose sevengill shark is frequently kept in temperate water aquariums and usually adapts readily to captivity. Both species are known to consume other elasmobranchs (including other cow sharks) housed with them.

D. W. Gotshall

1. Bluntnose sixgill shark *(Hexanchus griseus)*

Identification: Six gill-slits; broad, blunt snout; pale gray to black or brown above, slightly lighter below; eyes bright green. *Size:* Birth 70 cm (27.5 inches), maximum length 4.8 m (15.7 ft). *Range:* Wide ranging in all temperate and tropical seas. Most common in the abyssal depths (down to at least 1,875 m, 6,093 ft), but observed regularly by divers in the summer at Hornby Island in the northern Strait of Georgia, west of Vancouver and at the mouth of the Alberni Inlet, Barkley Sound, on the west coast of Vancouver Island, in water 25-70 m (81-227 ft) deep. *Reproduction:* One of the most fecund of all sharks, litter number 22-108. *Biology:* Eats hagfish, sharks (spiny dogfish, prickly sharks), rays, chimeras, bony fishes (anglerfish, hake, marlin, gurnards, herring, ling), shrimp, crabs, whale blubber, and seals; cannibalistic tendencies observed in captive specimens. Often with large copepod parasites streaming from the fins and body. Although not known to attack humans, its large size and varied diet make it worthy of great respect. Divers who have encountered this shark have reported some aggressive behavior in situations where the shark has been provoked. A possible threat display of circular swimming with mouth agape has been described for this species.

2. Broadnose sevengill shark *(Notorhynchus cepedianus)*

Identification: Seven gill-slits; broad snout; body peppered with black spots. *Size:* birth 50 cm (19.7 inches), maximum length 3 m (9.7 ft). *Range:* Found in most temperate seas. Depth range from intertidal zone to 50 m (163 ft). *Reproduction:* Litter number up to 82; gestation about 12 months. Nursery grounds usually shallow bays (e.g. San Francisco Bay). Breeds in spring and summer in California. *Biology:* Usually found in shallow water, close to shore, over sandy bottoms, sometimes near the edge of kelp beds. Feed on octopuses, lampreys, and rays (a major food is brown smoothhounds and bat rays in California waters; will also eat conspecifics), bony fishes (salmon, sturgeon, anchovies), snails, carrion, and seals. Sometimes found in association with seal rookeries; individuals have been observed hunting pinnipeds cooperatively. Moves into shallow bays with incoming tide. Apparent mating scars observed on females, but males also bare scars, possibly the result of male-male aggression. In the aquarium, it swims continuously. It has bitten divers in public aquariums and has behaved aggressively toward divers and spearfishermen in the wild. Possibly responsible for shallow water attacks on bathers in temperate coastal waters (human remains found in stomach of one specimen).

FAMILY SQUALIDAE (DOGFISH SHARKS)

This is one of the largest shark families (about 73 species), but most are deep water forms that do not frequent coral or rocky reefs; however, there is little doubt that the number of species that are transient in reef habitats is larger than represented in this book. These sharks are diverse in form, with most having spines in front of the two dorsal fins, no anal fin, and the first dorsal fin originating in front of the pelvic fins. A number of these sharks have light producing organs, known as photophores, that attract prey or may be used to communicate with conspecifics. The dogfish range in size from the diminutive lanternsharks, some of which reach maturity at less than 20 cm (7.9 inches), to the titanic sleeper sharks that attain lengths of 6 m (19.8 ft) or more. They are ovoviviparous (yolksac viviparity), with the spiny dogfish holding the record for the longest gestation period of any known vertebrate animal (i.e.

24 months). Some species in this family are known to hunt in large packs and several species are despised by commercial fishermen due to the destruction they cause to catch and equipment. They feed on a wide array of bony fishes and invertebrates. A few species (the cookie-cutter sharks, *Isistius* spp., and the Portuguese dogfish, *Centroscymnus coelolepis*) parasitize marine mammals and oceanic fishes by biting out small plugs of flesh. Dogfishes often fall prey to larger shark species, like the white shark (the stomach of one white shark contained eight dogfishes). In captivity, they often ram into the sides of the aquarium and cause severe, often lethal, injuries. However, they have been maintained in large public aquariums with some success.

3. Spiny dogfish *(Squalus acanthias)*

Identification: Spines present in front of dorsal fins; no anal fin; pointed snout; first dorsal originates behind pectoral fins; dorsal coloration brown to gray, usually with white spots. *Size:* Birth 22-33 cm (8.7-13 inches), maximum length 1.6 m (5.2 ft). *Range:* Worldwide, antitropical. Depth range from intertidal zone to 900 m (2,925 ft). *Reproduction:* Litter number 1-20; gestation 18-24 months. *Biology:* Common in a variety of habitats, including rocky reefs. Voracious predator that feeds on bony fishes (herring, hake, cod, blennies, flatfishes), fish eggs, squid, octopuses, crabs, krill, worms, snails, salps, and jellyfishes (adults feed more on fish than juveniles). Estimated annual food consumption rate for juveniles is five times the body weight, for adults it is two and a half times the body weight. Usually school, segregating by size and sex; observed to form mixed schools with leopard sharks and smoothhounds along California coast. Migrate in response to warming temperatures; some move into cooler, deeper waters in the spring. One tagged individual moved from Washington to Japan (6,500 km, 4,039 miles). Enemies include other sharks, killer whales, and seals. Dorsal spines can inflict painful puncture wounds; otherwise no threat to humans.

FAMILY SQUATINIDAE (ANGEL SHARKS)

Thirteen species of these ray-like sharks have been identified. They have flattened bodies, with terminal mouths, no anal fin, pectoral fins that are not attached to the head (as they are in rays), and no spines in front of the dorsal fins. Although these sharks are not usually found on reefs, they often occupy soft substrates near them. They are benthic, spending most of their day in repose, usually buried just under the sand or mud surface. If a prey item moves too close to the angelshark, it rapidly lifts its head from the substrate and throws its jaws forward to snatch its prey. This feeding mechanism is extremely fast, rivaling the speed of bony fish predators that ambush their prey. After the strike, the angelshark settles back down into the sediment and waits for its next victim. They are found singly or in aggregations. Angelsharks move over the bottom at night and hunt sleeping and dead fish and nocturnal invertebrates (squid, octopuses, crustaceans). All these sharks are ovoviviparous (yolksac viviparity), but nothing is known of their mating behavior. One species, that has yet to be formally described, from the Sea of Cortez, has spines on the edges of the pectoral fins like the alar spines of male skates. In skates, these spines help anchor the male to the female during copulation. They will bite if provoked or if a diver places a hand or foot near their head. Readily adapt to captivity in larger aquariums.

R. H. Kuiter

4. Australian angel shark *(Squatina australis)*

Identification: Broad body; nasal barbels and anterior nasal flaps with fringes; no lobes on side of head; dorsal tubercles small or absent; no ocelli on body, has numerous small white spots. *Size:* Birth 22-27 cm (8.7-10.6 inches), maximum length 1.5 m (4.9 ft). *Range:* Australia (New South Wales along south coast to western Australia). Depth range from intertidal zone to 256 m (832 ft). *Reproduction:* Litters number up to 20. Young born in the fall. *Biology:* Occurs inshore on sand and mud bottoms, often associated with sea grass beds and rocky reefs. Feeds on bottom dwelling fishes, crustaceans, and octopuses. Usually buried during the day, active at night.

5. Pacific angel shark *(Squatina californica)*

Identification: Broad pectoral fins; row of small tubercles on back; no ocelli, gray with brown flecks of varying size. *Size:* Birth 23 cm (9.1 inches), maximum length 1.5 m (4.9 ft). *Range:* Alaska, U.S.A. to Sea of Cortez, Ecuador to southern Chile (possibly a different species); abundant near California Channel Islands, where numbers decrease in the winter months. Depth range 3-100 m (9.8-325 ft) off California, in the Sea of Cortez down to 183 m (595 ft). *Reproduction:* Litters number 1-13; gestation 10 months. Most give birth in March and June. *Biology:* Usually found near rocky reefs, just under the sand or mud. Nocturnal, with activity peaking at dusk and midnight. Adults are nomadic, spending days in a limited area of 1 to 1.5 km (0.6 to 0.9 miles) then moving to a new area several kilometers away. Often aggregate. Feed on fishes (croakers, flatfish, corbina, blacksmith) and squid. Specimens examined by author in Sea of Cortez had eaten hake, croaker, peppered shark *(Galeus piperatus)* eggcases, and mantis shrimp. They are ambush predators. This shark may bite if provoked.

6. Japanese angel shark *(Squatina japonica)*

Identification: Pectoral fins broad with rounded rear tips; nasal barbels simple and spatulate, anterior nasal flaps weakly fringed or smooth; dermal flaps on side of the head without lobes; row of moderately large spines running down back; no ocelli, body blackish-brown with small dark and pale spots. The clouded angel shark *(S. nebulosa)* is a similar species that differs in having dermal flaps on the side of the head with two lobes, the distance between the spiracles shorter than the distance between the eyes, and a bluish-brown body with black and white dots (see figure in Pictorial Key to Families). The clouded angel shark occurs from Japan to Taiwan and attains 1.6 m (5.1 ft) in maximum length. *Size:* Maximum length 2.5 m (8.2 ft). *Range:* Japan to the Philippines. *Reproduction:* Litters number about 10. *Biology:* Usually found on sandy bottoms in shallow water, sometimes near rocky reefs. Food habits probably similar to preceding species.

7. Angel shark *(Squatina squatina)*

Identification: Pectoral fins very broad with broadly rounded rear tips; trunk broad; nasal barbels conical, anterior nasal flaps smooth or weakly fringed; dorsum gray or brown often with darker mottling, young have white lines. No ocelli. *Size:* birth 24-30 cm (9.4-12 inches), maximum length 244 cm (96 inches). *Range:* Eastern North Atlantic, from Norway to the Canary Islands, throughout the Mediterranean. Depth range 5-100 m (17-330 ft). *Reproduction:* Litter number 7-25, with larger females having larger litters. Birth occurs in summer in northern Europe and in winter in the Mediterranean. *Biology:* Found on sand and gravel bottoms, sometimes near rocky reefs. It feeds primarily on bony fishes (hake, argentine, flatfishes), but also eats skates, crabs, and squid.

FAMILY HETERODONTIDAE (BULLHEAD SHARKS)

The bullhead or horn sharks (eight species have been described) are characterized by a pig-like snout, spines in front of each of two dorsal fins, the presence of an anal fin, large ridges over the eyes (the supraorbital ridges), and large molariform teeth in the back of the jaws. The spines in front of the fins are an effective antipredation device, discouraging bonyfishes and other sharks from eating smaller specimens. There is one report of a dead wobbegong found with a Port Jackson shark stuck in its jaws. They are oviparous; the eggcase is cone shaped with an auger-like ridge spiralling around it. The cases of some species have tendrils at one end. There is an ontogenetic change in tooth form. In juveniles, the teeth are all of the grasping type, with 5-6 cusps in the case of the horn shark. But, as the shark grows, the rear teeth become molar-like, losing the cusps, and are better for grinding up invertebrate exoskeletons. The large and muscular pectoral fins are used to walk along the bottom. Although generally harmless to divers, they have been known to bite if harassed. Most of the bullhead sharks do well in large home and public aquariums; several species mate in captivity.

8. Horn shark *(Heterodontus francisci)*

Identification: Supraorbital crests moderately high; first dorsal origin over pectoral bases; spots on body small (less than 1/3 length of eye), sometimes spots absent, no light bars between eyes. *Size:* Hatch at 15 cm (5.9 inches), maximum length 1.2 m (3.9 ft). *Range:* Central California to Sea of Cortez, also possibly Ecuador and Peru. Depth range from intertidal zone to 150 m (488 ft), with juveniles residing in shallower waters. *Reproduction:* Pairs of 10 cm (4 inches) auger type eggcases laid every 11-14 days, 1-2 weeks after copulation. Eggs hatch in 7-9 months. Male grasps female's pectoral fin in his mouth and inserts one clasper into her cloaca for up to 40 minutes. *Biology:* Adults usually on rocky reefs or in kelp beds. Juveniles on sand bottoms, often sheltering near clumps of algae, rocks, debris, or in bat ray feeding depressions. Feeds on sea urchins, worms, crabs, anemones, and bony fishes. Feed on blacksmith at night when they rest among the rocks. Utilize a small area during the day, often spending daylight hours at one spot, usually a cave or crevice. Adults move onto the reef at dusk and utilize a home range of about 1,000 square meters (10,760 square feet). Return to the same daytime resting sites at dawn. Migrate into deeper water in winter. Spines in front of dorsal fins often worn in adults that utilize caves and crevices as a result of abrading them against the rocks. Usually solitary, sometimes aggregate. Long lived (up to 25 years) and known to mate in captivity.

R.H. Kuiter

9. Crested bullhead shark *(Heterodontus galeatus)*

Identification: Supraorbital crests very high; brown body with several dark bands on back. *Size:* Hatch at 17 cm (6.7 inches), maximum length 1.5 cm (4.9 ft). *Range:* Australia (Queensland and New South Wales). Depth range from intertidal zone to 93 m (302 ft). *Reproduction:* Eggs are about 11 cm (4.3 inches) long, auger type with long tendrils extending from the end that can be more than 2 m (6.5 ft) in length. Eggs are deposited in brown algae, which the tendrils become tangled around, at depths of 15 m (49 ft) or more and are most abundant in late winter; however, oviposition occurs all year round. Eggs hatch in about 5 months. *Biology:* Found on reefs, among large macroalgae, and in sea grass beds. Shoves head between rocks in search of sea urchins (which are major component of diet), crustaceans, molluscs, and small fishes. Teeth are often stained purple as a result of urchin-eating. Does well in captivity; females reach maturity in captivity at about 12 years of age.

R.H. Kuiter
M.D. Conlin

10. Japanese bullhead shark
(Heterodontus japonicus)

Identification: Supraorbital ridges low; first dorsal origin over pectoral bases; base color tan with darker bands (in juvenile) or saddles (in adult). The zebra bullhead shark *(H. zebra)* also occurs in Japanese waters south to Australia. This species has a distinct color pattern consisting of dark vertical stripes on a light background and high dorsal fins (see figure in Pictorial Key to Families). *Size:* Hatch at 18 cm (7 inches), maximum length 1.2 m (3.9 ft). *Range:* Japan to China (including Taiwan). Depth range 6-37 m (20-120 ft). *Reproduction:* Lays auger type eggs (about 12-18 cm, 4.7-7 inches long) among rocks and kelp, often with more then one female using same oviposition site, with as many as 15 eggs found in a single nest; female lays 2 eggs at a time, from spring to late summer in Japan, 6-12 times during a single spawning season. Eggs hatch in 1 year. During courtship, male grasps pectoral fin of female and wraps posterior part of body under her so single clasper can be inserted into her cloaca. In several mating bouts observed, copulation lasted as long as 15 minutes. *Biology:* Found in temperate waters where it frequents rocky reefs and kelp forests. Feeds on crustaceans, molluscs, small bony fishes, and sea urchins. Some specimens observed with hydroids growing on their teeth. Adapts well to captivity, even mating in aquariums.

11. Mexican bullhead shark
(Heterodontus mexicanus)

Identification: Supraorbital ridges low; first dorsal originates over pectoral base; large spots, larger than half of eye length (some specimens have no spots), a subtle bar between the supraorbital ridges. *Size:* Hatches at 14 cm (5.5 inches), maximum length 70 cm (2.3 ft). *Range:* From the upper Sea of Cortez (where it is common) to Peru. Depth range inshore to 50 m (163 ft) or more. *Reproduction:* Auger type eggcase, with tendrils on one end; length of case 8.3 cm (3.3 inches). *Biology:* Observed on sand, coral, and rocky reef areas, sometimes among large macroalgae. In Sea of Cortez, often captured in gill-nets with Pacific sharpnose shark, smoothhounds, and angel shark. Encountered on seamounts in southern Sea of Cortez. It is most abundant in this area in autumn, but is also observed in winter and spring. Feeds on crabs and benthic bony fishes (midshipman).

12. Port Jackson shark
(Heterodontus portusjacksoni)

R.H. Kuiter

Identification: Markings a unique black harness on back and flanks. *Size:* Hatch at 24 cm (9.4 inches), maximum length 1.7 m (5.5 ft). *Range:* Australia (Queensland south around the coast to western Australia); single specimen captured in New Zealand. Depth range from intertidal zone to 172 m (559 ft). *Reproduction:* Females lay 10-16 eggs on rocky reefs in water 1-30 m (3.2-98 ft) in depth. Auger type eggcase about 15 cm (5.9 inches) long. Mating is similar to Japanese bullhead shark. *Biology:* Juveniles utilize bays and estuaries as nursery grounds for several years of life then segregate by sex and move on to offshore reefs. Females migrate into shallow waters in winter to deposit eggs on rocky reefs, move back to deeper areas in spring; both sexes also make long range migrations of up to 850 km (527 mi) down the coast. They visit specific resting sites on reefs, usually caves or channels. Solitary or aggregate at resting sites, sometimes in large numbers. Feed on urchins, sea stars, molluscs, crustaceans, and benthic bony fishes. Nocturnal hunter; uncover prey hidden in sand by rapidly pumping water and sand through the gills. Does well in captivity, even breeds in aquariums. Adults observed eating their own eggcases.

13. Galapagos bullhead shark
(Heterodontus quoyi)

Identification: Supraorbital ridges low; first dorsal origin behind pectoral base; larger spots (over half of eye length), no light bands between supraorbital ridges. *Size:* Hatches at 17 cm (6.7 inches), maximum length 57 cm (22 inches). *Range:* Offshore islands off Peru, including the Galapagos Islands. *Reproduction:* Lays an egg similar to Mexican bullhead shark. *Biology:* Rocky and coral reef dweller, regularly encountered by divers near the Galapagos Islands. Often observed resting on the ledges of vertical rock faces at depths of 16-30 m (52-98 ft). Also observed in caves. Most active at night. Solitary. Crabs and green algae found in stomach contents. One small specimen taken from the stomach of a tiger shark.

14. Cortez bullhead shark *(Heterodontus sp.)*

Identification: Supraorbital ridges moderately high, with the height of the eye being equal to the distance between the top of the eye and the top of the surpaorbital ridge; the ridges are less squared off posteriorly and longer anteriorly than in *H. francisci*; snout longer than *H. francisci*; dorsal fins higher and more falcate than in *H. francisci* and *H. mexicanus*; dorsum and lateral surface brown, without spots and no pale line between the supraorbital ridges; ventrum lighter. *Range:* This is apparently an undescribed species that is known only from the accompanying photograph. The photo was taken in the southern Sea of Cortez.

FAMILY PARASCYLLIDAE (COLLARED CARPET SHARKS)

Five of the seven species in this family are known to occur on rocky reefs. They have long, slender bodies with a narrow head and an anal fin well in front of the lower tail lobe and partially in front of the end of the second dorsal fin. There are two genera in the family; all the species included in this book belong to the genus *Parascyllium* and are limited in their range to the more temperate waters of southern and western Australia. Color pattern is an important character to help identify the different species. Little is known about their biology; at least some of the species are oviparous and deposit tendril eggcases. They probably feed on worms, crustaceans, and small bony fishes; their narrow heads and slender bodies enable them to capture prey concealed in reef crevices. They are nocturnal and hide in caves and among large macroalgae stands during the day, and thus go unnoticed by most divers. They are harmless to divers, do well in large aquariums, and are good candidates for captive breeding programs.

15. Rusty carpet shark
(Parascyllium ferrugineum)

Identification: Inconspicuous collar around neck and dark spots on the pectoral fins and body; fewer spots than the Tasmanian carpet shark. *Size:* Hatch at approximately 15 cm (5.9 inches), maximum length 80 cm (31.5 inches). *Range:* Australia (Victoria, Tasmania). Depth range 5-55 m (16-179 ft). Common in shallow water around southern Tasmania, but found in deeper water off Victoria. *Biology:* Occurs in beds of macroalgae on rocky reefs and in deeper sea grass meadows. Hides in caves and under ledges during the day; forages for bottom dwelling crustaceans at night.

P. Humann
M.D. Conlin

P. Last

39

16. Tasmanian carpet shark
(Parascyllium multimaculatum)
Identification: Inconspicuous collar, dusky saddles on the back, dense covering of spots on the flanks and fins. *Size:* Maximum length 75 cm (29.5 inches). *Range:* Australia (Tasmania). Depth range 5-40 m (16-130 ft). *Reproduction:* Lays yellow, ribbed tendril eggcases, with long tendrils extending from all corners, during the summer months. *Biology:* Common shark on rocky reefs among macroalgae. Mollusc and crustacean predator.

17. Necklace carpet shark
(Parascyllium variolatum)
Identification: White-spotted, dark collar around its neck and black markings on its pectoral fins. *Size:* Maximum length 91 cm (35.8 inches). *Range:* Australia (New South Wales south to Victoria and Tasmania, common around King Island). Depth range from intertidal zone to 165 m (536 ft). *Biology:* Temperate water, rocky reef dweller, often observed in beds of large macroalgae and in sea grass meadows near reefs. Juveniles hide under rocks and debris in shallow water. Nocturnal, rarely observed during the day.

FAMILY BRACHAELURIDAE (BLIND SHARKS)
There are two species in this genus; only one of these, the blind shark, is regularly encountered. This shark was named for its habit of closing its eyelids when removed from the water. The blind shark is known to be ovoviviparous (yolk sac viviparity) and occurs only in temperate and tropical Australia. They are harmless, but may bite if provoked. The blind shark will breed in captivity.

18. Blind shark *(Brachaelurus waddi)*
Identification: Long nasal barbels; juveniles grayish with black bands, adults light to dark brown (bands inconspicuous in adults); all ages often have white flecks on body and tail. The only other species in the family, the bluegrey carpet shark *(Heteroscyllium colcloughi),* has been collected infrequently on the south Queensland coast of Australia. It differs from the blind shark in the placement of the anal fin (it does not reach back to the origin of the lower tail lobe), in the length of the snout (it is longer and more rounded), and in the relative sizes of the first and second dorsal fins (the second dorsal is noticeably smaller than the first dorsal). *Size:* Birth 17 cm (6.7 inches), maximum length 1.2 m (3.9 ft). *Range:* Australia (Northern Territory to New South Wales). Depth range from intertidal zone to 150 m (488 ft). *Reproduction:* Litter number to eight; gives birth in the summer months. *Biology:* Warm temperate to tropical shark; juveniles often found in shallow, surgy waters hiding under ledges and in crevices. Adults in caves and under ledges during the day (they are rarely observed at this time). Hunt on shallow reefs and sea grass beds at night. Feeds on anemones, cuttlefish, crabs, and shrimp. They can live for as long as 18 hours out of the water. This adaptation may enable a blind shark caught in a shallow tide pool at ebb tide to survive! Secretive, but adapts readily to captivity.

FAMILY ORECTOLOBIDAE (WOBBEGONGS)

Their are seven described species (and apparently several undescribed species) within this unusual family, all of which are found on coral and/or rocky reefs. Wobbegongs are characterized by a somewhat flattened body, a very broad head with a large mouth positioned near its end, long barbels, and flaps of skin around the mouth. The color pattern, presence of tubercles along the back, and number of skin flaps on the upper jaw are all features that can be used in separating the various species. Their ornate color patterns help the wobbegongs disappear among coral, rocks, and algae, where they lie in repose. From daytime resting sites, they ambush prey that come into striking range. They hold large prey items until they are subdued, then manipulate the catch so it is swallowed head first. At night, they actively stalk octopuses, squid, crabs, sharks (including other wobbegongs), rays, and reef fishes. The flattened anterior end of the wobbegongs enables them to shove their heads into crevices and extract hiding prey items. All species, where data are available, are ovoviviparous (yolk sac viviparity). Juveniles are cryptic, living in deep crevices, under rocks, and in tide pools. They may be reclusive to avoid larger wobbegongs! One species gives birth in shallow areas away from the areas frequented by adults. Unlike some of their close relatives, the wobbegongs do not crawl about on their pectoral fins, instead they swim in a sinuous, polliwog-like fashion. Individuals have been observed moving from one tide pool to another in water so shallow their backs were completely exposed. Wobbegongs have a dubious reputation. Many divers consider them harmless unless provoked, but there are reports of wobbegongs biting divers for no apparent reason. Apparently these fishes have poor visual acuity and will strike at any movement near their head; therefore, it is unwise to place a hand or foot near the biting end of even a smaller wobbegong. They adapt readily to life in captivity and two species have even mated in public aquariums.

19. Tasselled wobbegong
(Eucrossorhinus dasypogon)

Identification: Very wide head, the edge of which is covered by a "beard" of dermal flaps; unlike the other wobbegongs, this species has dermal lobes on its chin; color pattern a network of dark lines on a lighter background. *Size:* Birth 22 cm (8.7 inches), maximum length over 3 m (9.8 ft). *Range:* Indonesia, Papua New Guinea, Australia (Queensland along northern coast to western Australia). Depth range from intertidal zone to depths of 40 m (130 ft) or more. *Reproduction:* Anecdotal report of a pair mating at night in a cave. *Biology:* Tropical shark that is an obligatory coral reef dweller. Observed in reef channels and on reef faces. Solitary; usually found resting in caves or under ledges during daytime and may leave these resting sites at night to forage. Also feeds during the day on other nocturnal species that share caves with them (squirrelfish, soldierfish, sweepers). Known to use several daytime resting sites within a small home range. Rests on sea floor with its tail curled up. Cleaner shrimp observed living on and picking at the skin of this wobbegong. Possibly the most aggressive of the wobbegongs, it is responsible for several unprovoked attacks on divers.

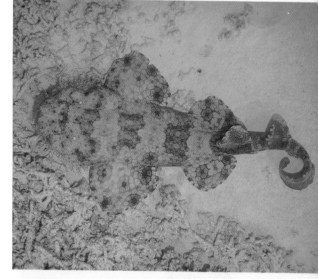

D.J. Wrobel

20. Japanese wobbegong *(Orectolobus japonicus)*

Identification: Five to six dermal lobes under the eyes of each side of head; dark saddles with network of dark lines in light areas between saddles. Most similar to ornate wobbegong. One albiro specimen recorded. *Size:* Birth 20 cm (7.9 inches), maximum length 1 m (3.3 ft) or more. *Range:* Japan to Vietnam and the Philippines. *Reproduction:* Litter number 1-27; gestation about 1 year. Makes inshore migration to give birth and mate; apparently anorexic during the breeding season. Mating observed in captivity; male bites and holds gill region while laying alongside the female during copulation; inserts single clasper. *Biology:* Rocky and coral reef dweller. Feeds almost entirely on benthic fishes (skates, lizardfishes, cutlassfish, horse mackerel, jacks, goatfishes, groupers, tilefishes, weeverfishes, whiting, parrotfishes, scorpionfishes, flatfishes, sea robin, sea bream, croakers); occasionally ingest shark eggcases, cephalopods, and shrimp. Nocturnal. Rarely observed by divers, but disposition probably similar to other wobbegongs. Kept for over 5 years in captivity.

41

R.H. Kuiter
© G. Bell

21. Spotted wobbegong
(Orectolobus maculatus)

Identification: Has more dermal lobes on the side of the head than ornate wobbegong (8-10 on each side of the head under and in front of eyes); has distinct ocelli on the body. *Size:* Birth 20 cm (7.9 inches), maximum length 3.2 m (10.5 ft) *Range:* Australia (New South Wales south to Western Australia), possibly also occurs in Japan, and South China Sea (may be different species). Depth range from intertidal zone to 100 m (325 ft). *Reproduction:* Litters number to 37. Before and during copulation, the male bites and holds the female's gill area. *Biology:* Primarily found in temperate waters on rocky reefs and in coastal bays. Juveniles occur in estuaries, sea grass beds, or on low profile reefs. By day it is often found resting in caves, under overhangs, in channels, and among the wreckage of sunken ships, sometimes in aggregations of a dozen or more individuals. Occasionally makes short forays up into water column. It feeds on crabs, lobsters, octopuses, bony fishes (groupers, scorpionfishes, sea chubs), as well as on other sharks (including its own species) and rays. Can be very aggressive, with reports of unprovoked attacks on divers near and well above the bottom.

22. Ornate wobbegong *(Orectolobus ornatus)*

Identification: Five to six dermal lobes under and in front of eyes on each side of head (unlike spotted wobbegong) and dark and light areas between saddles on the back that have spots with light centers, but no reticular pattern of lines (as in Japanese wobbegong). An unidentified wobbegong, that has been confused with *O. ornatus*, has been reported from Japan. This species has a greenish-gray dorsum with black reticulations on the back, head and fins (see figure in Pictorial Key to Families). *Size:* Birth 20 cm (7.9 inches), maximum length 2.9 m (9.5 ft). *Range:* Australia, Papua New Guinea, Indonesia, and possibly Japan. Depth range from intertidal zone to 30 m (99 ft). *Reproduction:* Litter number of at least 12. *Biology:* Coral and rocky reef inhabitant, found in tropical and temperate waters. In lagoons, on reef flats, reef channels, and reef faces. This species is more often found in less turbid bays and near offshore islands than the spotted wobbegong. Often observed in aggregations (sometimes piled on top of one another) in gutters, under ledges, and in caves during the day. Solitary individuals often rest in large "dish" corals. Increased activity at night. Will consume bony fishes, sharks, rays, cephalopods, and crustaceans that come within striking distance. Aggressive if provoked; large male wobbegongs more aggressive during the breeding season. They will sometimes swim off the bottom to confront an intruding diver.

N. Coleman

23. Ward's Wobbegong *(Orectolobus wardi)*

Identification: Two dermal lobes below and in front of eyes on each side of head; nasal barbels are not branched; large ocelli-like saddles on back with few spots and no lines between saddles. *Size:* Maximum length 1 m (39 inches). *Range:* Australia (Queensland along north coast to western Australia). Observed on shallow water reefs in less than 3 m (9.8 ft) of water. *Biology:* Found in tropical areas, often in turbid water. Not active during the day, sometimes observed with only its head under a ledge. Although said to be common in northern Australia, virtually nothing is known about its natural history.

24. Western wobbegong *(Orectolobus sp.)*

Identification: Four dermal lobes on each side of head under and in front of eyes; dark cross bands with lighter splotches (not ocelli) on saddles; juveniles have two rows of bumps on back. The cobbler's wobbegong *(Sutorectus tentaculatus)* is a similar species that differs from all other wobbegongs in that it has large, rounded tubercles (bumps) on its head and body (present in adults and juveniles), a low first dorsal fin that originates before the midbase of the pelvic fins, nasal barbels that lack prominent flaps, and large black spots on the fins and body. (see drawing in Pictorial Key to Families). This species is common off south Australia (its range is restricted to western and south Australia), but I could find no information on its biology. *Size:* Maximum length 2 m (6.6 ft). *Range:* Known only from western Australia, where it is the most common wobbegong observed. *Biology:* Nothing is known of its natural history, but probably similar to other large wobbegongs. Will bite if provoked.

N. Coleman

FAMILY HEMISCYLLIDAE (BAMBOO SHARKS AND EPAULETTE SHARKS)

This family has 13 species, 8 of which occur in reef habitats. The physical attributes they share include nasoral grooves, perinasal grooves, small mouths positioned in front of the eyes, no dermal flaps on the sides of the head, and a low rounded anal fin that is distinct from the caudal fin. They are ideally adapted to life in a highly structured environment; their muscular paired fins enable them to walk along the sea floor and their slender bodies allow them to slip between coral branches and into tight reef fissures. Some species are known to be oviparous. Young members of this family are rarely observed in the wild; they apparently live deep in coral crevices and in dense staghorn coral beds where they are safe from most predators (including other sharks). The color pattern of all but one of the hemiscyllids changes as they grow. Bamboo shark juveniles usually have distinct bands that fade or disappear with age, while young epaulette sharks possess bands that transform into spots as they grow. The color patterns of the epaulette sharks provide effective camouflage, especially when they are viewed from above, while the eye-spots (or ocelli) may function to dupe would-be predators. Paired eye spots may serve to intimidate predators by mimicking the head-on perspective of a piscivorous fish. Since many predators would approach the bottom oriented epaulette shark from above they would look down and see both of the ocelli. These sharks are harmless but may bite if harassed. Because these sharks are adapted to live in confined areas, they do well in public and larger home aquariums. Three members of the family regularly breed in captivity.

J. Randall

25. Arabian bamboo shark
(Chiloscyllium arabicum)

Identification: Posterior edge of dorsal fins rounded (not concave); second dorsal base longer than first dorsal base; juveniles and adults uniform in color. In the similar gray bamboo shark *(C. griseum)* the first dorsal base is longer than the second dorsal base, and the distance between the first and second dorsal fin origins is usually more than 9.3% of total length. The gray bamboo shark occurs from Iran to Papua New Guinea. *Size:* Hatch at 12 cm (4.7 inches), maximum length 78 cm (30.7 inches). *Range:* Arabian Gulf to India. Said to be common in the Arabian Gulf, especially in the summer months. Depth range 3-100 m (9.8- 328 ft). *Reproduction:* A tendril adhesive eggcase that adheres to coral. Lays four eggs in time period ranging from 20 minutes to 2 days, eggs hatch in 70-80 days. Reproductive phase about 6 months long. Mating behavior observed in captivity; male grasps pectoral fin of female in mouth and inserts a single clasper; interfering males have been observed to bite the clasper of courting male; copulation lasts from 5-15 minutes. *Biology:* Coral reef dweller, observed in crevices and caves. Crustaceans and molluscs main components of diet, also takes fishes (snake eels) and squid.

26. Whitespotted bamboo shark
(Chiloscyllium plagiosum)

Identification: Dorsal fin posterior edges rounded (not concave); bands and white spots on a gray to dark brown background. Hasslet's bamboo shark *(C. hassleti)* is similar, but is uniform in color as an adult and the distance from the first to second dorsal fin is less than 9.3% of the total length, the first dorsal height is less than 6.6% of the total length, and the second dorsal fin height is less than 5.8% of the total length. The juveniles have black bordered, gray-brown band (see figure in Pictorial Key to Families). Hasslet's bamboo shark has been reported from Thailand, Malaysia, and Indonesia. *Size:* Birth 15 cm (5.9 inches), maximum length 95 cm (37.4 inches). *Range:* Japan to Indonesia, Thailand to India. *Biology:* Tropical reef inhabitant, occurring in reef crevices during the day, moves out to feed at night. Feeds on fishes and crustaceans. Does well in captivity, reported to survive as long as 25 years in public aquariums.

27. Brownbanded bamboo shark
(Chiloscyllium punctatum)

Identification: Dorsal fin posterior edges concave; juvenile with dark bands on light background, in adults these bands are less distinct or absent. *Size:* Hatch at about 16 cm (6.3 inches), maximum length 104 cm (40.9 inches). *Range:* Japan to Australia (Queensland around north coast to western Australia), Indonesia to India. *Reproduction:* Atendril adhesive eggcase. Reproduces in captivity; male bites female's pectoral fin before and during mating. Also may bite gill area during courtship. *Biology:* Found on coral reefs, observed in tidepools, on tidal flats, and reef faces. Nocturnal. Solitary. These sharks (especially the juveniles) are very cryptic, hiding deep in crevices at the base of coral heads. I have observed adults hiding under table corals during the day. Forages with its snout for invertebrates in coral rubble and sand. May bite if provoked.

28. Epaulette shark
(Hemiscyllium ocellatum)

Identification: Snout swollen and longer than other hemiscyllid sharks; large black spot surrounded by white just behind pectoral fins, numerous dark spots that are smaller than ocelli. Two color morphs observed; one with golden base color and more, darker, smaller spots and very pronounced ocelli; the other is tan with fewer, larger spots and less distinct ocelli. Hallstrom's epaulette shark *(H. hallstromi),* which is known only from the waters of Papua New Guinea, is similar to *H. ocellatum.* Hallstrom's epaulette has spots that are equal to or larger than the ocelli and has no spots in front of the eyes (see figure in Pictorial Key to Families). These may be present or lacking in the epaulette shark. *Size:* Hatch at 15 cm (5.5 inches), maximum length 107 cm (42.1 inches). *Range:* Australia (Queensland around north coast to western Australia) and New Guinea. Depth range from intertidal zone to 10 m (33 ft). *Reproduction:* Atendril adhesive eggcases are deposited at night, usually two eggs are laid at a time. When mating, the male grasps the female's pectoral fin and inserts a single clasper. Mating lasts about 2 minutes. *Biology:* An obligatory reef dweller, most abundant in staghorn coral stands on reef faces and on reef flats (often in tide pools). Eats worms, shrimp, and crabs dug out of sand or sucked from crevices. Solitary. Primarily nocturnal, but I have observed considerable activity (including mating) in this species during the day. Inactive individuals are sometimes observed hiding, with their heads stuck under a ledge. Harmless, but will bite if provoked.

29. Freycinet's epaulette shark
(Hemiscyllium freycineti)

Identification: Spots on head, in front of the eyes, slightly smaller or equal to the eye diameter; in specimens of approximately 30 cm (12 inches) or more, body covered with a honeycomb of rusty-brown spots on a cream background, inconspicuous eye-spots present over each pectoral fin; juveniles have alternating dark brown and tan bands that break up into spots as the shark grows. *Size:* Maximum length 72 cm (28.3.in); matures at less than 61 cm (24 inches). *Range:* Indonesia and Papua New Guinea (apparently common in certain areas). *Biology:* Shallow water, coral reef species. During the day, hides in reef crevices, sometimes with only its tail visible. At night, moves over reef and surrounding rubble, sea grass, and sand bottoms looking for food. Food and behavior probably similar to epaulette shark.

J. Stafford-Deitsch

30. Hooded epaulette shark
(Hemiscyllium strahani)

Identification: Ventral surface of head has dark markings, in some specimens entire head has hooded appearance; eye-spots present, but less conspicuous. *Size:* Reported maximum length 80 cm (31.5 inches), although a 75-cm (29.5-inch) male I collected was still immature. *Range:* Indonesia and Papua New Guinea. All the specimens I observed were at depths of 3-13 m (9.8-39 ft), although reported as deep as 18 m (59 ft). *Biology:* A coral reef dweller that is nocturnally active. Fairly common along the northeastern coast of Papua New Guinea, where I observed six specimens during night dives (none was seen during the day). On reef flats and reef faces. Found in areas with abundant hard coral growth. Hides in crevices and under table corals during day. Does well in aquariums; one specimen was kept for over 7 years. Harmless.

G. Allen

31. Speckled epaulette shark
(Hemiscyllium trispeculare)

Identification: Spots present in front of eyes are much smaller than eye diameter; two or three larger dark spots behind ocellus; flanks and dorsal surface covered with small spots. *Size:* Maximum length 79 cm (31.1 inches). *Range:* Indonesia, Australia (Queensland around northern coast to Western Australia). *Biology:* Coral reef dwelling shark; encountered in shallow waters, including tide pools. Often observed under table corals.

FAMILY STEGOSTOMATIDAE (ZEBRA SHARKS)

The only member of this family is resident to coral and rocky reefs in tropical to warm temperate regions. It is characterized by a tail almost as long as its body, ridges on the sides of the

body, a small mouth, and a banded color pattern (in juveniles; see figure in Pictorial Key to Families) or spotted color pattern (subadults and adults). This shark is usually observed resting on the bottom, sometimes standing on its pectoral fins with its open mouth facing into the current. This behavior probably facilitates respiration while the animal is at rest. These sharks are often accompanied by discfishes and are also cleaned by blue-streak cleaner wrasses. At Phuket Island, Thailand, they are commonly hand fed and some individuals allow divers to handle them and rub their stomachs, sometimes for extended periods of time. This shark is commonly encountered near Phuket Island as well as Lady Elliot Island on the Great Barrier Reef. The zebra shark is oviparous and does well in large public aquariums.

A. Klapfer

32. Zebra Shark *(Stegostoma varium)*

Identification: Tail almost as long as the body; specimens greater than 90 cm (35.4 inches) have dark spots on yellow to cream background, smaller individuals with yellow stripes and spots on a dark brown background. Albino specimen recorded. *Size:* Hatching 25 cm (9.8 inches), maximum length 3.5 m (11.5 ft). *Range:* Samoa to Australia, north to Japan; Indonesia to South Africa, also the Red Sea. Depth range from intertidal zone to 65 m (214 ft). *Reproduction:* A tendril adhesive eggcase purple or brown and about 20 cm (7.9 inches) long. May lay as many as four eggs at a time. Juveniles are rarely encountered; they may occur in deeper water (greater than 50 m, 165 ft). *Biology:* Sluggish bottom dweller that is inactive during the day (where it is found on sand, rubble, or coral substrates) and hunts the reef and adjacent sandy areas at night. Observed in lagoons, reef channels, and on reef faces. Feeds primarily on snails and clams; eats crabs, shrimps, and bony fishes on occasion. Its long, flexible body and tail enable it to enter reef crevices and caves to capture concealed prey. Usually solitary, rarely aggregates. It is inoffensive, never having been reported to attack a diver.

FAMILY GINGLYMOSTOMATIDAE (NURSE SHARKS)

This family has three species, all of which are rocky and coral reef dwellers. These sharks have nasal barbels, nasoral grooves, small mouths positioned in front of the eyes, fourth and fifth gill-slits that are very close together, a second dorsal fin origin well in front of the anal fin origin, and a short tail. Nurse sharks are ovoviviparous (yolk sac viviparity) and the reproductive behavior of one species is well known. By day, the members of this family laze around on the sea floor, but at night they hunt torpid fishes and invertebrates. In tight spaces, these sharks will walk forward or backwards on their pectoral fins. When they locate a prey item hiding in a crevice or amid coral rubble, they place their small mouth near it and inhale it by rapidly expanding the pharynx. Barbels near the front of the mouth are covered with taste receptors and help nurse sharks locate food items, while the powerful jaws enable them to crush hard shelled invertebrates. There are reports of several unprovoked attacks on divers by nurse sharks; however, in most cases these sharks will not attack unless provoked. Nurse sharks have powerful jaws and are often reluctant to release their victim if they do attack. These sharks thrive in large public aquariums; some specimens have lived in captivity for more than 25 years.

33. Nurse shark *(Ginglymostoma cirratum)*

Identification: Pectoral and dorsal fins rounded; second dorsal origin in front of anal origin; barbels long (extend to mouth); color tan to dark brown, juveniles have small black spots. The shorttailed nurse shark *(G. brevicaudatum)* has an anal fin that is almost as large as the first and second dorsal fins, rounded fins, and a shorter caudal fin (less than 25% of the total length). This shark is known only from Tanzania, Kenya, and possibly Mauritius and the Seychelles (see figure in Pictorial Key to Families). *Size:* Birth 27 cm (10.6 inches), maximum length 4.3 m (14 ft). *Range:* Western Atlantic from Rhode Island to Brazil; eastern Atlantic from Senegal to Gabon; eastern Pacific from southern Baja California to Peru. Depth range from intertidal zone to 50 m (163 ft). *Reproduction:* Litters number up to 28. *Biology:* Found on lagoon patch reefs, reef flats, reef faces, and mangrove swamps. Inactive during the day, often found in aggregations on sea floor at this time. At night, hunts benthic invertebrates (spiny lobsters, crabs, octopuses, sea urchins), stingrays, and benthic bony fishes. Digs under coral chunks with head in search of concealed invertebrate prey. Has a fixed home range; tagged individuals have been recaptured in same area, even after 4 years at liberty.

34. Tawny nurse shark *(Nebrius ferrugineus)*

Identification: Dorsal fins and pectoral fins are sharply pointed, pectoral fins falcate. Albino specimen, with only one dorsal fin, reported. *Size:* Birth 40 cm (15.7 inches), maximum length 3.2 m (10.5 ft). *Range:* Society Islands east to South Africa; north to the Red Sea, south to Australia. From intertidal zone down to 70 m (228 ft). *Reproduction:* Litters number up to eight. *Biology:* Sluggish, coral reef dweller. Juveniles frequent shallow lagoons, where they hide in reef crevices, while adults are found in a variety of habitats (lagoons, reef flats, channels, reef faces). Larger individuals are often seen moving over the reef or resting in caves during the day. Sometimes aggregate on the sea floor, with individuals laying on or next to one another. It has a limited home range; individuals usually return to the same area every day. At night, it leaves its daytime resting place and hunts octopuses, squid, crabs, lobsters, sea urchins, and bony fishes (queenfish, surgeonfish, rabbitfish). Also eats sea snakes on occasion. This species is placid, but there have been several provoked attacks attributed to this species and, when it bites, it does so with remarkable tenacity.

M. Strickland

FAMILY RHINCODONTIDAE (WHALE SHARKS)

This family is comprised of a single mammoth species, the whale shark, which is the world's largest fish. The whale shark has a terminal mouth, ridges or keels on the side of its body and caudal peduncle, a broad head and a semilunate tail. The jaws are lined with 300 rows of minute teeth and the inside of the gill slits supports a spongy connective tissue. This shark is a filter feeder and the spongy material associated with the gill arches helps sieve food items from the water. Whale sharks have been observed to adopt a vertical orientation at the water's surface when feeding. The sharks hang in a tail-down position and thrust themselves up through schools of feeding tuna and baitfish until their heads break the water's surface. Frenzied tuna have been observed to leap into the mouths of whale sharks feeding in this manner. Whale sharks have also been observed to adopt this vertical orientation to ingest air bubbles emitted from scuba tanks! Whale sharks regularly associate with schools of scombrid fishes (i.e. mackerel and tuna). By swimming with schools of scombrids, the shark may benefit from the acute sensory system of the bony fish and their ability to locate aggregations of small baitfish. The feeding activity of the scombrids may also cause their prey to form a more concentrated mass and this in turn would be a productive target for the filter-feeding whale shark. In turn, the bony fishes may use the whale shark as a surface to chafe off parasites or to hide from larger, open ocean predators. The whale shark will purge undigestible objects from the alimentary tract by everting its gut out its mouth. The reproductive mode of this shark is still in question. An eggcase was dredged from the sea floor in the Gulf of Mexico that was 30 cm (12 inches) long and 14 cm (5.5 inches) wide and contained a 36 cm (14 inches), fully formed embryo. The eggcase, which was amber colored and extremely thin, was similar to those of the nurse shark, an ovoviviparous species whose eggcases hatch in utero just before birth. This eggcase was probably aborted prematurely and otherwise would have hatched inside the mother's oviduct. Female whale sharks may carry up to 16 of these eggcases at a time. This species has been maintained with some success in a large oceanarium in Okinawa and comes to the surface to have krill shoveled into its mouth! It is regularly encountered by divers at Cocos Island, Costa Rica, the island of Hawaii, the Bismarck Sea, Papua New Guinea, Phuket, Thailand, Okinawa, Japan, and in the southern Sea of Cortez, Baja California. Some researchers merge the preceding two families (the nurse and zebra sharks) into the family Rhincodontidae.

35. Whale shark *(Rhincodon typus)*

W. Hasson

Identification: Unmistakable! Terminal mouth; ridges or keels on side of body; checkerboard color pattern, with light stripes and spots on a dark background. *Size:* Born (or hatched ?) at 45 cm (17.7 inches), maximum length 14 m (46 ft), possibly larger. Individuals from 1-4 m (3.3-13.2 ft) in length virtually unknown in the literature. The few juveniles reported captured in tuna schools. *Range:* Found in all tropical to warm temperate oceans. *Biology:* Oceanic and coastal shark that is encountered near reefs (often in the vicinity of upwellings) and occasionally enters atoll lagoons. Usually solitary or in small loose groups, but has been observed in large aggregations, numbering over 100 individuals! They occasionally associate with other sharks, dolphins, and pilot whales. It is a filter feeder that sucks squid, planktonic crustaceans, and sardines into its capacious mouth. Tuna and jacks are also eaten as they feed on the sardines, while shark suckers may be accidently ingested. Some specimens wary and difficult to approach, other individuals indifferent, even allowing divers to hold on to their fins and ride them. Harmless to divers, but there are several reports of unprovoked attacks on boats.

47

FAMILY ODONTASPIDIDAE (SANDTIGER SHARKS)

There are four species currently recognized in this family. The sandtiger shark *(Eugomphodus taurus)*, is commonly encountered in reef channels (or gutters) off New South Wales, Australia, near rocky reefs off South Africa, and around ship wrecks off North Carolina; these groupings may be reproductive in nature. The smalltooth sandtiger *(Odontaspis ferox)*, has been observed infrequently by divers near the Kermadec Islands, north of New Zealand. Members of this family have long, dagger-like teeth that protrude from their jaws, large dorsal and anal fins, small pectoral fins, small eyes, and no nictitating membrane. Sandtiger sharks are quite sluggish, but are capable of quick lunges at prey. The sandtiger is ovoviviparous and embryophagous (i.e. developing young engage in intrauterine cannibalism). No data exists on the reproductive mode of the smalltooth sandtiger, but development is probably similar to the sandtiger.

M. Cufer

36. Sandtiger shark *(Eugomphodus taurus)*

Identification: Bulky; snaggle-toothed appearance; dorsal fins set back on body, closer to pelvic base than pectoral base, both dorsal fins about the same size; anal fin large (similar in size to dorsal fins); base color brown, often with small spots. *Size:* Birth 1 m (3.3 ft), maximum length 3.2 m (10.5 ft). *Range:* Wide ranging species; includes western and eastern Atlantic, western Indian Ocean, and western Pacific. Depth range from surface to 200 m (660 ft). *Reproduction:* Litter number usually two; said to aggregate in specific areas for mating. Courtship and copulation have been observed in captivity; male bites and holds female gill region and they maintain a parallel orientation during copulation. Females cease to feed during pregnancy; hydroids grow on teeth due to a lack of use! *Biology:* Temperate to tropical seas; has been observed on or near coral and rocky reefs. Solitary and aggregates. Often found amid large schools of smaller baitfish (which it occasionally eats). Feeds on bony fishes (herrings, croakers, bluefish, eels, remoras, wrasses, mullets, sea robins, groupers, jacks, flatfishes), sharks and rays (spotted eagle ray, sharpnose and dusky sharks). It uses its stomach as a buoyancy compensator; it ingests air at the water's surface and can achieve neutral buoyancy. They often float motionless in the water column. Solitary or aggregates. This species is not aggressive toward divers, with the possible exception of spearfishermen. Adult males are reported to be more aggressive during the mating season.

37. Smalltooth sandtiger *(Odontaspis ferox)*

Identification: Bulky; conical snout; first dorsal fin larger than second dorsal, closer to the pectoral fin base than to the pelvic fin base; gray overall with a lighter, often blotchy belly, some individuals have small reddish spots scattered over body. *Size:* Birth 1 m (3.3 ft), maximum length 3.6 m (11.8 ft). *Range:* Eastern Atlantic from Gulf of Gasconey into the Mediterranean; western Indian Ocean from South Africa and Madagascar; western Pacific from Japan, Australia, New Zealand, and the Kermadec Islands; also Hawaii, southern California, and the Sea of Cortez. Depth range 13-420 m (43-1,386 ft). *Biology:* Inhabits deeper waters in warm temperate and tropical areas and has been observed by divers on coral reefs near drop-offs. Known to aggregate. Like sandtiger shark, this species has been observed swimming amid large schools of baitfish. Feeds on bony fishes, squid, and shrimp. No aggression shown towards divers, but encounters with this shark are no doubt rare.

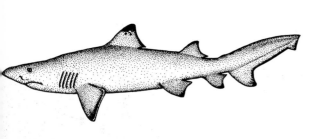

FAMILY ALOPIIDAE (THRESHER SHARKS)

Three species compose this family of unusual sharks. One of these, the pelagic thresher, is occasionally observed by divers around coral reef drop-offs and seamounts. The common thresher *(Alopias vulpinus)* is a circumglobal species that has been encountered near rocky reefs and kelp beds. It differs from *A. pelagicus* in the shape of the pectoral fins (they are pointed in the common thresher) and in the color pattern (the white found on the ventral surface extends up and over the pectoral fin bases in the common thresher). This species is shy and difficult to approach underwater, but there is one report of a specimen attacking a spearfisherman in New Zealand. The third species, the bigeye thresher *(A. superciliosus)*, is generally found in open ocean environments, although it has been caught by fishermen nearshore. All of the thresher sharks are characterized by a long upper caudal lobe that is nearly as long as the body. This exaggerated tail is used to herd and stun schooling fishes and there is an old report of a common thresher tail-slapping a loon that was sitting on the water's surface. These sharks are often foul hooked on long lines when they swat the bait with their caudal fin. At least one species (i.e. *A. vulpinus*) is known to segregate by sex. These sharks are ovoviviparous, and oophagous. The author has observed one species (i.e. the bigeye thresher) with sea lampreys adhereing to the skin near the cloaca. The thresher sharks do poorly in aquariums.

Schmidt

38. Pelagic thresher shark
(Alopias pelagicus)

Identification: Long upper caudal lobe, as long as body; pectoral fins straight with rounded tips; flanks dark colored, white coloration of ventrum does not extend onto sides above pectoral fins. *Size:* Birth 96 cm (3.1 ft), maximum length 3.3 m (10.8 ft). *Range:* Wide ranging in the Indo-Pacific; from Sea of Cortez and the Galapagos Islands to the Red Sea and South Africa. Depth range from surface to 150 m (495 ft). *Reproduction:* Litter number two. *Biology:* Generally oceanic, epipelagic shark that is sometimes observed near coral reef drop-offs or seamounts in the Red Sea, Indonesia, Micronesia, and in the Sea of Cortez. In the Tuamotu Islands, it sometimes enters large lagoons (misidentified there as the common thresher, *A. vulpinus*). Feeds on bony fishes and possibly squid. It often leaps out of water; I observed one specimen breach five times in succession. It is usually shy and difficult for divers to approach.

FAMILY CETORHINIDAE (BASKING SHARKS)

This family contains one large, plankton feeding species. The basking sharks have a conical snout, extremely long gill slits, hair-like gill rakers, pronounced keels on the caudal peduncle, and a lunate tail. They also have a huge liver that makes them almost neutrally buoyant. The basking shark is found in open ocean and inshore environments and occasionally visits rocky reefs. They are migratory and are seasonally abundant. For example, off the coast of Scotland they are most common, in inshore waters in the spring and summer months, while off southern California, they make their appearance during the fall and winter. By swimming through the water with their huge mouths agape, the basking sharks push water and small planktors over their erect gill rakers. The plankton adheres to these mucus covered structures and are squeezed into the mouth when the gill rakers are collapsed. It has been suggested, but not confirmed, that when plankton stocks are low, the basking sharks shed their gill rakers, sink to the ocean floor, and remain torpid until the gill rakers grow back. However, basking sharks without gill rakers have been taken near the surface, apparently feeding. The gill rakers are replaced in approximately 4 to 5 months. Little is known about their reproduction, but basking sharks are thought to be ovoviviparous and oophagous. The females only have one functional ovary and it may contain as many as 6,000,000 ova measuring up to 5 mm (0.2 inches) in diameter! These sharks often have crustacean parasites (copepods), and sometimes lampreys, adhering to their skin.

39. Basking shark *(Cetorhinus maximus)*

M. Kerr

Identification: Conical snout; large gill rakers that almost meet on the ventral surface of head; a lunate, or half-moon, caudal fin; dorsal color brown to slate gray or black, often mottled with lighter areas. The snout is longer and more pointed in young specimens. *Size:* Birth 1.7 m (5.4 ft), maximum length 15 m (48 ft). *Range:* Circumtemperate. Usually observed on the surface. *Reproduction:* Litter number unkown. Mating has not been observed, but courtship may involve males following females. After mating, both sexes have abrasions near the vent region caused by their rough skin contacting one another. From scar patterns in the vagina it has been suggested that females mate more than once in a breeding season. In parts of their range (Scotland) mating occurs in inshore waters in the early summer. After mating, females move offshore where they give birth to their young. *Biology:* This shark occurs in bays and fjords, near offshore islands, and in the open ocean. They are observed singly, in small groups or large aggregations (numbering over 100 individuals). They often swim, and feed, with their first dorsal and upper caudal fins projecting above the water's surface. They filter planktonic crustaceans and fish eggs from the water. They are not aggressive to divers.

FAMILY LAMNIDAE (MACKEREL SHARKS)

Five species make up this group, collectively known as the mackerel shark family. The mackerel sharks have conical snouts, one or two lateral keels on the caudal peduncle, lunate (half-moon shaped) tail fins, large gill-slits, and small second dorsal and anal fins. This group includes the infamous white shark that frequents rocky reef environments and the shortfin mako shark that is known to visit reef drop-offs and kelp beds. Mackerel sharks maintain their body temperature higher than the surrounding water by conserving metabolic heat with a specialized circulatory system (i.e., the rete mirabilia). The white shark maintains its muscle at 3-5° C higher than the ambient water temperature, while the shortfin mako's body temperature is 7-10° C higher. With an elevated body temperature, these sharks increase their digestive rates, metabolic reactions occur more rapidly, and muscles contract faster, which results in a greater predatory efficiency. These sharks most often feed on bony fishes, elasmobranchs, and marine mammals. Stomach content analyses reveal that mako sharks occasionally chase down and eat billfish, but not without risk. For example, one longfin mako *(Isurus paucus)* was captured that had a swordfish rostrum broken off in its abdomen and a shortfin mako was taken that had the fractured bill of a small sailfish embedded in its eye! The mackerel sharks are ovoviviparous and oophagous. Both the white shark and the shortfin mako have attacked swimmers and divers and the white shark is considered to be the most dangerous shark. Public aquariums have little success in long term maintenance of these active animals.

M. Snyderman ▲
▼

40. White Shark *(Carcharodon carcharias)*

Identification: One keel on each side of caudal peduncle; large, serrated, triangular teeth; long gill slits; grayish above, whitish below with sharp demarcation between dorsal and ventral coloration, often with black spot at pectoral fin axil and underside of pectoral fins blacktipped. *Size:* Birth 1.1 m (3.6 ft), adults to at least 6.5 m (21.5 ft) and maybe to 8 m (26.4 ft) in length. *Range:* Found in most temperate and some tropical areas world wide. Depth range from surface to 1,280 m (4,224 ft). *Reproduction:* One litter of nine and another of seven reported. Full term embryos have bulging stomachs; eggs released in the uterus are eaten by the developing young. *Biology:* Found in coastal areas (usually near rocky reefs, rarely near coral reefs), adults are more common in warmer seas than juveniles, but all are more abundant in warm temperate to temperate waters. Solitary individuals, pairs, or sometimes aggregations (especially where prey is abundant) are encountered. Feed on seals, sea lions, dolphins, other sharks, rays, bony fishes, and invertebrates. This is the most fearsome of all sharks and for good reason; has attacked divers, snorkelers, surfers, and bathers.

41. Shortfin mako *(Isurus oxyrinchus)*

Identification: One keel on each side of caudal peduncle; tail lunate; teeth long and curved for grasping prey; dorsal coloration blue, white ventral surface. *Size:* Birth 65 cm (25.6 inches), maximum length 3.9 m (12.9 ft). *Range:* Worldwide in all tropical and temperate seas. Depth range from surface to 152 m (501 ft). *Reproduction:* Litter size 4-16. Courtship and copulation apparently includes biting of the female (on the belly, flanks, pectoral fins, and gill region) by the male. *Biology:* An oceanic shark that has been encountered in kelp beds and near reef drop-offs. Active, thought to be fastest of all shark species. It will leap clear of the water's surface by several body lengths. Diet varies in different locations; off New South Wales, Australia and the northeastern U.S.A. feeds primarily on bony fishes (mackerels, tuna, bluefish, anchovies, lancetfish, cod, sea bass, swordfish), while off South Africa feeds most on small sharks and rays. Remains of marine mammals, squid, and salps also found in mako stomachs. Teeth of large adults have broader cusps and are better suited for cutting up larger prey items than those of juveniles. When bait not present, usually very wary; even in baited situations it can be hesitant to approach and take a bait. It is quick and frenetic, and may makes close passes at the diver when bait is present; it should be treated with considerable caution. Possible threat display consists of jaw gaping and figure eight swimming. Implicated in attacks on divers and swimmers.

FAMILY SCYLIORHINIDAE (CATSHARKS)

The catsharks are the largest shark family, with over 103 described species. These sharks have nictitating membranes, elongated eyes, a first dorsal fin that originates over or behind the pelvic fins, no precaudal pit, a strongly developed lower caudal lobe, and large spiracles. Although many catshark species occupy deep water habitats (e.g. deepwater ghost catsharks, genus *Apristurus*, comprise about 1/3 of the family) a number of these sharks are coral and rocky reef dwellers. These species (e.g., *Atelomycterus* spp.), have elongate bodies and narrow heads that allow entry into interstices, in which they hunt and refuge. Many reef varieties bear attractive color patterns consisting of stripes, spots, saddles, and/or blotches. These color patterns disrupt the catshark's outline against the varied background of the reef. A number of catsharks are nocturnal, spending their days resting on the sea floor. The reef-dwelling species feed on a wide range of food items, including worms, snails, crustaceans, bony fishes, and elasmobranchs. The swell sharks of the genus *Cephaloscyllium* may wedge themselves into reef crevices and inflate the abdomen by swallowing large volumes of water so that it difficult for a large predator to eat. However, inflating does not always work; for example, a balloon shark *(Cephaloscyllium sufflans)* was taken from the stomach of a coelacanth! While the majority of catsharks are oviparous, a few are ovoviviparous. None of the shallow reef dwelling species are live bearers. Copulation has been observed in several species. In many catsharks, the males have longer teeth than the females. This is probably an adaptation to aid them in biting and holding a prospective mate. All these sharks are harmless to divers, but may bite if sufficiently aggravated. Most catsharks adapt readily to captivity and some even breed in public aquariums.

42. Australian spotted catshark
(Asymbolus analis)

Identification: Nasoral grooves absent; nasal flaps do not reach mouth; anal fin about same size or slightly larger than second dorsal and positioned far in front of its origin; color pattern consists of light brown with scattered brown spots, also faint saddles. *Size:* Maximum length 90 cm (35.4 inches). *Range:* Australia (New South Wales around the southern coast to western Australia). Depth range 10-175 m (33-578 ft). *Reproduction:* Deposits brown, tendril eggcase. Eggcases often found in groups, with their tendrils all tangled around a common holdfast. *Biology:* Temperate water shark found on mixed sand and rock substrate. Has also been recorded from bays and estuaries.

R.H. Kuiter

43. Gulf catshark *(Asymbolus vincenti)*

Identification: Similar to proceeding species, but color pattern consists of white spots on a dark brown background and the ventral surface is lighter and unspotted. *Size:* Maximum length 60 cm (23.6 inches). *Range:* Australia (Victoria around southern coast to western Australia). Depth range 2-200 m (7-726 ft), but usually at depths of 130 m (429 ft) or more. *Reproduction:* Two tendril eggcases are deposited at a time. *Biology:* Occurs in temperate waters on mixed reef and sea grass habitats.

44. Coral catshark
(Atelomycterus marmoratus)

Identification: Nasoral grooves present; nasal flaps reach mouth; no distinct saddles with light spots and bars on a dark background and a white belly (the color pattern is extremely variable); dorsal fins with white tips; males have long, narrow claspers. The Australian marbled catshark *(A. macleayi)* is a similar species that differs in color, which consists of gray bands (or saddles) with spots in the light areas between them (see figure in Pictorial Key to Families). *Atelomycterus macleayi* occurs near Australia (western Australia around the northern coast to Queensland). An undescribed *Atelomycterus* sp. has been reported from western Austrailia that has distinct dark brown bands on a lighter background (see figure in Pictorial Key to Families). *Size:* Hatch at about 10 cm (3.9 inches), maximum length of 70 cm (27.6 inches) with one report of 1.5 m (4.9 ft) specimen that was probably erroneously identified. *Range:* Pakistan to New Guinea, Philippines, Thailand, and China. Commonly observed on Indonesian reefs at night. *Reproduction:* Two tendril eggcases deposited at a time. *Biology:* A shallow water, coral reef species with an elongate body which allows movement into reef crevices and among branching corals; however, does not move on paired fins like bamboo sharks. Reported to prey on benthic invertebrates and bony fishes. Nocturnal.

A. Kuiter

45. Blackspotted catshark
(Aulohalaelurus labiosus)

Identification: Nasoral grooves absent; nasal flaps do not reach mouth; anal fin smaller than second dorsal and positioned under it; interdorsal distance 9.7% of total length; color brownish-gray with small dark blotches and a few light spots, with a few obscure saddles, and white-tipped dorsal fins. The only other member of the genus, the Kanakorum catshark *(A. kanakorum)*, was recently described from a specimen collected in New Caledonia. It differs from *A. labiosus* in having large blotches that are fused and form a dark brown reticulated pattern around numerous white blotches, white posterior and anterior fin margins, and an interdorsal distance fo 13.8% of total length (see figure in the Pictoral Key to Families). The kanakorum catshark reaches a maximum length of at least 79 cm (31 inches). *Size:* Maximum length 67 cm (26.4 inches). *Range:* Western Australia. A shallow water species that has been recorded at depths to only 4 m (13.2 ft). *Biology:* Common, but rarely observed due to its nocturnal habits. Hides during day in reef crevices.

R.H. Kuiter

46. Draughtsboard shark
(Cephaloscyllium isabellum)

Identification: Large, broad head with wide mouth; no labial furrows; nasal flaps do not reach mouth; second dorsal fin much smaller than first dorsal; color pattern of dark saddles and blotches (checker board pattern, hence the name) on a brown, sometimes golden background, with ventral surface light and not spotted. *Size:* Hatch at 16 cm (6.3 inches), maximum length commonly 1 m (3.3 ft), possibly up to 2m (6.6 ft). *Range:* New Zealand; common around Stewart Island. Depth range of 18-220 m (59-726 ft). *Reproduction:* Deposits two tendril eggcases at a time. Eggcase is cream color and 12 cm (4.7 inches) long. *Biology:* Occurs in crevices and caves of rocky reefs during the day, but may move onto adjacent sandy areas at night. It eats a wide range of fishes (spiney dogfish, cod, sand perch, blennies) and invertebrates (octopuses, squids, snails, innkeeper worms, krill, hermit crabs, brachyuran crabs, spiny lobster). May suck innkeeper worms out of their burrows. One of the most unusual components of their diet are tunicates (sea squirts). When large lobsters are eaten, the shark will often swim around with the antennae protruding from its mouth for hours. Adults segregate by sex.

47. Australian swell shark
(Cephaloscyllium laticeps)

Identification: Similar to draughtsboard shark (may be the same species). The color pattern is slightly different, with fewer saddles and numerous blotches, of varying sizes between them, and a background color gray to brown. *Size:* Hatching size of 16 cm (6.3 inches), maximum 1.5 m (5 ft). *Range:* Australia (New South Wales around the southern coast to south Australia. Common around Tasmania). Depth range 6-650 m (20-2,145 ft). *Reproduction:* The tendril eggcase of this species differs from that of the draughtsboard shark in that it has transverse ridges across it. Breeds in the Australian summer. *Biology:* Found on sand and mud bottoms, as well as rocky reefs. It feeds on fishes and large crustaceans. Harmless.

N. Coleman

48. Blotchy swell shark
(Cephaloscyllium umbratile)

Identification: Similar to draughtsboard shark, but the color pattern is different. Overall color is lighter, with irregular saddles and numerous blotches and a ventral surface that is not spotted. *Size:* Hatch at 16-22 cm (6.3-8.7 inches), maximum length 1.2 m (4 ft). Females larger than males. *Range:* Japan to the South China Sea and possibly to New Guinea. Depth range 20-200 m (66-660 ft). *Reproduction:* Two tendril eggcases deposited at one time. Reproductive season not well defined. Eggs hatch after about 1 year. *Biology:* A rocky reef dweller. Bony fishes are the primary component of their diet (mackerel, sardines, filefishes, moray eels, dragonets, flatfishes, cowfishes). They also eat elasmobranchs. Eight species of sharks (including juvenile swell sharks), skates, electric rays, and the eggcases of a catshark and a skate have been found in their stomachs. Squid are also commonly eaten. Harmless. Thrives and even breeds in public aquariums.

R.H. Kuiter
D. Gotshall

49. Swell shark
(Cephaloscyllium ventriosum)

Identification: Nasal flaps reach the mouth; ventral surface is spotted. *Size:* Hatch at 14 cm (5.5 inches), maximum 1 m (3.3 ft). *Range:* Central California to southern Mexico, and also reported near central Chile. Depth range 5-457 m (16-1,508 ft). *Reproduction:* Females lay amber colored, tendril eggcases that hatch in 7.5-10 months. Developing embryos are occasionally consumed by snails that bore through the protective casing. Young have enlarged denticles along the back that aid in escaping from the eggcase; the denticles disappear soon after hatching. Mate and lay eggs in captivity. *Biology:* A rocky reef dweller, most common in kelp forests. Solitary or aggregations of individuals found in crevices during the day. Active at night, when they have been observed moving onto adjacent sand bottom to feed on blacksmith. Use a sit-and-wait strategy to capture these fish. Feeds on bony fishes and crustaceans. Along the California coast this species has disappeared from areas where it once was common, possibly as a result of changes in sea temperatures. Harmless. Does well in captivity.

Debelius

50. Smallspotted catshark (*Scyliorhinus canicula*)

Identification: Second dorsal fin smaller than first dorsal fin; no upper labial furrows; no nasal barbels, nasal flaps broad, extending to mouth; has nasoral grooves; many small dark and sometimes light spots over body; 8 to 10 dusky saddles sometimes present. *Size:* Hatch at 10 cm (3.9 inches), maximum length 1 m (3.3 ft). *Range:* Norway, British Isles, Mediterranean, to Ivory Coast. Depth range from intertidal zone to 400 m (1,320 ft). *Reproduction:* Two tendril eggcases (4-7 cm, 1.6-2.8 inches, long) deposited at one time, 18-20 in a breeding season. Female swims around algae, or other suitable anchoring sites, until extruding tendrils catch and the egg is pulled from the cloaca. Hatch in 5-11 months. Copulation observed in the wild and in captivity; the male coils around the female and inserts one clasper during mating. Other males have been observed to interfere, biting the copulating female. *Biology:* Common temperate water, rocky reef shark, also found on sand and mud bottoms. Adults segregate by sex and move into deeper water during the mating season. Inactive during daytime and hunt at night. Primary components of diet are molluscs (squid, whelks, scallops, clams) and crustaceans (hermit crabs, swimming crabs, lobsters, shrimp), but they also eat bony fishes (sea horses, dragonets, goatfishes, hake, gobies, flatfishes), worms, and sea cucumbers. Harmless. Does well in captivity.

A. Purcell
Soichi Hagiwara

51. Nurse hound *(Scyliorhinus stellaris)*

Identification: Stocky build; nasal flaps narrow and do not extend to mouth, no nasoral grooves; large and small dark spots on the fins and body, sometimes has white spots. *Size:* Hatch at 16 cm (6.3 cm), maximum length 1.6 m (5.3 ft). *Range:* Scandinavia, British Isles to Mediterranean, possibly to West Africa. Depth range from intertidal zone to 125 m (413 ft). *Reproduction:* Two tendril eggcases (12 cm, 4.7 inches long) are deposited in algae during spring and summer. Eggcases are often found in tide pools. Eggs hatch in 9 months. *Biology:* Rocky reef dweller. Diurnally quiescent, active at night. Diet consists of crustaceans (hermit crabs, swimming crabs, shrimp), squid, octopuses, bony fishes (mackerel, dragonets, gurnards, flatfishes) and other sharks (small-spotted catshark). Harmless. Has lived as long as 19 years in captivity.

52. Cloudy catshark *(Scyliorhinus torazame)*

Identification: Narrow head; small nasal flaps that do not extend to mouth, no nasoral grooves; color consists of dark saddles on the back with a few dark and light spots of varying size. The skin is very rough. A similar species, the Izu catshark *(S. tokubee)*, has been described from near the Izu Pennisula of southern Japan. It differs from the cloudy catshark in having an interdorsal distance shorter than the mouth width, and dark reddish brown saddles and blotches on the dorsal and lateral surfaces with numerous yellowish spots. *Size:* Hatch at 9 cm (3.5 inches), maximum length 50 cm (19.7 inches). *Range:* Japan to the Philippines. From shallow water to 100 m (330 ft). *Reproduction:* Deposit two tendril eggcases at one time in specific nesting areas. Eggcases 6 cm (2.4 inches) in length hatch in 15 months at 11.3° C (52.4° F) and 7-9 months at 14.5° C (58.1° F). Copulation observed in captivity, in this species and the Izu catshark. Male bites the female's side, coils around her, and inserts a single clasper. Mating lasts about 4 minutes. Breeds all year round. *Biology:* Known from rocky reef areas. Nonmigratory. Harmless. Does well in captivity, with longevity records of over 12 years.

53. Leopard catshark (*Poroderma pantherinum*)

Identification: Second dorsal fin smaller than first dorsal; long nasal barbel; variable color pattern of dark spots or broken rings on a white to gray background. The sympatric pajama catshark (*P. africanum*) has dark longitudinal stripes and attains 1 m (3.3 ft) in lenth. *Size:* Maximum length 74 cm (29 inches). *Range:* South Africa. Depth range from intertidal zone to 256 m (845 ft). *Reproduction:* Deposits two tendril egg cases at one time. In *P. africanum* eggcases are deposited every three days during the breeding season and hatch about 5.5 months. *Biology:* Common on rocky reefs. Solitary specimens or aggregations found in caves and crevices by day. Actively hunts at night. Feeds predominantly on bony fishes, also eats some worms, cephalopods, crustaceans. the related *P. africanum* feeds predominantly on mantis shrimp, shrimp, crabs, but also consumes bony fishes (anchovies, gurnards, hake), squid, octopuses, cuttlefish, worms, and clams. this is a hardy aquarium shark.

S. Chater

54. Tiger catshark (*Halaelurus natalensis*)

Identification: Tip of snout pointed and upturned; head broad; dorsal color yellowish-brown with broad bars and dusky saddles and no spots on body. *Size:* Maximum length 47 cm (18.5 inches). *Range:* South Africa and Mozambique. Depth range from shallow water to depths of 172 m (568 ft). *Reproduction:* Lays 12-22 eggcases at one time. Tendril eggcase about 4 cm (1.6 inches) which remains in female's oviducts for most of the embryo's development. *Biology:* Occurs on sand bottoms and reefs. Feeds on crabs, shrimp, squid, bony fishes, and small sharks.

R. Van Der Elst
S. Chater

55. Puffadder shyshark (*Haploblepharus edwardsii*)

Identification: Dorsal fins about equal in size; nasal flaps broad and extend to mouth, nasoral grooves present; color pattern of reddish-brown saddles that have darker margins and light spots about the size of the spiracles. The sympatric brown puffadder shark (*H. fuscus*) is similar to this species morphologically, but is plain brown in color. *Size:* Hatch at 10 cm (3.9 inches), maximum length 60 cm (23.6 inches). *Range:* South Africa. Depth range from intertidal zone to 130 m (429 ft); more common at shallower depths in the more southern part of its range. *Reproduction:* Two eggcases about 5 cm (2 inches) in length are deposited simultaneously. Eggs have hair-like filaments that anchor them to reef structure. *Biology:* Occurs on sand and rock bottoms. Feeds on bony fishes (anchovies, jacks, gobies, gapers), crustaceans (mysids, shrimp, mantis shrimp, crabs, hermit crabs), squid, and worms.

FAMILY TRIAKIDAE (SMOOTHHOUND SHARKS)

The smoothhound shark family is composed of 34 species that have well developed dorsal fins, with the first dorsal fin positioned well ahead of pelvic fins, elongated eyes, no precaudal pits, short anterior nasal flaps that are not barbel-like (except in the whiskery shark), and nictitating eye lids. Although most smoothhounds occur near continental coastlines, few are resident to reef environments. They are active sharks that spend most of their time swimming just above the bottom. Occasionally, they rest motionlessly on the ocean floor, but only for short periods of time. Most of the smoothhounds are drab colored without markings, however there are some exceptions. Members of the genus Mustelus are either viviparous or ovoviviparous, while those of the genera *Furgaleus, Galeorhinus,* and *Triakis* are ovoviviparous. Most of these sharks form large reproductive aggregations at specific times of the year. In an old account, captive male dusky smoothhound (Mustelus canis) were observed to try and mate with each other in the absence of females! In this same study, males were reported to insert both claspers simultaneously during copulation. Several smoothhounds are commonly eaten by other sharks species (sevengill sharks and white sharks). Scuba divers have a difficult time getting near these fish, but smoothhounds are readily approached by snorkelers. Many of these sharks *(Mustelus spp.)* are considered good for aquarium display, but because they often fall prey to larger sharks, they are best mixed with smaller sharks and rays.

56. Whiskery shark *(Furgaleus macki)*

Identification: No nasoral grooves and nasal flaps that are long and slender (barbel-like); has a hump-backed appearance; dorsal fins about equal in size; body color gray above with light saddles that are more distinct in juveniles. *Size:* Birth size 20 cm (7.9 inches), maximum length 1.6 m (5.3 ft). *Range:* Australia (Victoria around southern coast to western Australia). *Reproduction:* Litter number 9-11. *Biology:* Commonly associates with kelp beds and rocky reefs. Active shark that feeds on octopuses, squid, small lobsters, and bony fishes. Harmless.

CSIRO

57. School shark *(Galeorhinus galeus)*

Identification: Nasal flaps small; second dorsal fin smaller than first dorsal; terminal lobe of tail long, about half of the length of entire caudal fin. *Size:* Birth 35 cm (13.8 inches), maximum length 2 m (6.6 ft). *Range:* Circumtemperate. Depth range from the surface to 471 m (1,554 ft). *Reproduction:* Litter number 6-52, with larger females having bigger litters. *Biology:* Active, schooling species sometimes found on rocky reefs. Sexual segregation known in some populations, with males occurring closer inshore than females. Regularly frequent nursery areas. In spring and early summer, females give birth in shallow bays and estuaries. Juveniles may remain in these areas for up to 2 years before moving offshore in schools. Feed predominantly on bony fishes (herring, salmon, cod, croakers, wrasses, damselfishes, gobies, kelpfishes, scorpionfishes). Also eat squid, octopuses, crabs, shrimp, snails, worms, echinoderms, and other elasmobranchs (small sharks, stingrays, skates). In turn, eaten by larger sharks. Males mature at 8 years, females 11 years. Harmless. Swims constantly in captivity. Will adapt to captivity if carefully captured and handled.

58. Starry smoothhound *(Mustelus asterias)*

Identification: Snout moderately long; distance between nostrils narrow (2 to 2.6% of total length); upper labial furrows longer than lower ones; pectoral and pelvic fins small; color gray with white spots on flanks and dorsum, light ventrum. The only spotted smoothhound that occurs around Europe. A similar species, the starspotted smoothhound *(M. manazo)*, occurs in the western North Pacific and western Indian Ocean. It differs from the starry smoothhound in the number of vertebrae and its smaller size (it attains a maximum length of 1.2 m, 3.8 ft). The whitespotted smoothhound *(M. palumbes)* is also similar, and differs in having larger pectoral and pelvic fins. This species occurs around the coast of southern Africa. *Size:* Birth 30 cm (12 inches), maximum length 1.4 m (4.5 ft). *Range:* British Isles to the Mediterranean and the Canary Islands. Depth range from intertidal zone to 100 m (330 ft). *Reproduction:* Litter number 7-15, number is dependent on the size of the female; gestation about 12 months. *Biology:* Occurs over sand, mud, and gravel bottoms. Feeds mainly on crustaceans (crabs, hermit crabs, slipper lobsters, lobsters). The closely related *M. manazo* also feeds heavily on crustaceans, but also eats fish (jacks, herring, filefish, mackerel), worms, and clams.

M. Kerr

59. Gray smoothhound
(Mustelus californicus)

Identification: First dorsal closer to pelvic fins than pectoral fins; dorsal fins triangular; ventral lobe of tail poorly developed; no spots, uniform gray color. Albino specimens reported. *Size:* Birth 20-30 cm (7.9-11.8 inches), maximum length 1.2 m (4 ft). *Range:* Coastal waters of northern California, south to Sea of Cortez. Depth range from intertidal zone to 90 m (300 ft). *Reproduction:* Litter number 2-16 young. *Biology:* Common in temperate waters in muddy bays and over sand bottoms. Occasionally visit rocky reefs, often associating with schools of leopard sharks. Feed primarily on crabs, but also eat innkeeper worms, squid, shrimp, mantis shrimp, and bony fishes (midshipmen, croaker, herring). I examined gray smoothhound stomachs in the Sea of Cortez that were packed with krill. This is a schooling species that is difficult to approach underwater. Harmless.

D.J. Wrobel

60. Brown smoothhound *(Mustelus henlei)*

Identification: Similar to **gray** smoothhound, but the posterior edges of dorsal fins are frayed and the origin of the first dorsal fin is over pectoral fins. Color bronze to gray above, lighter below, without spots. *Size:* Birth size 20 cm (7.9 inches), maximum length 95 cm (3.1 ft). *Range:* Northern California, south to the Sea of Cortez, Ecuador, and Peru. Depth range from intertidal zone to 200 m (660 ft). *Reproduction:* Litter number 3-9. *Biology:* Active, temperate water shark most often found over muddy or sandy substrates. Occasionally visits rocky reefs. Crabs are this shark's primary food, but also eats shrimp, mantis shrimp, squid, tunicates, and bony fishes (adults eat more fish than juveniles). In a study I carried out, 97% of 37 individuals examined from a "single net sample" contained large numbers of krill. Will grasp and rip the claws off large crabs before ingesting them. Solitary or in schools. Important prey for broadnose sevengill shark. Harmless.

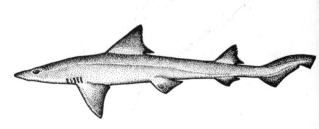

61. Spotted estuary smoothhound (Mustelus lenticulatus)

Identification: Upper labial furrows much longer than lower ones; gray to brown above with white spots. Closely related to the gummy shark *(M. antarcticus)* of Australia. Differs in size of the pelvic fins (smaller in *M. antarcticus)* and the number of vertebrae centra. These two species are similar to *M. asterias.* *Size:* Birth 31 cm (12.2 inches), maximum length 1.4 m (4.6 ft). *Range:* New Zealand. Depth range from intertidal zone to 220 m (726 ft). *Reproduction:* Litter number 2-23; gestation period about 11 months. Females give birth in offshore waters and return to shallow coastal areas to mate. *Biology:* Temperate water shark most often encountered over sand and mud substrates. Occasionally occurs on rocky reefs. Their winter habitat is not known (possibly deep waters of continental slope), but in spring and summer these fish aggregate in shallow areas. Females make longer migrations than males at this time and utilize energy reserves stored in their livers. Predator on benthic invertebrates. Major prey of both sexes include hermit crabs, brachyuran crabs, and snails, but males feed more on innkeeper worms than females. The related gummy shark feeds heavily on fish. Fed upon by groupers, cod, and porbeagle sharks. Will rest on the sea floor. Harmless. Does well in large public aquariums.

62. Smoothhound shark *(Mustelus mustelus)*

Identification: Snout short and broad; upper labial furrows longer than lower ones; usually uniform brown or gray, some individuals have dark spots. This species is closely related to the dusky smoothhound *(M. canis)* from the western Atlantic (ranges from Massachusetts to Argentina). It differs in having less distance between the nostrils and shorter upper labial furrows. The Arabian smoothhound *(M. mosis),* which has been observed on coral reefs, ranges from India to South Africa, including the Red Sea. It differs from *M. mustelus* in having upper labial furrows that are about equal in length to the lower ones. *Mustelus mosis* is not sympatric with any other smooth-hound over most of its range. *Size:* Birth 39 cm (15 inches), maximum length 1.6 m (5.2 ft). *Range:* France and the British Isles south to southern Africa. *Reproduction:* Litter number 4-15; gestation 10-11 months. *Biology:* Found nearshore, sometimes around rocky reefs, from intertidal zone to 350 m (1,120 ft). Preys primarily on crustaceans (lobsters, crabs, hermit crabs, mantis shrimp), but also eats cephalopods and bony fishes (snake eels). Swims just over, or lies, on the bottom. This species adapts readily to captivity.

M.J. Smale ▲
▼

63. Sharptooth houndshark (Triakis megalopterus)

Identification: Second dorsal fin about equal in size to first dorsal; dorsal fin rear margins vertical, not inclined forward; broad snout; pectoral fins falcate; dorsal coloration gray, lighter ventrally, often (but not always) has irregular-sized black spots over body and fins. The spotted houndshark *(T. maculata)* is a similar species that occurs from Peru to Chile, and around the Galapagos Islands. In the spotted houndshark the rear margins f the dorsal fins are inclined forward (see figure in Pictorial Key to Families); it attains a maximum length of 2.4 m (7.7 ft) *Size:* Birth 31 cm (12.2 inches), maximum length 1.7 m (5.6 ft). *Range:* South Africa. Depth range from intertidal zone to 50 m (165 ft). *Reproduction:* Litter number up to 12. In summer, females congregate in bays to give birth. *Biology:* Temperate water shark that favors sandy bottoms and rocky reefs. Most often swims just above bottom, but also found resting in reef crevices. Preys on crabs, bony fishes, and catsharks.

64. Leopard shark *(Triakis semifasciata)*

Identification: Color distinct, with black saddles and spots on a gray-bronzy background. One albino specimen reported. *Size:* Birth 20 cm (7.9 inches), maximum length 1.8 cm (5.9 ft). *Range:* Oregon to central coast of Mexico. Depth range from intertidal zone to 90 m (300 ft). *Reproduction:* Litter number 4-29; gestation 12 months. It gives birth in spring, with coastal bays serving as nursery grounds. Courtship includes the male biting the female. *Biology:* Usually found in coastal areas, it frequents rocky reefs (often in vicinity of kelp beds) and muddy and sandy bays. Often aggregate in shallow water, sometimes in mixed schools with smoothhound sharks and spiny dogfish. Will rest on bottom, but usually swims just above it. Diet includes crabs, shrimp, clams, innkeeper worms, octopuses, bony fishes (anchovies, herring, surf perches, gobies, rockfishes, sculpins, flatfishes), fish eggs, and elasmobranchs (smoothhounds, guitarfishes, bat rays). Feed on several types of infaunal invertebrates that are sucked or dug from the substrate. Generally shy underwater, although large aggregations sometimes oblivious to snorkelers. Scuba divers can more easily approach these sharks at night. Harmless, although there is a report of a leopard shark charging a diver with a nose bleed. Long lived in captivity, with longevity reports of over 20 years.

M.D. Conlin (bottom)
R.H. Kuiter

65. Banded houndshark *(Triakis scyllium)*

Identification: Pectoral fins are broad and triangular; first dorsal fin rear edge almost vertical; young specimens with dusky saddles and small dark spots on body, these may fade or disappear in adults. *Size:* Birth 23 cm (9 inches), maximum length 1.5 m (5 ft). *Range:* Siberia to China, Japan, and the Koreas. *Reproduction:* Litter number 9-26; gestation 11-12 months. Mating occurs with the male and female in a parallel orientation while the male grasps the female's pectoral fin in his mouth. Breed in the summer in Japan. *Biology:* Found in temperate water on rocky reefs, also in estuaries and eelgrass beds. Aggregations sometimes found piled on top of one another in caves. Feed on bony fishes and crustaceans. Nocturnal. Harmless. Does well in captivity with specimens surviving for over 5 years in public aquariums.

FAMILY CARCHARHINIDAE (REQUIEM SHARKS)

This family is familiar to divers, because a number of its members are frequently encountered on coral reefs. There are 50 described species in this family. Many of these, especially members of the genus *Carcharhinus*, are difficult to differentiate underwater and are most easily separated on the basis of tooth morphology and dental counts, characters that are not easy for divers to examine. Fin position, fin form, fin markings, fin size, build, and snout shape are all characteristics helpful for identification in the field. Features shared by all members of this family include a circular eye, nictitating eyelids, a first dorsal fin positioned well ahead of the pelvic fins, precaudal pits, and a well developed lower caudal lobe. Most of these sharks are active predators on large invertebrates, bony fishes, and other elasmobranchs. Members of this family are viviparous (placental viviparity) except for tiger sharks, which are ovoviviparous (yolk sac viviparity). They range in length from 70 cm (27.6 inches) to over 5 m (16.5 ft), and a number of requiem sharks reach over 2 m (6.6 ft) in length. Many of these sharks make long, seasonal migrations, moving to warmer waters in cooler months. Because of the large size of these sharks and their affinity for areas frequented by humans (i.e., tropical, shallow, coastal areas), they are probably responsible for more attacks on people (including divers) than any other family of sharks. Even though certain species are potentially dangerous, many of the carcharhinids are difficult to approach underwater and baiting is often necessary to bring them into camera range. They vary in suitability for display at public aquariums; some, like the lemon, whitetip reef, bull, oceanic whitetip, Caribbean reef, and sandbar sharks do well in large shark tanks while others, like the tiger shark, rarely acclimate to aquarium life.

66. Sicklefin lemon shark
(Negaprion acutidens)

Identification: Dorsal, pectorals, and pelvic fins falcate; dorsal fins about the same size; a broad head; overall color yellowish-brown. *Size:* Birth 45-80 cm (17.7-31 inches), maximum length 3.1 m (10.2 ft). *Range:* Wide ranging in the central Pacific, western Pacific, and Indian ocean. Depth range from intertidal zone to 30 m (99 ft). *Reproduction:* Litter number 1-18; gestation period 10 months. *Biology:* Frequents lagoons, estuaries, and reef face habitats. Will rest on the sea floor. Juveniles move onto tidal flats at high tide to feed and seek refuge from larger sharks. Have relatively small home range, with tagged individuals being recaptured in same area after 4 years at liberty. Feeds most on bony fishes (triggerfish, parrotfish, bream, mullet, batfish, jacks, porcupinefish), but also eats crabs, shrimp, octopuses, and stingrays. Never provoke this fish and give it wide berth if encountered. I have snorkeled with aggregations of juvenile and adolescent specimens on a number of occasions and found them to be shy and difficult to approach, but there are reports of smaller individuals attempting to bite waders and of larger specimens fervently attacking divers after being harassed.

D. Perrine

67. Lemon shark *(Negaprion brevirostris)*

Identification: Fins less falcate and the teeth of larger individuals are more deeply serrated than the sicklefin lemon shark. *Size:* Birth 63 cm (24.8 inches), maximum length 3.4 m (11.2 ft). *Range:* Atlantic coast of U.S.A. to southern Brazil, east African coast, Sea of Cortez to Ecuador. Depth range from intertidal zone to 92 m (303 ft). *Reproduction:* Litter number 4-17. A male and female swam side by side during presumed mating in captivity. Females bear tooth marks, indicating biting during courtship. *Biology:* Juveniles common on sand flats and mangrove areas in lagoons, while adults are found in lagoons as well as off reef faces in deeper water. Solitary or aggregate, commonly associate with schools of jacks. Home range about 18-93 square km (7-36 square miles), with younger sharks ranging over a smaller area than adults. Activity peaks at twilight. Primary food of juveniles is bony fishes (toadfish, pinfish) and shrimp. Adults feed mainly on fishes (catfish, mullet, jacks, croaker, spiny boxfish, cowfish, guitarfish, stingrays, sharks), but also crabs, sea birds, and conchs. Will bite if provoked and suspected of being involved in unprovoked attacks. Not generally aggressive toward divers, but deserves respect.

68. Whitetip reef shark *(Triaenodon obesus)*

Identification: Very broad snout; pectoral fins and dorsal fins have pointed tips, and the first dorsal and caudal fins bear white tips; color gray to brown above (sometimes with darker blotches). *Size:* Birth 56 cm (22 inches), maximum length 2.1 m (6.9 ft). *Range:* Most of the tropical Indo-Pacific; in eastern Pacific near Cocos and Galapagos Islands, Islas de Revillagigedo, and Panama to Costa Rica. Depth range from intertidal zone to 40 m (132 ft). *Reproduction:* Litter number 1-5; gestation period 13 months. During copulation male seizes female pectoral fin in his mouth and inserts a single clasper while in a parallel orientation. Copulation lasts from 1.5 to 3 minutes. Male may also bite female's gill area during courtship. *Biology:* Rests in caves, under ledges, or in reef gutters (often in groups) during the day. Found in lagoons, on reef flats, and reef faces (where it is most abundant). Most active at night. Individuals might return to the same cave or crevice every day, sometimes for years. Feeds on bony fishes (eels, parrotfishes, goatfishes, snappers, damselfishes, surgeonfishes, triggerfishes) crabs, lobsters, and octopuses. Indifferent toward divers; however, may become aggressive when mistreated or when food is present (when spearfishing).

"BLACKTIP" SHARKS (genus *Carcharhinus*)

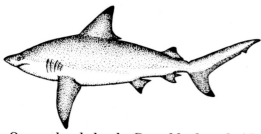

Queensland shark, *C. amblyrhnychoides*
(see species account number 71)
Range: Gulf of Aden to Australia and Gulf of Thailand.

Blacktip shark, *C. limbatus*
(see species account number 79)
Range: Circumglobal, in tropical and subtropical seas.

Whitecheek shark, *C. dussumieri*
(low interdorsal ridge, first dorsal triangular and erect, with a sloping rear margin, dorsal fin not falcate)
Range: Arabian Sea to Java and Japan

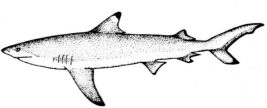

Blacktip reef shark, *C. melanopterus*
(see species account number 81)
Range: Widespread in Indian and Pacific Oceans.

Pondicherry shark, *C. hemiodon*
(first dorsal rear tip long, 5.9-6.5% of total length)
Range: Oman to New Guinea, to China and Australia.

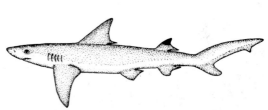

Blackspot shark, *C. sealei*
(large eyes; small falcate dorsal and pectoral fins)
Range: East Africa to China and Australia.

Smoothtooth shark, *C. leiodon*
(pointed snout, first dorsal origin over middle of the pectoral inner margin)
Range: Gulf of Aden.

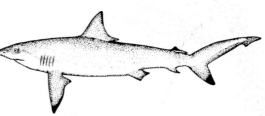

Spottail shark, *C. sorrah*
(see species account number 85)
Range: East Africa to China and Australia.

69. Blacknose shark
(Carcharhinus acronotus)

Identification: Origin of second dorsal near origin of anal fin; small first dorsal and pectoral fins; second dorsal fin origin over or slightly in front of anal fin origin: anal fin posterior margin deeply notched: black blotch usually present on underside of snout; second dorsal fin and tip of tail with dark markings. *Size:* Birth 43 cm (16.8 inches), maximum length 2 m (6.6 ft). *Range:* North Carolina to southern Brazil. Depth range from intertidal zone to 38 m (125 ft). *Reproduction:* Litter number 3-6; gestation 10-11 months. Pregnant females found in Florida waters from November to January. *Biology:* Occurs near coral reefs. Adults segregate during parts of the year. A fast, active species that feeds on small bony fishes (pinfish, croakers, porgies, spiny boxfishes, porcupinefishes) and octopuses. In turn, it is often eaten by larger sharks. Often associates with schools of small fishes (mullet, anchovies). Shows possible threat display similar to gray reef shark: arches back, lowers tail, and raises snout. Apparently harmless.

70. Silvertip shark
(Carcharhinus albimarginatus)

Identification: Stocky build; edges and tips of first dorsal, pelvic, and caudal fins white; fins not broad but taper at the ends. *Size:* Birth 65 cm (25.6 inches), maximum length 3 m (9.9 ft). *Range:* Red Sea to Southern Africa, Japan to New Guinea and Australia (common on the northern Barrier Reef and in the Coral Sea), east to Colombia. Depth range from intertidal zone to 10 m (33 ft). *Reproduction:* Litter number 1-11. Females observed with mating wounds; sometimes with the top of first dorsal bitten off. *Biology:* Found around coral reefs, usually in deeper water (greater than 30 m, 99 ft) on the reef face. Young occur in shallow areas, occasionally in lagoons. Adult home range may extend for 5 km (3 miles) along the reef face. Solitary individuals, pairs, and aggregations observed. An active species that feeds on pelagic and benthic bony fishes (scorpionfishes, lanternfishes, flyingfishes, tuna, wrasses, wahoo, parrotfishes, porcupinefishes), other sharks, eagle rays, and octopuses. Clouds of rainbow runner observed swimming beside and chafing against this shark. When bait is not present, this species is generally shy and rarely approaches too near to a diver. Juveniles are often more inquisitive than adults. In a feeding situation, it may make close, persistent approaches; they have chased divers out of the water. Attacks on divers reported in Micronesia and New Guinea in baited situations.

CSIRO

71. Queensland Shark
(Carcharhinus amblyrhynchoides)

Identification: Second dorsal, pectorals, and lower caudal black tipped; thick bodied; wedge shaped snout (shorter and less pointed than blacktip shark); first dorsal origin just behind or over pectoral axil. *Size:* Birth 53 cm (21 inches), maximum length 1.6 m (5.1 ft). *Range:* Gulf of Aden to Australia, north to Gulf of Thailand. *Biology:* This is a coral reef shark, observed on mud flats near mangrove swamps, in lagoons, reef passes, and on the reef face. Intertidal zone to depths of at least 10 m (32 ft). Solitary, or in aggregations. Feed primarily on small to medium sized bony fishes (anchovies, catfishes, halfbeak, barramundi, groupers, threadfins, mudskipper, tuskfish) and to a lesser degree on crustaceans (shrimps, crabs, lobsters and cephalopods). Move into nearshore areas to feed at night. Will approach divers and may attempt to steal speared fish. Not usually aggressive, but local New Guinea spearfishermen leave the water when there are several Queensland sharks in the area that begin to swim rapidly or erratically.

72. Gray reef shark
(Carcharhinus amblyrhynchos)

Identification: Prominent black band along trailing edge of tail; no black marking on first dorsal fin; snout moderately long; no interdorsal ridge; dorsal color gray. In some geographical areas (Indian Ocean) the posterior first dorsal margin is white. Considered here to be synonymous with the blacktail reef shark *(C. wheeleri)*. *Size:* Birth 50 cm (19.7 inches), maximum length 1.8 cm (5.9 ft). *Range:* Madagascar and Red Sea to Easter Island, north to Hawaiian Islands, south to Lord Howe Island. Depth range from intertidal zone to 274 m (904 ft). *Reproduction:* Litter number 1-6; gestation about 12 months. *Biology:* Often observed on the reef face and in reef channels, especially in areas with strong current. Sometimes in loose groups or schools (with as many as 100 individuals in a group) during the day in a limited area. At night, individuals disperse and move over large area, often enter the shallow part of the lagoon. Average home range is 4.2 square km (1.6 square miles). Individuals may also move into reef passes at ebb tide. Major components of this shark's diet are small bony fishes, (morays, needle fishes, coronetfishes, soldierfishes, surgeonfishes, butterflyfishes), cephalopods, and crustaceans. Groups of these sharks have been observed herding schooling fish up against the reef before attacking. It is a curious species that should not be rapidly approached by a diver; if they are threatened they exhibit the well studied threat display. This species is probably responsible for more attacks on divers than any other coral reef species.

73. Bronze whaler shark
(Carcharhinus brachyurus)

Identification: Fins have no distinct markings (sometimes with dusky pectoral tips); small dorsal fins; long pectoral fins; long, sharply rounded snout; no interdorsal ridge; bronze to gray dorsal coloration, white band on side, lighter ventrally. *Size:* Birth 64 cm (25.1 inches), maximum length 2.9 m (9.6 ft). *Range:* Wide ranging in warm temperate and subtropical seas of both hemispheres; especially common around southern Australia, northern New Zealand, Japan, South Africa, southern California, and Peru. Depth range from intertidal zone to 100 m (330 ft). *Reproduction:* Litter number 13-20. *Biology:* Rocky reef species, found inshore in shallow bays, harbors, and around offshore islands. Migrate into warmer waters in the winter. This shark feeds on bony fishes (sardines, kahawai, gurnards, sea catfishes, hake, sole), sharks, rays (torpedo rays, stingrays, sawfish), sea snakes, and squid. Follows and feeds on schooling fish species, sometimes in shallow water. Usually indifferent to divers, but when feeding stimulus is present, it can become aggressive. Reported to attack bathers and surfers. Often does not adapt to aquarium life, abrading nose on sides of the tank.

R.H. Kuiter
CSIRO

74. Nervous shark *(Carcharhinus cautus)*

Identification: Short, rounded snout; no interdorsal ridge; dorsal fin low with sharply rounded or pointed apex; pectoral fins short; no interdorsal ridge; similar in overall morphology to blacktip reef shark, but fins not edged or tipped with black. *Size:* Birth 35 cm (13.8 inches), maximum length 1.5 m (5 ft). *Range:* Australia (Queensland, around northern coast to western Australia) and Solomon Islands. *Reproduction:* Litter number 1-5; gestation period 8-9 months. *Biology:* Shallow water, coral reef, and estuarine species that feeds primarily on bony fishes (jacks, sea catfishes, sardines, mojarras, needle fishes), but also feeds on crabs, mantis shrimp, shrimp, molluscs, and sea snakes. A shy species that apparently avoids divers.

A. Klapfer

75. Silky shark *(Carcharhinus falciformis)*

Identification: Sleek looking shark; snout relatively long; interdorsal ridge present; dorsal fin low, with a rounded apex, and originating behind pectoral fins; second dorsal with long free tip (usually two times the height of this fin); long pectoral fins; ventral surface of pectoral and pelvic fins may have dusky tips, dorsal color variable, from dark brown to blue gray. *Size:* Birth 70-87 cm (27.6-34.2 inches), maximum length 3.3 m (10.9 ft). *Range:* Circumtropical. Depth range from surface to 500 m (1,650 ft). *Reproduction:* Litter number 2-14. *Biology:* An oceanic shark that is observed near reef drop-offs (adjacent to deep water), offshore islands (e.g., Cocos, Costa Rica), and seamounts. Feeds primarily on fishes (scad, chubs, tuna, jacks, mackerel, mullets, porcupine fishes), but also eats squid. On three occasions I have examined stomachs packed with pelagic crabs. Often associated with schools of tuna and is observed among scalloped hammerhead schools in the Sea of Cortez. Young specimens occur in shallower areas than the adults and are sometimes found in loose groups. This species is known to arch the back, raise the snout, and lower the tail in an apparent threat display. Divers should treat larger individuals with extreme respect, especially in baited situations (they have chased divers out of the water). Usually indifferent toward divers except when initially encountering them. I have found that subadult and small adult specimens are curious in nonbaited situations, making slow, close passes.

76. Creek whaler shark *(Carcharhinus fitzroyensis)*

Identification: Long pointed snout; no interdorsal ridge; relatively large second dorsal fin set over anal fin; large, broad pectoral fins; no fin markings. *Size:* Birth 50 cm (19.7 inches), maximum length 1.5 m (5 ft). *Range:* Australia (northern Queensland along northern coast to western Australia). Depth range from intertidal zone to 30 m (99 ft). *Reproduction:* Litter number 3-7; gestation period 7-9 months. *Biology:* Common in estuarine and shallow inshore areas. Feeds mainly on bony fishes and crustaceans (shrimps, mantis shrimps), also on some molluscs.

CSIRO
M. Bacon

77. Galapagos shark *(Carcharhinus galapagensis)*

Identification: Snout long and rounded; low interdorsal ridge present; first dorsal origin over pectoral axil, first dorsal fin relatively high with pointed or sharply rounded tip; pectoral fins large, often ventral surfaces have dusky tips. *Size:* Birth 57-80 cm (22.4-31.5 inches), maximum length 3 m (9.9 ft). *Range:* Circumtropical, usually around oceanic islands (the similar dusky shark is most often found near continental coastlines). Depth range from surface to 180 m (594 ft); juveniles in the shallower part of this range. *Reproduction:* Litter number 6-16. *Biology:* Found near rocky and coral reefs, often common around drop-offs and steep reef slopes. Food includes reef fishes (moray eels, parrotfishes, surgeonfishes, squirrelfishes), octopuses, squid, and crustaceans. Feeds more on sharks, rays, porcupine-fishes, and cetaceans than smaller requiem sharks. Prey on sea lions off the Galapagos Islands. Performs apparent threat display, which consisits of head swinging and exaggerated swimming. Very curious, often aggregates around an anchored boat. Potentially dangerous; young specimens can be particularly brazen, persistently approaching and even charging divers. Responsible for at least one attack on a swimmer. Adults should be treated with extreme respect. Does well in captivity.

78. Bull shark *(Carcharhinus leucas)*

Identification: A stocky body; very broad, short snout; eyes are small; no interdorsal ridge; large, triangular dorsal fin with sharp apex; no distinct markings on the fins, although fin tips and the trailing edge of the caudal fin are sometimes dusky, especially in juveniles. *Size:* Birth 56-81 cm (22-31.9 inches), maximum length 3.4 m (11.2 ft). *Range:* Found in all tropical and subtropical seas, being most abundant near continental coastlines. Depth range from intertidal zone to 150 m (495 ft), usually near bottom. *Reproduction:* Litter number 1-13; gestation period 10-11 months. Move into estuaries and even lakes to give birth. *Biology:* Well known for its habit of entering rivers and lakes around the world. Segregation of different sizes occurs, with juveniles in shallower areas than adults. Feeds on a wide range of prey items, including bony fishes, sea turtles, marine mammals, crabs, and squid. Adults known for their dietary predilection for other elasmobranchs. Observed lying torpid ("sleeping") on the ocean floor. Although there are no verified attacks on divers (except spearfishermen and aquarists) on record, this species, because of its varied diet and sheer bulk, is potentially dangerous. It has attacked bathers.

D. Perrine

79. Blacktip shark *(Carcharhinus limbatus)*

Identification: Tips of pectoral, second dorsal, and lower lobe of caudal fin fins black; anal, first dorsal, upper caudal and pelvic fin tips may also be black; white band on side; snout long and pointed; no interdorsal ridge; first dorsal large with pointed apex. *Size:* Birth 38- 72 cm (15-28.3 inches), maximum length 2.6 m (8.6 ft). *Range:* Found throughout tropical and subtropical seas. Depth range from intertidal zone to 30 m (99 ft). *Reproduction:* Litter number 1-10; gestation 11-12 months. Females give birth in shallow, often turbid, coastal waters. *Biology:* Inhabits turbid inshore waters (e.g. lagoons, mangrove swamps, and estuaries), and reef channels, reef faces, and seamounts. At Rangiroa Atoll, this species occurs in the lagoon and moves out through the pass onto the reef face during slack tide. Primarily fish eater (sardines, menhaden, anchovies, sea catfishes, jacks, croakers, snook, boxfishes, sharks, rays), but also consumes snails, squid, and crustaceans. More active during the day than at night. Jumps out of the water, spinning as it falls back in the water. In unbaited situations behavior toward divers varies. Sometimes shy, circling at a distance, at other times bold and aggressive. Known to be aggressive in baited situations, especially in turbid water.

Debelius

80. Oceanic whitetip shark *(Carcharhinus longimanus)*

Identification: Rounded dorsal and pectoral fins with conspicuous white tips; pectoral fins broad; dorsal coloration in Pacific gray, in Red Sea brown. Newborns have dusky fin tips rather than white tips. *Size:* Birth 63 cm (24.8 inches), maximum length 3.5 m (11.6 ft). *Range:* Circumglobal in tropical and warm temperate seas. Depth range from surface to 150 m (495 ft). *Reproduction:* Litter number 1-15; gestation period about 12 months. *Biology:* Primarily oceanic (usually over water 180 m, 594 ft, in depth), but encountered near reef drop-offs. Migrates to warmer waters in winter. Solitary, loose groups, sometimes aggregate around food source. This shark feeds on squid, bony fishes (lancetfishes, marlin, oarfishes, barracuda, tuna, dolphinfishes), and pelagic stingrays. Associates with pods of pilot whales, feeding on remains resulting from whale attacks on schooling fish. A bold shark known to persistently circle divers (sometimes for hours), and make occasional slow, close passes. They have attacked divers. Their behavior is generally deliberate, they are not frenetic like some of the reef shark species.

81. Blacktip reef shark
(Carcharhinus melanopterus)

Identification: First dorsal and lower caudal fins always have distinct black markings, other fins also with black tips or margins; snout bluntly rounded; no interdorsal ridge. *Size:* Birth 33-52 cm (13-20.5 inches), maximum length 1.8 m (5.9 ft). *Range:* Red Sea to the Society Islands, north to Japan and south to New Caledonia and Australia. Also reported from the eastern Mediterranean. Depth range from intertidal zone to usually no deeper than 10 m (33 ft). *Reproduction:* Litter number 3-4; gestation period 8-9 months. Pair observed copulating in venter-to-venter posture in shallow water. *Biology:* Observed in lagoons and on the reef flat. Will aggregate in reef channels at low tide and move on to the reef flat at high tide. Feeds on fishes (wrasses, triggerfishes, parrotfishes, goatfishes), squid, octopuses, crabs, mantis shrimp, and sea snakes (feed on them heavily in some areas). A fast swimming predator that has been observed chasing down surgeonfishes and stingrays. Has been observed attacking aggregations of spawning surgeonfish. Utilizes a limited home range of several square kilometers (about 1 square mile). Eaten by other sharks and groupers. In nonbaited situations, usually nonaggressive to divers and difficult to approach. Larger specimens are potentially aggressive when fish are speared and smaller specimens have attacked waders (if attacked while wading lie down in the water).

82. Dusky shark *(Carcharhinus obscurus)*

Identification: Snout moderately long and broadly rounded; low interdorsal ridge; fin tips often dusky; first dorsal over or slightly behind inner pectoral corner, tip of this fin pointed or sharply rounded; pectoral fins moderately large and falcate, often with dusky tips. Similar in external morphology to Galapagos shark, differs in the dorsal fin heights (the first and second dorsal are lower in the dusky shark) and in distribution (dusky more often found around continental coastlines). Depth range from intertidal zone to 400 m (1,320 ft). *Size:* Birth 69-100 cm (27.1-39 inches), maximum length 4.2 m (13.9 ft). *Range:* Circumtropical. *Reproduction:* Litter number 3-14. *Biology:* Utilize shallow waters of specific geographical areas for nursery grounds. As individuals grow, they move into deeper water. Bulk of diet consists of bony fishes (eels, lizardfishes, cuskeels, spadefishes, jacks, tuna, mackerels, flatfishes, gurnards), sharks (angel sharks, sawsharks, catsharks, requiem sharks), skates, and rays, but also eats some crustaceans, squid, octopuses, and sea snakes. Feeds actively during the day. Large, potentially dangerous species involved in several persistent attacks on swimmers.

83. Caribbean reef shark
(Carcharhinus perezi)

Identification: Short, bluntly rounded snout; low interdorsal ridge; first dorsal fin tip acute; pectoral fins moderately long and narrow; tips of pectoral, pelvic, anal, and lower lobe of caudal fins dusky, upper caudal fin margin dusky. Often misidentified as the bull shark, but more similar to Galapagos and dusky. *Size:* Birth around 70 cm (27.6 inches), maximum length 3 m (9.9 ft). *Range:* Florida to Brazil; most common large reef shark in the Caribbean. Depth range from the surface to at least 30 m (99 ft). *Reproduction:* Litter number 4-6. *Biology:* Usually observed on the reef face. Feeds on bony fishes and probably also large motile invertebrates. Commonly observed laying on the bottom in caves and under ledges, often in an apparent torpor as if sleeping. A dangerous species that has been responsible for a number of attacks on divers, many in the presence of speared fish. Most common participant in Bahamian "shark feeds," it is usually not aggressive in these situations, but will make close passes.

84. Sandbar shark *(Carcharhinus plumbeus)*

Identification: Origin of first dorsal fin over or anterior to pectoral fin axil; first dorsal fin large; low interdorsal ridge; large, broad pectoral fins. *Size:* Birth 56-75 cm (22-29.5 inches), maximum length 2.4 m (7.9 ft). *Range:* Worldwide in subtropical and tropical waters. Depth range from intertidal zone to 280 (924 ft). *Reproduction:* Litter number 1-14; gestation period 8-12 months. Nursery areas in shallow bays. *Biology:* Found most often over sand and mud bottoms in surf zone, but also encountered near reefs. Swims near bottom and feeds on benthic bony fishes (goosefishes, menhaden, flounders, porcupinefishes, eels, parrotfishes, surgeonfishes, goatfishes), skates, skate eggcases, sharks, crustaceans (mantis shrimp, crabs, shrimp), and squid and octopuses. Increase in feeding activity in the early morning. In coastal bays, young sharks move with tidal currents and remain in a relatively small area during slack tide. Observed singly and in large schools, the adults segregate by sex. Usually not aggressive, but there are several reports of these sharks making close passes at divers.

Post

85. Spottail shark *(Carcharhinus sorrah)*

Identification: Moderately long, rounded snout; moderately large eyes; interdorsal ridge; small pectoral fins; first dorsal fin of moderate size while second dorsal fin is low with long rear tip; black tips on second dorsal fin and lower lobe of caudal fin. *Size:* Birth 45-60 cm (17.7-23.6 inches), maximum length 1.5 m (5 ft). *Range:* Indo-West Pacific, South Africa north to Red Sea, east to China and Australia. Juveniles reported from calm, shallow waters, while adults occur down to 70 m (231 ft). *Reproduction:* Litter number 1-6; gestation period less than 1 year. Near India, this species gives birth between April and May. *Biology:* Found near coral reefs, usually in shallow areas outside of lagoons. Fast swimming species that pursues small reef fishes. Feeds equally on benthic and pelagic bony fishes (eels, herring, mackerel, jacks, filefishes, porcupinefishes, boxfishes), and to lesser extent on sharks, rays, crustaceans (shrimp, mantis shrimp, and crabs), and cephalopods. Smaller specimens feed more on benthic prey, while adults take both benthic and pelagic items. Preyed upon by other sharks and not known to be aggressive toward divers.

J.E. Randall
W.R. Strong, Jr.

86. Tiger shark *(Galeocerdo cuvier)*

Identification: Large blunt snout; well developed caudal keel; dark vertical stripes on body (less conspicuous or absent on adults). *Size:* Birth 51-76 cm (20-29.9 inches), maximum length 5.5 m (18.2 ft). *Range:* Circumtropical. Depth range from intertidal zone to 305 m (1,007 ft). *Reproduction:* Litter number 10-82; gestation period 12-13 months. *Biology:* Occurs in a wide range of habitats, from clear waters around coral reefs to turbid estuaries and bays. Eats a wide range of prey, including horseshoe crabs, slipper lobster, conch, squid, demersal bony fishes (goosefishes, walking batfishes, sea robins, lizardfishes, flounders, porcupinefishes, pufferfishes), sharks, skates, rays, and marine mammals (including the endangered Hawaiian monk seal). Feeds more frequently on sea turtles (which are swallowed whole or bitten into smaller pieces), sea snakes and birds (both sea and land species) than any other shark. Appears sluggish, but it is capable of fast attacks on prey. Nocturnal, moving into shallower areas at night to feed. Solitary, will aggregate near a rich food source. One of the most dangerous sharks, has attacked divers, surfers, swimmers, and boats. More people die when attacked by the tiger shark than by the white shark and there are several cases where a single tiger has attacked more than one person. Rarely encountered by divers, but if a large specimen is spotted one would be best advised to leave the water.

67

87. Caribbean sharpnose shark
(Rhizoprionodon porosus)

Identification: Long snout; long labial furrows; anal fin origin in front of second dorsal fin origin; anal fin posterior margin straight or slightly concave; small pectoral fins; color gray-brown, can have white spots on flanks and white fin margins. Similar to the Atlantic sharpnose *(R. terraenovae)* from which it differs in the number of precaudal vertebrae. *Size:* Birth 35 cm (13.8 inches), maximum length 1.1 m (3.6 ft). *Range:* Bahamas to Uruguay. Depth range from intertidal zone to 500 m (1,650 ft). *Reproduction:* Litter number 2-6; gestation 10-11 months. *Biology:* Inshore species found in lagoon grass beds, coral reef slopes, and estuaries (may swim up rivers). Eats bony fishes, squid, snails, and shrimp. Difficult to approach underwater, harmless. Successfully kept in large public aquariums.

D. Perrine

88. Blue shark *(Prionace glauca)*

Identification: Long snout; long, narrow pectoral fins; eyes relatively large; dark blue dorsally, lighter ventrally. *Size:* Birth 40 cm (15.7 inches), maximum length 3.8 m (12.5 ft). *Range:* Circumglobal in tropical and temperate seas. In more tropical areas they are found at greater depths (tropical submergence); for example, in tropical Indian Ocean most common between 80-220 m (264-726 ft). Depth range from surface to 220 m (726 ft). *Reproduction:* Litter number 4-135; gestation 9-12 months. Males bite the females during courtship and possibly copulation. *Biology:* Oceanic, but sometimes they move inshore near offshore islands where they have been observed in kelp beds. Feeds heavily on smaller prey (krill, squid, schooling fishes). The gill rakers have elongate papillae that apparently prevent smaller, slippery prey from escaping out of the gill slits. They also eat small sharks, sea birds, and mammalian carrier. More active at night; around the Channel Islands off California, it moves into shallow inshore areas at night, possibly in response to changes in prey distribution. In the north Atlantic blue sharks make regular dives, from the surface to depths greater than 400 m (13,200 ft). These vertical movements usually occur several times each day and occur most often during the daylight hours. Usually curious of divers, but not aggressive. In baited situations it has bitten divers.

M. Snyderman

FAMILY SPHYRNIDAE (HAMMERHEAD SHARKS)

The hammerheads are conspicuous members of the shark clan because of the lateral extensions of the head (sometimes dubbed the cephalofoil). Otherwise, these sharks are similar in form to the requiem sharks. There is much speculation concerning the function of the unusual head morphology. It may aid in locomotion, serving as a bow plane to increase lift and maneuverability. It may enhance electroreceptive, olfactory, and visual perception by spreading the sense organs over a broader area. It is also used to pin stingrays to the ocean bottom. There are eight hammerhead species currently recognized that range in size from 1 m (3.3 ft) to over 5 m (16.5 ft) in length. They are found in temperate and tropical coastal habitats, with several species occurring on or near reefs where they take refuge, hunt, and are cleaned (this has been observed in one species) by resident cleaner fishes. These sharks are viviparous (placental viviparity); the near term embryos have flexible "hammers" that are bent back toward the tail. Some species move from deeper water into the shallows to give birth. These sharks feed on squid, crustaceans, other elasmobranchs (two species feed heavily on rays), and bony fishes. Several species form large schools and undergo long north-south, seasonal migrations. The larger species, like the great hammerhead, can be bold and even dangerous to divers, while the smaller species, such as the bonnethead, are shy and difficult to approach underwater. The bonnethead shark does well in larger aquariums, while the larger species suffer capture and handling stress and rarely adapt to life in the oceanarium.

89. Scalloped hammerhead shark
(Sphyrna lewini)

Identification: Head hammer shaped, with broad head extensions arched posteriorly and an indentation in the middle of the head; pelvic fins not falcate; pectoral fins black tipped or dusky. *Size:* Birth 42-55 cm (16.5-21.7 inches), maximum length 4.2 m (13.9 ft). *Range:* Found in most warm temperate and tropical seas. Most abundant hammerhead species. Depth range from surface to 275 m (908 ft). *Reproduction:* Litter number 15-31. Nursery areas in shallow, turbid coastal areas. One mating bout observed in large school in the Sea of Cortez. Male grasped female pectoral fin and curled posterior part of body around female (parallel orientation). The pair dropped through the water column until they collided with the reef below, at which time they separated. *Biology:* Adults occur in pelagic and inshore waters, sometimes observed near coral reef drop-offs and often around seamounts. Feeds mainly on bony fishes (mackerel, dolphinfish, squirrelfish, scorpionfish, snake eels, groupers), sharks, rays, squid, crustaceans, and octopuses; rarely on sea snakes. Juveniles feed more on benthic bony fishes and crustaceans, while squid are a more important food source for adults. Although usually indifferent and inoffensive toward divers, it may become aggressive in baited situations. It will occasionally make close approaches to the diver, even when feeding stimuli are not present.

M. Snyderman

90. Great hammerhead shark
(Sphyrna mokarran)

Identification: Head hammer shaped, with front edge of the head nearly straight with an indentation in the center; falcate pelvic fins; high dorsal fin (orca-like); free tip of dorsal fin in front of pelvic fin origin; no fin markings. *Size:* Birth 50-70 cm (19.7-27.6 inches), maximum length 6 m (19.8 ft). *Range:* Occurs in most tropical oceans. Depth range from intertidal zone to 80 m (264 ft). *Reproduction:* Litter number 13-42, with larger females more fecund. Birth occurs in late spring and summer. *Biology:* Feeds on sharks, bony fishes (catfishes, toadfishes, jacks, herring, groupers, boxfishes), squid, and crustaceans that occur on or near the bottom. Preys heavily on rays (guitarfishes, whiptail stingrays, cownose rays, eagle rays) and skates. Specimens reported with up to 50 stingray and catfish spines broken off in the jaws, throat, and sides of the head. Most feeding occurs at dusk. Solitary. Reported to be avoided by other shark species, possibly because it has superior maneuverability. Although usually not aggressive, it will make close and unnerving passes toward divers. Its large size makes it worthy of respect; it has been reported to attack bathers.

D. Perrine

91. Bonnethead shark *(Sphyrna tiburo)*

Identification: Head shovel shaped with no indentation. The scoophead shark *(S. media)* is a similar species that has a mallet shaped head, a dorsal fin free tip that is over or behind the orgins of the pelvic fins, and unnotched posterior pelvic fin margins (see figure in Pictorial Key to Families). The scoophead ranges from Panama to southern Brazil in the western Atlantic and from the Sea of Cortez to Ecuador in the eastern Pacific. It attains 1.5 m (5 ft) in maximum length. *Size:* Birth 37 cm (14.6 inches), maximum length 1.5 m (5 ft). *Range:* Western Atlantic, from North Carolina to Brazil; eastern Pacific, from southern California to Ecuador. Depth range from intertidal zone to 80 m (264 ft). *Reproduction:* Litter number 11-14. Often give birth in estuarine waters. *Biology:* Diurnal. Feeds mainly on swimming crabs and shrimp, but also eats mantis shrimp, bivalves, barnacles, isopods, cephalopods, and small fishes. Segregates by sex, with females moving into shallow water during the birthing season. Harmless and difficult to approach underwater.

92. Smooth hammerhead shark
(Sphyrna zygaena)

Identification: Head hammer shaped with no indentation in front edge, but is rounded; free tip of the first dorsal fin does not extend back to pelvic fin origin. *Size:* Birth 50-61 cm (19.7-24 inches), maximum length 4 m (13.2 ft). *Range:* Worldwide, in warm temperate and tropical seas. Depth range from surface to 20 m (66 ft). *Reproduction:* Litter number 29-32. *Biology:* Usually over deeper water in oceanic habitats. However, it also occurs in shallow coastal waters, including areas around rocky reefs. Its primary prey are squid and bony fishes (herring, mackerel, groupers, jacks, mullet, barracuda, needlefishes, filefishes), but in certain areas it also feeds heavily on small sharks, rays (whiptail stingrays, spotted eagle rays), and skates. Solitary or in huge migratory schools. It engages in migrations to warmer waters in the winter. Usually indifferent toward divers, it may make close passes, but can be aggressive in baited situations.

R.H. Kuiter

FAMILY PRISTIDAE (SAWFISHES)

This family of unusual rays has four or more species. They all have elongated rostrums that bear teeth on each edge, no rostral barbels (as found in the saw sharks - family Pristiophoridae), and gill slits on the ventral surface of the body. Two species not included in the species accounts that could be encountered by divers are the large tooth sawfish *(Pristis microdon)* and the green sawfish *(Pristis zijsron)*. The large tooth sawfish is circumtropical in distribution, has 14 to 22 very large teeth on each side of a thick rostrum, a dorsal fin originating in front of the pelvic fins, and broad, pointed pectoral fins. The green sawfish occurs in the Indian and western Pacific oceans, has 23 to 32 pairs of teeth on a narrow rostrum, a first dorsal that originates over the pelvic fins, and pectoral fins that are rounded (see figure in Pictorial Key to Families). These two sawfishes are found in estuaries and rivers and are probably rare visitors to reefs. The largest sawfish (i.e. green sawfish) reaches 7.3 m (24.1 ft) in total length. Sawfishes are ovoviviparous (yolk sac viviparity) and several species utilize river mouths as communal parturition sites. The rostral teeth of full-term embryos are covered with a membranous sheath and the saw is flexible; these features prevent the rostrum from damaging the female during the birthing process. There are reports of these animals slashing humans and damaging shark tankmates with their tooth-studded rostrums. There is one account of a dugong mortality that was possibly the result of a sawfish inflicted wound and there is an old report of battles between crocodiles and sawfish in an estuarine environment. The rostral teeth grow throughout the sawfish's life, but if they are lost, they are not replaced. In the sawsharks new rostral teeth promptly grow in if old ones are lost. Sawfishes do well in larger public aquariums.

D. Perrine

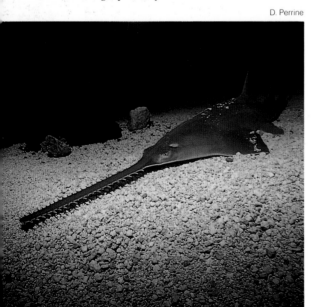

93. Smalltooth sawfish *(Pristis pectinata)*

Identification: Pectoral fin bases broad with bluntly pointed tips; first dorsal fin over pelvic fins; saw narrow, with 21-34 small rostral teeth on each side. *Size:* Birth 61 cm (24 inches), maximum length 6 m (19.8 ft). *Range:* Circumtropical. *Reproduction:* Litter number 15-20. Gives birth in shallow bays and estuaries. Born with flexible saw and with the rostral teeth covered with skin. *Biology:* Most common in bays, lagoons and estuaries, but also in rivers and lakes. Observed in shallow water with fins breaking the water surface. Feeds mainly on slow and schooling bony fishes, which it incapacitates with its saw. It also uses saw to dig crabs and bivalves out of the mud. This species is often aggressive towards sharks in captivity. In one account, a large specimen was reported to inflict blows with the rostrum to any shark tankmate that came near, although it ignored guitarfish and whiptail stingrays housed with it. In other situations, specimens were observed to approach resting sharks and smack them with their rostrums. It can deliver rapid blows in quick succession. Sharks also taken in the wild with apparent "rake marks" inflicted by sawfish rostrum. Not known to be aggressive to divers, but encounters with this fish in the wild are rare. A captive sawfish was cleaned of trematode flatworms by the bannerfish (*Heniochus acuminatus*).

FAMILY RHINIDAE (SHARKFIN GUITARFISHES)

The sharkfin guitarfish family consists of five species that have the first dorsal fin over the pelvic fin base and a well developed lower caudal lobe. The anterior part of the body and the large dorsal fins are shark-like in appearance and neophytes to elasmobranch identification often mistake it for its more notorious relative. Two species within the family are regularly encountered on sandy bottoms around coral and rocky reefs. These batoids are ovoviviparous (yolk sac viviparity). Both of the species mentioned in this book do well in large public aquarium and one is known to breed in captivity.

94. Bowmouth guitarfish
(Rhina anclyostoma)

Identification: Snout broad and rounded; pectoral fins shark-like, triangular and far forward on the body; heavy ridges above eyes and down middle of head. Color changes as animal grows, adults gray with small white spots, juveniles brown to blue-gray with partial eye spots (ocelli) over pectoral fins and black bars between eyes (faint in adult), also white spots are larger. *Size:* Birth 45 cm (17.7 inches), maximum length 2.4 m (7.9 ft). *Range:* South Africa to Red Sea, east to Australia, north to southern Japan. *Reproduction:* Litter number four. *Biology:* Little known species observed near coral reefs and ship wrecks, sometimes high in the water column. Feeds on crabs and shrimp. Observed being cleaned by bluestreak cleaner wrasses (see accompanying photograph). One specimen kept almost 7 years in captivity.

95. White-spotted shovelnose ray
(Rhynchobatis djeddensis)

Identification: Pointed snout; first dorsal fin over pelvic fins; eye-spots (ocelli) often at base of pectoral fins; body color tan to black, usually with distinct white spots on dorsum. *Size:* Birth 43-60 cm (16.9-23.6 inches), maximum length 3.1 m (10.2 ft). *Range:* South Africa to Red Sea, Japan to New South Wales, Australia. Depth range from intertidal zone to 50 m (165 ft). *Reproduction:* Litter number to 10. Birth occurs in summer in South African waters. In some areas, young are born in estuarine habitats. *Biology:* Occurs in the surf zone, in estuaries, lagoons, and on sandy bottoms near coral and rocky reefs. Swims onto reef flat to feed and find refuge at flood tide, sometimes with groups of roundnose stingrays. Feeds on crabs, lobsters, clams, and small fishes; some prey are excavated from the sand. Difficult for divers to approach. Does well (kept for over 5 years) in public aquariums.

G.L. Chesnut
M. Snyderman

FAMILY RHINOBATIDAE (GUITARFISHES)

The guitarfish are identified by the placement of the first dorsal fin (which is behind the base of the pelvic fins) and the absence of a lower caudal lobe. There are 43 species in this family. A number of these (more than are identified in this book) are found near reef habitats. To the untrained eye many of the guitarfish are indistinguishable, but characteristics like snout shape and length, spiracle shape, nostril morphology, presence or absence of spines along the back and tubercles on the snout, color pattern, and orientation of nostrils relative to the mouth can assist in identification of various species. The largest guitarfishes reach lengths of around 2 m (6.6 ft) and all are ovoviviparous (yolk sac viviparity). No information is available on their mating behavior, but males have been observed to closely follow females. They spend much of their time lying on sand or sea grass. When startled they race away, not by undulating the disc like a stingray, but by using lateral, shark-like strokes of their tail fin. The guitarfishes are common near continental coastlines, but rarely near oceanic islands. Several species occur in estuaries and even in freshwater, and some segregate by sex and make seasonal migrations. Several species do well in public aquariums, while others fail to adapt.

96. Short-snouted shovelnose ray
(Aptychotrema bougainvillii)

Identification: Nostrils oriented parallel to mouth; distance between tip of snout and eyes three times the distance between the spiracles; mouth slightly curved; dorsal surface yellowish-brown, often with dark blotches on body and fins. The similar Southern shovelnose ray *(A. vincentiana)* has a shorter snout and usually has darker blotches on the dorsum. *Size:* Birth 10 cm (3.9 inches), maximum length 1 m (3.3. ft). *Range:* Australia (southern Queensland and New South Wales). Usually 20 m (66 ft) or deeper. *Reproduction:* Litter number to 8. Uterine lining with numerous club-shaped villi that provide nutrients for the developing embryo. *Biology:* Found in bays, seagrass beds, and on sand bottoms near rocky reefs.

R.H. Kuiter

97. Long-snouted shovelnose ray
(Aptychotrema rostrata)

Identification: Nostrils oriented parallel to mouth; distance between tip of snout and eyes almost four times the distance between the spiracles; mouth obviously curved. *Size:* Birth approximately 13 cm (5.1 inches), maximum length 1.2 m (4 ft). *Range:* Australia (Queensland to Victoria). Depth range from intertidal zone to 60 m (198 ft). *Reproduction:* Litter number up to four. *Biology:* Common on sandy bottoms in bays, sea grass beds, and sometimes near rocky reefs.

R.H. Kuiter

98. Fiddler ray *(Trygonorhina fasciata)*

Identification: Pectoral fins broad; snout obtusely rounded; network of white lines on dorsum. Color pattern on the head distinguishes this species from the southern fiddler ray. There is some debate on how many species of fiddler rays exist. There is an apparent color morph with white margined fins and an overall bluish-black body color from south Australia, known commonly there as the magpie fiddler. *Size:* Birth 25 cm? (9.8 inches), maximum length 1.3 m (4.3 ft). *Range:* Australia (southern Queensland to Victoria). Depth range from intertidal zone to 180 m (594 ft). *Reproduction:* Egg capsules, which hatch in the uteri, are golden in color and each can contain up to three embryos. *Biology:* Occurs on sandy bottoms and in seagrass beds, often near rocky reefs. Does well in large public aquariums.

99. Southern fiddler ray
(Trygonorhina guaneria)
Identification: Pectoral fins broad; snout obtusely rounded; network of white lines on the dorsum; Color pattern on head distinguishes this species from the fiddler ray. *Size:* Maximum length 1.2 m (3.9 ft). *Range:* Australia (south Australia to western Australia, including Tasmania). Depth range from intertidal zone to 50 m (160 ft). *Biology:* Occur in estuaries, bays, sea grass beds, and near rocky reefs.

R.H. Kuiter

100. Banded guitarfish
(Zapteryx exasperata)
Identification: Moderately rounded snout; rostral ridges parallel, do not converge; prominent spines on back; dorsal fin posterior margins shorter than their bases; grayish-brown with dark brown bands transvering the dorsum. Some specimens have yellow spots, as big as the pupil, outlined in black. The short-nosed guitarfish *(Z. brevirostris)* is known from Brazil, and differs in having rostral ridges that converge near the tips, dorsal fin posterior margins that are longer than their bases, and no dorsal bands. *Size:* Maximum length 91 cm (35.8 inches). *Range:* Southern California to Panama. Depth range from intertidal zone to 22 m (73 ft). *Biology:* Common on rocky reefs, often in caves and under ledges. Also reported from tide pools. Rarely buries in the sand.

R. Steene

101. Green guitarfish *(Rhinobatus batillum)*
Identification: Nostrils oblique and long; distance from tip of snout to the eyes four times the distance between the spiracles; snout not expanded at tip; dorsal color sandy brown to olive green, with no markings. The spiny guitarfish *(R. armatus)*, is a similar species that occurs in the Indian Ocean, from the Malay Peninsula to the Solomon Islands. It differs from the green guitarfish in that the distance from the tip of the snout to the eyes is three times the distance between the spiracles. *Size:* Maximum length 2 m (6.6 ft). *Range:* Australia (Queensland around north coast to western Australia) and New Guinea. *Biology:* Common in lagoons on sand bottoms. Moves into shallow water at flood tide to feed. Feeds on shrimp and benthic fishes (flatheads). Enters freshwater where it has been reported to reproduce. Harmless.

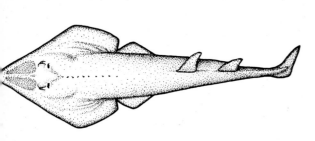

102. Halav's guitarfish *(Rhinobatus halavi)*

Identification: Snout bluntly pointed; snout to eye length 2.75 to 3 times the distance between the spiracles; rostral ridges converge near posterior ends, run side by side to end of snout, and separate towards the anterior end; eyes are small, eye length goes 5 or 6 times into snout to eye length; spiracles have low ridges; distance from pelvic fin axil to origin of first dorsal fin up to twice the distance between the dorsal fins; large thorns on rostrum, over eyes, on shoulders, and down middle of back; color plain, dorsum yellowish-gray to brown, edges of pelvic and caudal fins edged with white, ventrum white. The whitespotted guitarfish *(R. punctifer)* differs from this species in having no thorns (only minute denticles) on the snout, shoulders or back, rostral ridges broadly separated over entire length, large eyes (eye length goes 3.2 times into snout to eye length), and white spots on head, back, pelvic fins, and tail. This species is endemic to the Red Sea. *Size:* Maximum length 2 m (6.6 ft). *Range:* Wide ranging; reported from Red Sea (common around Egypt) and the Persian Gulf to China. Also reported from the Mediterranean. *Biology:* Feeds on small molluscs and bony fishes.

103. Atlantic guitarfish
(Rhinobatus lentiginosus)

Identification: Disc close to being as broad as long; rostral cartilage expanded at the tip; snout with tubercles on the tip; the origin of the first dorsal fin is posterior to the tips of the pelvic fins by a distance equal to the origin of the first dorsal fin to its free tip; gray to brown dorsal surface with many (several hundred) small white spots (rarely individuals will lack spots). A similar species, the southern guitarfish *(R. percellens)*, differs in having no enlarged tubercles on the end of the snout in adults, the rostral cartilage is narrower towards the tip, and when spots are present they are fewer in number (40-45), larger, and occur along each side of the trunk (see figure in Pictorial Key to Families). The southern guitarfish ranges from the Caribbean to western Argentina. The Brazilian guitarfish *(R. horkelii)* is plain in color, it has no enlarged tubercles on the expanded snout tip, and the origin of the first dorsal is posterior to the tips of the pelvic fins by a distance about equal to the base of the first dorsal fin. The Brazilian guitarfish ranges from Brazil north to the Lesser Antilles. *Size:* Birth about 20 cm (7.9 inches), maximum length 76 cm (29.5 inches). *Range:* North Carolina to Yucatan, Mexico, including Gulf of Mexico. Depth range from intertidal zone to 20 m (66 ft). *Reproduction:* Litter number six. *Biology:* Found on sand and mud bottoms, in sea grass beds, and near lagoon patch reefs. Feeds on molluscs and crustaceans.

M. Bacon
D. Gotshall

104. Shovelnose guitarfish
(Rhinobatus productus)

Identification: Disc longer than wide; rostral cartilage narrow at tip with no large tubercles; row of spines down middle of back; dorsum color brown, occasionally with gray spots. The flathead guitarfish *(R. planiceps)* is a similar species from the Galapagos Islands and Peru. It has an olive green dorsum, often with numerous dark blotches, and a single spiracular fold *(R. productus* has two spiracular folds). *Size:* Birth 15 cm (5.9 inches), maximum length 1.7 m (5.6 ft). *Range:* Central California to the Sea of Cortez. Depth range from intertidal zone to depths of 13 m (43 ft). *Reproduction:* Litter number up to 28. *Biology:* Found on sand bottoms in bays, sea grass beds, and near rocky reefs. During the day, partially buries in sand. Feeds at night on worms, clams, crabs, and benthic and mid-water fishes. Clams are apparently masticated, spit out, and only the meat is reingested. Solitary or aggregates, sometimes in large numbers. Juveniles are eaten by leopard sharks. Harmless, although one report of an apparently amorous male biting a diver.

105. Common guitarfish
(Rhinobatus rhinobatus)

A. Purcell

Identification: Rostral ridges separated by a considerable interspace over their entire length, converge slightly at tip; spiracle with two folds; small spines on midline of back and tail, between the eyes, and on the shoulders; dorsal color brown, gray, or yellowish; dorsal fins often with white rear margins; ventrum white. The blackchin guitarfish *(R. cemiculus)* occurs from Portugal, throughout the Mediterranean, and south to Angola. It differs from *R. rhinobatus* in having rostral ridges that are narrowly separated over the entire length and converge near the snout tip, and a black blotch on the snout (this is most conspicuous in juveniles). *Rhinobatus cemiculus* is more similar to *R. halvai* (see species account 102) and differs from it in having a distance from the pelvic axil to the first dorsal fin origin, which is about equal to the distance between the dorsal fins. *Size:* Maximum length 1 m (3.3 ft). *Range:* Eastern Atlantic from Portugal, the Mediterranean, and east Africa. Depth range from intertidal zone to 100 m (330 ft). *Reproduction:* Litter size 4-10. One or two litters born each year. Parturition in February and June in Mediterranean. *Biology:* Found on mud and sand bottoms, sometimes near rocky reefs. Often buries in substrate. Feed mostly on clams and squid, but also consumes benthic bony fishes (conger eels, sea bass, flatfishes, blennies, gobies, goatfish, sardines), gastropods (nudibranchs, snails), worms, and crustaceans (mantis shrimp, pistol shrimp, hermit crabs). Many of these prey items are dug from the sand or mud.

FAMILY PLATYRHYNIDAE (THORNBACK RAYS)

There are five species in the thornback ray family. They are similar in overall appearance to the guitarfish, but differ by having two slender pieces of cartilage extending from the skull to the tip of the snout (rhinobatids have only one), a broadly rounded snout, and one or three rows of large, curved tubercles (i.e., thorns) running down the back and the tail. As far as their systematic standing is concerned, the thornback rays are thought to be intermediate between the torpedo rays and the guitarfishes. Thornbacks do not exceed 1 m (3.3 ft) in total length. All of these rays are benthic, occurring on soft sand and mud bottoms and, although at least one species inhabits shallow coastal areas, most occur in deeper offshore waters. They eat infaunal invertebrates and most are ovoviviparous (yolk sac viviparity). However, one species is reported to be oviparous, laying skate-like eggcases (this needs to be verified). They occur in the eastern Pacific, and near Japan, China, India, and West Africa. Thornback rays kept in public aquariums are reported to be hardy.

D. Gotshall

106. Thornback ray
(Platyrhinoides triseriata)

Identification: Disc wider than long; rounded snout; three rows of large spines down back and tail; dorsal coloration brown with no markings. A similar species, the Japanese thornback ray *(Platyrhina sinensis)*, has spines down its back, two pair of light colored spines on each shoulder, and spines near its eyes (see figure in Pictorial Key to Families). This species ranges from Japan to the south China Sea and attains a maximum length of 70 cm (2.8 ft). The Japanese thornback is rarely observed by divers. *Size:* Maximum length 91 cm (35.8 inches). *Range:* Central California to Baja California, Mexico. Depth range from intertidal zone to 50 m (165 ft). *Reproduction:* In California parturition and mating occur in late summer. *Biology:* Found on sand and mud bottoms, sometimes in kelp beds. During the day, often found partially buried in the substrate. Solitary or in small groups. Feeds on worms, molluscs, and crustaceans (crabs, shrimp, isopods). Harmless.

FAMILY TORPEDINIDAE (TORPEDO RAYS)

This family has one genus and 14 to 17 species that are characterized by a round or oval flabby disc, two dorsal fins, slender jaws, lack of labial cartilages, a straight or notched anterior disc margin, and a short tail with a well developed caudal fin. Characters that can aid in identifying the species within this family include the position of the first dorsal fin relative to the pelvic fins, the presence of papillae on the spiracle margins, the number of spiracle papillae when present, and the color pattern (this may vary in some species). The family is currently in need of taxonomic revision, especially those representatives from the western Indian Ocean, where it appears there may be several different species, each endemic to one of the island groups there. The torpedos possess two kidney-shaped electric organs, embedded under the skin on each side of the head, that are capable of producing an electrical discharge of over 220 volts in some species. These electrogenic organs are used to capture prey, to ward off predators, and, possibly, to communicate among conspecifics. People who have "stumbled onto" these animals while wading or diving have reported a shock similar to being hit by a very large fist! Electrical discharge could result in unconciousness of a diver. Torpedos are found in all temperate and tropical seas, inshore and offshore, with several species regularly occurring on or near reefs. They are ovoviviparous, being nourished by a yolk sac and secretions exuded by the uteri. In gravid females, the uteri secrete a nutrient-rich liquid ("uterine milk") which is ingested by the developing embryos. No information exists on courtship and mating behavior in these rays. Fishes make up the bulk of their diets. The small jaws are distensible and enable the torpedos to eat large prey items relative to their body size, for example a 1.2 m (4 ft) California torpedo has eaten a 60-cm (2-ft) silver salmon. They employ several strategies to capture prey. Lying just beneath the sand, or mud, surface they lunge from the substrate when a victim comes within striking distance. Most emit an electrical discharge to immobilize or disorient the prey just prior to attacking. They also stalk their quarry by slowly drifting over the reef or by creeping along the sea floor. Despite their strong electrogenic organs, torpedos are occasionally preyed upon by requiem sharks. Some of these rays have been successfully maintained in public aquariums (e.g. *Torpedo nobiliana*), but they will usually take only moving food, whether live prey or a piece of fish manipulated on a line or stick. Others (e.g. *Torpedo californica*) often refuse to eat in aquarium confines.

D. Gotshall
CSIRO

107. Pacific torpedo ray
(Torpedo californica)

Identification: Posterior base of first dorsal fin well behind the posterior end of pelvic fin base; first dorsal fin much larger than second dorsal fin; caudal fin posterior margin straight or concave; spiracle margins smooth, with no papillae; the distance between spiracles and snout about 2.5 times the distance between spiracles; color gray dorsally with scattered black spots and no ocelli. The Japanese torpedo *(T. tokionis)* is a similar species that differs in having a disc that is about as wide as it is long. The Japanese torpedo is dark brown or black, with no spots, and is only known from Japan. *Size:* Maximum length 1.4 m (4.6 ft). *Range:* British Columbia to Baja California Depth range 3-196 m (10-647 ft). *Biology:* Feeds exclusively on fishes (anchovies, kelp bass). During the day, it buries in the sand and ambushes its prey. At night, it emerges from the substrate to stalk fish, which it stuns with an electrical discharge. Solitary, but several specimens may bury in the same area during the day. Nomadic, not home ranging. They are almost neutrally buoyant and can suspend in the water with minimal swimming. Has been reported to swim at divers with jaws agape when provoked and will deliver an electric shock when annoyed.

108. Macneill's torpedo ray
(Torpedo macneilli)

Identification: Posterior end of first dorsal base considerably posterior to the rear end of pelvic fin base; first dorsal fin much larger than second dorsal fin; caudal fin posterior margin straight or concave; edges of spiracles smooth, without papillae; color dark gray, black, or brown, sometimes with dark brown spots, ventrum white. This species is similar and probably synonymous with *T. fairchildi* from New Zealand and India. In *T. fairchildi*, the posterior end of the first dorsal fin base is over or in front of the posterior pelvic fin base. *Size:* Maximum length 1 m (3.3 ft). *Range:* Austrailia (New South Wales around the southern coast to western Australia) and India. Collected as deep as 600 m (1,980 ft). *Biology:* Found near rocky reefs over sand and mud bottoms. Feeds on fishes and crustaceans. Fairchild's torpedo known to arch and twist its body when approached by a diver in an apparent threat display.

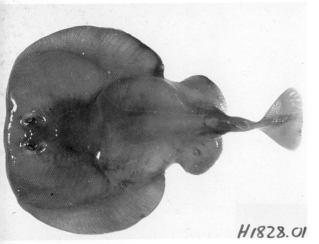

H1828.01

109. Marbled torpedo ray
(Torpedo marmorata)

Identification: Posterior first dorsal fin base behind posterior base of pelvic fin; first dorsal fin only slightly larger than second dorsal; spiracles with six to eight long papillae; eyes very near to spiracles; light brown to cream dorsum with dark brown mottling, an occasional specimen has a uniform brown dorsum. *Size:* Birth 20 cm (7.9 inches), maximum length 60 cm (23.6 inches); females grow to larger size than males. *Range:* Eastern Atlantic, from Britain and France, throughout Mediterranean, south to the Atlantic coast of southern Africa. Depth range from 2-200 m (7-660 ft). *Reproduction:* Litter number 5-32; gestation period 8-10 months. *Biology:* Found in sea grass meadows, on rocky reefs and soft bottoms adjacent to them. It feeds predominantly on bony fishes (conger eels, hake, sea bass, goatfish, mackerel, gobies, sole), and occasionally eats shrimp and squid. One 41- cm (16-inches) specimen speared off England had a 34-cm (13-inches) three-bearded rockling in its stomach! Solitary. When threatened, this ray will bend the body, propel itself upwards with the disc margins, which results in the ray looping in the water column, and emit an electrical discharge. By bending the body, the ray places a predator that grasps its tail in the maximum gradient of its electrical field.

A. Klapfer

110. Atlantic torpedo ray
(Torpedo nobiliana)

Identification: First dorsal fin considerably larger than second dorsal fin; caudal fin posterior margin straight or concave; spiracles smooth, without papillae; dorsal color uniform dark violet, black, or brown, sometimes with black blotches and small white spots; ventrum white. *Size:* Birth 23 cm (9 inches), maximum length 1.8 m (5.9 ft). *Range:* East Atlantic from Britain to South Africa, including the Mediterranean, and west Atlantic from Nova Scotia to the Florida Keys. Depth range 2-450 m (7-1,489 ft). It is most common in temperate waters. *Reproduction:* Litter number up to 60; gestation period 1 year. *Biology:* Juveniles primarily benthic in inshore habitats, usually on soft bottoms and sometimes near reefs. Adults are more pelagic, swimming in the water column over deep water, and may migrate over long distances. Feeds primarily on pelagic and benthic bony fishes (flatfishes, conger eels, salmon, goatfish) and sharks (catsharks). This species feeds to a lesser degree on crustaceans. Electrical discharge, which can reach 220 volts, could possibly cause diver unconsciousness.

G. Van Ryckevorse
Debelius

111. Panther torpedo ray *(Torpedo panthera)*

Identification: First dorsal fin only slightly larger than second dorsal fin, the tips of both are rounded; entire base of the first dorsal fin is over or in front of the posterior base of the pelvic fins; eyes well in front of spiracles, in some specimens half way between the front of disc and spiracles; spiracles with seven papillae; interdorsal distance equal to that between the posterior base of the second dorsal fin and the caudal fin origin; dorsal color uniform tan or rusty brown with pale blotches, or white spots. The blackspotted torpedo ray *(T. fuscomaculata)* is similar to this species and could be encountered on or near reefs off South Africa, Zanzibar, the Seychelles, Mauritius, Madagascar, Mozambique, and south-western India. The blackspotted torpedo differs in having its eyes much nearer to the spiracles than to the front of the disc, an interdorsal space greater than the distance between the posterior base of the second dorsal fin and the origin of the caudal fin, and a dark brown to light gray dorsum with or without black spots, black lines, or white flecks. The blackspotted torpedo attains a maximum length of 64 cm (25 inches). *Size:* Maximum length around 1 m (3.3 ft). *Range:* Red Sea; reported from other areas in the western Indian Ocean, but these probably refer to the similar blackspotted torpedo ray.

112. Peruvian torpedo ray
(Torpedo peruana)

Identification: First dorsal considerably larger than second dorsal; posterior margin of caudal fin roundish and convex; posterior base of first dorsal fin directly above the posterior base of the pelvic fins; length of upper caudal fin 2.8-3.5 times greater than the distance from the end of the second dorsal fin to its origin; spiracles smooth, without papillae; dorsum uniform dark gray or dark chocolate-brown, lighter ventrum. *Size:* maximum length to at least 50 cm (19.7 inches). *Range:* Peru, including the Galapagos Islands. Depth range 24-168 m (79-554 ft). *Biology:* The Peruvian torpedo ray is common on sand and mud bottoms as well as in the water column over deep water. It is one of the few semipelagic torpedo rays.

113. Spotted torpedo ray
(Torpedo sinuspersici)

Identification: First dorsal fin slightly larger than second dorsal fin; at least half of the base of the first dorsal fin is behind the posterior base of the pelvic fins; eyes very near to spiracles; spiracles with 9-10 papillae; attractive color pattern consists of golden or cream circles or marbling on a dark red, brown, or blackish background. Juveniles sometimes have up to seven large, pale-edged, dark spots (ocelli) on the dorsum. *Size:* Maximum length 1 m (3.3 ft). *Range:* Persian Gulf to India, south to South Africa, also in the Red Sea. Depth range from intertidal zone to 200 m (660 ft). *Reproduction:* Litter number 9-22. In South Africa, females give birth in shallow waters, including estuaries, in the summer and newborn specimens are occasionally stranded on the beach when the tide goes out. *Biology:* Found inshore on sandy bottoms and on or near coral reefs. Feeds on bony fishes. Usually solitary, but may aggregate during the breeding season. Reported to live out of the water for hours when stranded by an ebb tide.

114. Torpedo ray *(Torpedo torpedo)*

Identification: First dorsal only slightly larger than second dorsal; spiracle papillae small, knob-like; dorsum uniform dark to light brown, usually with five (sometimes one to seven) blue-centered ocelli. *Size:* Birth 9 cm (3.5 inches), maximum length 60 cm (23.6 inches). *Range:* Bay of Biscay south to Angola, also in Mediterranean. Depth range 2-70 m (7-231 ft). *Reproduction:* Litter number 3-21; gestation period 6-7 months. In Mediterranean, migrates into shallow water in the fall to mate and moves offshore in the summer to give birth. *Biology:* Eats bony fishes (gobies, goatfishes, chinchards). Ambush hunter that buries in sand and attacks prey that comes within striking distance. Shocks prey to immobilize it and then manipulates it into the mouth. At birth, the amplitude of electrical discharge is about 4 volts; this increases to 26 volts by the end of the 4th month. It can be maintained in captivity if fed live fish (blennies).

115. Ocellated torpedo ray *(Torpedo sp.1)*

Identification: First dorsal fin considerably larger than second dorsal fin; entire first dorsal fin base is ahead of posterior pelvic fin bases; second dorsal fin short, with round apex and a broad base; papillae present on spiracle margins (number unknown); color light brown or tan with dark brown mottling, and five large, dark brown spots. *Range:* Single specimen photographed near Sanganeb Atoll off Port Sudan. *Remarks:* This is apparently a new species known only from the accompanying photograph. It differs from the spotted torpedo in the position of the first dorsal, the size and shape of the second dorsal, and the color pattern. Although juvenile spotted torpedo rays have been reported with large dark spots, the specimen in the photo of ocellated torpedo ray is an adult male (note the length of the claspers). It differs from the black-spotted and panther torpedos in having eyes near to the spiracles, a low, rounded second dorsal fin, and a marbled color pattern with five large black spots. Specimens of ocellated torpedo ray are wanted by the author.

J.E. Randall

116. Caribbean torpedo ray *(Torpedo sp.2)*

Identification: First dorsal fin much larger than second dorsal fin, about 3-3.5 times the area; first dorsal tall, pointed apex, and a straight posterior margin; second dorsal low (the base length greater than the fin height) and rounded with a straight posterior margin; caudal fin posterior margin convex; disc width greater than its length; spiracle margins appear to have papillae; front edge of disc scalloped; posterior edge of disc thin with frill-like edges; color of dorsum light tan with brown blotches. *Size:* The only known specimen is about 31 cm (1 ft) in total length. *Range:* Single specimen photographed near Grand Cayman Island. *Remarks:* This undescribed species is one of two torpedo rays known from the western Atlantic and the only one reported from the Caribbean. It has been encountered by Captain Wayne Hasson on numerous dives, always near the same location. It is usually observed at a depth of about 11 m (35 ft), among hard coral and gorgonians. It differs from the Atlantic torpedo ray in having a tall, pointed, first dorsal fin, a scalloped anterior disc margin, a caudal fin with a convex posterior edge, spiracle papillae, and a mottled color pattern. The Atlantic torpedo is also more common in temperate waters. The Caribbean torpedo will shock a diver if provoked. Specimens of the Caribbean torpedo are wanted by the author.

W. Hasson

FAMILY HYPNIDAE (SHORTTAILED ELECTRIC RAY)

The shorttailed electric ray has a vestigial tail, small dorsal and caudal fins, tricuspid teeth, and a disc that is pear shaped. It occurs in coastal areas near temperate and tropical Australia. Electrical discharge strength in this species can reach about 200 volts; this is apparently used to capture food and discourage predators. This species is ovoviviparous. The shorttailed electric ray can live out of water for extended periods of time and has been observed to survive for hours after being stranded on shore by an ebb tide. Like the torpedos, the shorttailed electric ray feeds on relatively large prey items. For example, one 60-cm (23.6-inches) specimen had the tail of a 70-cm (27.6- inches) flathead fish *(Platycephalus sp.)* protruding from its mouth. This ray is common on coral and rocky reefs in parts of its range. Little is known of its suitability for captivity.

117. Shorttailed electric ray
(Hypnos monopterygium)

Identification: Oval, flabby body; short tail; tan to brown in dorsal color, no markings. Some ichthyologists recognize a second species, *H. subnigrum. Size:* Birth about 8 cm (3.1 inches), maximum length 69 cm (27 inches). *Range:* Australia (Queensland south, around south coast to western Australia). Depth range from intertidal zone to 240 m (792 ft). *Biology:* Occurs on sand, mud, in grass beds, on coral and rocky reef sand patches, and on reef flats. It is a weak swimmer that buries itself deep in the sand during the day. The only trace of it when it is buried are the two holes where the spiracles take in water. Feeds mainly on bony fishes, but also eats molluscs, crustaceans, and polychaete worms. Gives birth in the summer. I used a plastic slate to unbury a specimen hidden in the sand. The ray suddenly emerged and swam in a loop in the water column with its mouth open. This is possibly an antipredation response.

FAMILY NARCINIDAE (ELECTRIC RAYS)

This family of electric rays has 4 genera, and approximately 18 species. They have oval discs that are usually longer than they are wide, the anterior edge of which is broad and rounded. They also have two dorsal fins, a well developed caudal fin, lateral folds on the tail, stout jaws, and strong labial cartilages. The narcinids possess electric organs and can emit shocks of up to 37 volts. More provocation is usually necessary to elicit electrical discharge than in the torpedo rays. These rays are found on soft mud and sand substrates, but several are residents of, or visitors to, reef environments. The electric rays are ovoviviparous. The uterine wall of the gravid female is covered with villi that secrete uterine milk for the developing embryos and the yolk sacs also provide nourishment. These rays are harmless to divers, although they will shock if provoked. Most electric rays do poorly in captivity unless provided with their natural prey (e.g. annelid worms).

M. Snyderman

118. Bulls-eye electric ray
(Diplobatus ommata)

Identification: Dorsal and caudal fin tips rounded; dorsal color light brown often with many small black spots or marbled with dark brown, always has conspicuous ocelli in middle of back. The painted electric ray *(D. pictus)* is a similar species reported from reef habitats near the Atlantic coast of South America, from Brazil to Colombia. This ray has a subcircular disc, a fan-like caudal fin with a distinct upper corner, and sharply pointed dorsal fin tips. The painted electric ray is highly variable in color, but is often tan with scattered brown and white spots (see figure in Pictorial Key to Families). It reaches a total length of 20 cm (7.9 inches). *Size:* Maximum length 25 cm (9.8 inches). *Range:* The Sea of Cortez to Panama. Depth range from intertidal zone to 64 m (211 ft). *Biology:* Found on sandy and rocky bottoms, in bays, and on rocky reefs. Inactive during the day, moves just over or on the bottom at night. Moves along bottom by "hopping" on pelvic fins. Feed on amphipods, shrimp and, worms. Usually solitary.

119. Lesser electric ray
(Narcine brasiliensis)

Identification: Disc almost circular; spiracles positioned right behind eyes; caudal fin fan-shaped; dorsal color pattern often plain background with dark markings, but sometimes no markings present. *Size:* Birth 11 cm (4.3 inches), maximum length 45 cm (17.7 inches). *Range:* North Carolina, also Gulf of Mexico, to northern Argentina. Depth range from intertidal zone to 40 m (132 ft). *Reproduction:* Litter number 2-17. In Florida waters, females move into the surf zone to give birth in late summer. *Biology:* Common along sandy shorelines, sometimes near coral reefs. Feeds almost exclusively on worms, occasionally eats juvenile snake eels, anemones, and small crustaceans. They uncover infaunal prey by undulating the posterior disc margin. Nocturnal, they bury under substrate during the day. Move from shallow inshore waters to deeper areas in the winter, where they aggregate at preferred sites.

D. Gotshall (bottom)

120. Cortez electric ray *(Narcine entemedor)*

Identification: Similar to lesser electric ray (may be the same species); adult dorsal coloration tan to brown, adults have no distinct markings, juveniles may have up to four pair of faint ocelli on the dorsum. *Size:* Maximum length 76 cm (29.9 inches). *Range:* Sea of Cortez to Panama. *Biology:* Common in shallow water on sandy bottoms, sometimes adjacent to reefs. Feed mainly on polychaete worms and rarely on sea squirts. Nocturnal, move into shallow bays to feed at night. Bury in sand during the day. When threatened, this species will arch its back and explode off the bottom and do a loop in the water column. This is apparently an antipredation strategy which may serve to warn (back arch) and then confuse (loop) a would-be predator. There is one case where a diver received a mild shock after he provoked one of these rays to do a loop and it landed on his back.

R.H. Kuiter

121. Tasmanian electric ray
(Narcine tasmaniensis)

Identification: Distance between spiracles and eyes longer than the horizontal diameter of the eye; dorsal color brown, no markings. The related western electric ray *(N. westraliensis)* can be distinguished from this species by its color, which consists of a light brown dorsum with ornate brown markings (see figure in Pictorial Key to Families). The western electric ray is only known from Shark Bay, Western Australia (depth range 11-32 m, 36-102 ft) and attains 29 cm (11.4 inches) in total length. *Size:* Maximum length 46 cm (18 inches). *Range:* Australia (New South Wales to Tasmania). Depth range 5-100 m (17-330 ft). *Biology:* Usually found on sand or mud bottoms, sometimes near rocky reefs. Feeds on amphipods, shrimp, and worms.

FAMILY NARKIDAE (SHORTNOSE ELECTRIC RAYS)

This family contains three genera and four species. Members of the genus *Narke* and *Typholonarke* have one dorsal fin and those species in the genus Temera have none. These rays are electrogenic, have a rounded disc, a short, thick tail, a large caudal fin, a shallow groove around the mouth, short transverse jaws, and a short snout. Some family members have minute eyes; in others they are concealed under a ridge of skin. Most of the numbfish occupy temperate seas, and are usually found in deeper waters on the continental shelf and slope; however, at least one species is encountered in shallow water near rocky reefs. The diet of one species (the blind numbfish, *Typholonarke aysoni*) consists of shrimp, crabs, and small fish, while that of another (the onefin electric ray, *Narke capensis*) includes polychaete worms.

R. Pyle

122. Japanese numbfish *(Narke japonica)*

Identification: Has one dorsal fin; base of dorsal fin behind the pelvic fins, the pelvic fins are rounded; dorsal color reddish or chocolate brown, may have black or white spots, ventrum brown or white. *Size:* Birth size 10.2 cm (4 inches), maximum length 40 cm (16 inches). *Range:* Japan south to the South China Sea. *Reproduction:* Litter number up to five. Give birth in early summer. *Biology:* Found on sand, often near rocky reefs, in some areas not uncommon. Often buries under the sand. In Izu Marine Park in Japan it is found in water 12-23 m (40-75 ft) in depth. A friend of mine found that this species was aggressive when prodded with a plexiglass camera housing. When harassed, the ray would rub its back against the cameraport. It can produce an electrical discharge of 30-80 volts. It is eaten by the blotchy swell shark. This species usually does not fare well in captivity (reported longevity record 119 days).

FAMILY DASYATIDAE
(WHIPTAIL STINGRAYS)

This family has 6 genera and approximately 62 species, many of which are found in association with coral and rocky reefs. Some dasyatids have distinctive morphologies, while others are difficult to distinguish from one another underwater. Characteristics like disc and snout shape, color, the presence or absence of a dorsal or ventral finfold or a dorsal keel, tail length, the presence of tubercles (thorn-like spines) on the disc and/or tail, sting position, and number of stings can aid the diver in identifying whiptail stingrays. It is not uncommon for the tails of these stingrays to be damaged, thus tail length can be an unreliable character in species identification. There are six genera in the family, five are represented in reef habitats. They are as follows: *Dasyatis* (35 species), with rhomboid shaped disc, and ventral tail finfold height less than tail height above it; *Himantura* (18 species?), with rhomboid to oval shaped disc, and long, slender tail without tail folds; *Hypolophus* (1 species), with disc rhomboid-shape, and ventral tail finfold much greater than tail height above it; *Taeniura* (4 species), with oval or round disc, and ventral tail finfold reaching tip of tail; *Urogymnosus* (2 species?), with large tubercles (thorns) on a round or oval disc, and no caudal sting. Several of these genera (e.g. *Himantura*) are in need of taxonomic revision. The dasyatid rays are better known than their batoid relatives because of the interactions, both good and bad, that occur between them and humans. Recent popularization of dive sites where large southern stingrays envelope divers in their huge pectoral fins and feed from their hands give these animals a positive image. But, most of these rays also present a potential hazard to humans. The large sting(s) on the tail, which is ensheathed in venomous tissue, is used as a defensive weapon. When provoked, these fish thrust the tail over their bodies and into the offender, whether the offending party is a hammerhead shark or a human foot. A number of fatalities have resulted from physical damage or loss of blood caused by the sting, but few of these victims were diving. Many whiptail stingrays bury in the substrate, with only their eyes protruding, to conceal themselves from potential predators and can go unnoticed by waders or even a diver. A number of whiptail stingrays migrate up rivers (e.g. feathertail stingray) and several species are known only from freshwater (e.g. Laos stingray, *Dasyatis laosensis*). The whiptail stingrays are ovoviviparous (uterine viviparity). Two different mating postures have been described for these rays. Three species have been described to mate venter-to-venter, while in another species a male mounted a female dorsally. These rays eat a variety of invertebrates and fishes and most dig for infaunal animals. Stingrays are not considered voracious predators, but some are. For example, the stomach of one honeycomb stingray (disc width 145 cm, 4.8 ft) contained eight threadfin bream, three mackerel, eight ponyfish, eight cardinalfish, three sardines, three anchovies, two flatfish, one mojarra, four flatheads, three pufferfish, five squids, two crabs, and two mollusc shells! Several of the whiptail stingrays visit cleaning stations, where reef fishes remove parasites and ingest the ray's body mucus. They vary in hardiness in public aquariums. Several species have reproduced in captivity.

123. Red stingray *(Dasyatis akajei)*

Identification: Rhomboid disc, with straight anterior margin and convex posterior margin; snout triangular and slightly produced; pre-sting length longer than 125% of disc width; dorsal keel present on tail and about same length as ventral finfold; small spines present on disc and posterior part of tail in adults, also one to six tubercles before sting; dorsal color brown, some specimens with orangish coloration on the pectoral fin margins, on a small area in front of the eyes, behind the spiracles, and especially just anterior to the sting on the sides of the tail; the ventrum is also orangish red. *Size:* Maximum disc width around 40 cm (16 inches). *Range:* Japan, Korea, Taiwan, and China. *Reproduction:* Litter number up to 10. Mate in a venter-to-venter posture. *Biology:* Found on sand and mud bottoms, in estuarine and coral reef habitats. Feeds on bivalves, crustaceans, worms, and bony fishes.

S. Hagiwara

124. Southern stingray *(Dasyatis americana)*

Identification: Rhomboid disc; row of small tubercles running down the back; low dorsal keel present on tail, ventral finfold long; dorsal coloration gray to brown, without markings. *Size:* Birth 20 cm (7.9 inches) disc width, maximum disc width 1.5 m (5 ft). *Range:* New Jersey to Brazil. Depth range from intertidal zone to 25 m (82 ft). *Reproduction:* Litter number three to five. In presumed copulation event, male mounted female dorsally. *Biology:* Observed on sandy bottoms, in sea grass beds, lagoons, and on the reef face. Feeds equally on bony fishes (toadfishes, jawfishes, surgeonfishes, scorpionfishes), crabs, and worms. Occasionally eats clams, shrimp, tunicates, and mantis shrimp. Clams are apparently crushed with the dental plate and the shell fragments are spit out. Observed singly, in pairs, and in aggregations. Inactive during the day, often burying in the sand; actively feed at night, often in sea grass beds. Swim over or rest near cleaning stations, where they are cleaned by the bluehead wrasse and Spanish hogfish. Will allow divers to hand feed and handle them (e.g. "Stingray City," Cayman Islands); they have been known to bite divers in this context, but they do minimal damage. When threatened, they will raise the tail and sting over the body like a scorpion.

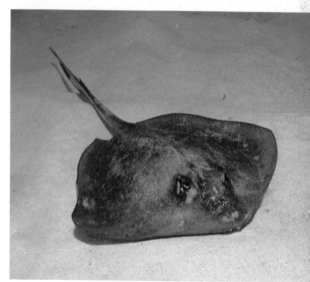

M. Bacon

125. Shorttail stingray *(Dasyatis brevicaudatus)*

Identification: Rhomboid disc, anterior and posterior margin of disc slightly convex, with rounded tips; disc is smooth; tail has small dorsal finfold and long ventral finfold; tail shorter than the disc, with a thick base; usually has two stings on tail, the first one small, the second large; scattered white spots on base of pectoral fins. *Size:* Birth 15 cm (5.9 inches) disc width, maximum disc width 2 m (6.6 ft). *Range:* Australia, New Zealand, and east and south Africa. Depth range from intertidal zone to 476 m (1,571 ft). *Reproduction:* During courtship, one or more males will grasp pectoral margin of female and hold on, sometimes for hours, as she swims through the water. Male flips under female and inserts a single clasper. Beats his tail rhythmically from side to side, causing clasper to move backward and forward in the cloaca. The pair swims off the bottom during mating. Copulation lasts from three to five minutes. During parturition, males have been observed nudging the females abdomen; this behavior is thought to facilitate birthing. *Biology:* Found on sandy bottoms, in bays, harbors, and near rocky reefs. Also in deeper water near edge of continental shelf. Feeds on fishes (nannegai), bivalves, squid, and crustaceans. Move into the shallows at flood tide. Often aggregate in large numbers.

M. Snyderman

126. Diamond stingray *(Dasyatis brevis)*

Identification: Rhomboid disc, its length is longer than 85% of disc width, anterior margin of disc slightly convex, posterior margin convex; pectoral tips rounded; dorsum of adults with row of tubercles down the midline of the back and on each shoulder, these are lacking in young specimens; snout blunt and not produced; finfolds on dorsal surface of tail are short (33% of disc width) and high (tail of specimen in accompanying photograph is broken off); tail less than 1.5 times the disc length; eyes large, eye diameter about 1/3 of interorbital width; dark brown or black dorsum, white ventrum. *Size:* Maximum disc width 1.2 m (4 ft). *Range:* Southern California, the Sea of Cortez, to Peru and the Galapagos Islands. Depth range from intertidal zone to 17 m (56 ft). *Biology:* Found in bays, in sea grass meadows, kelp beds, and near reefs on sand and mud bottoms. Food includes crabs (e.g. one 69-cm or 27-in, specimen had 30 small crabs in its stomach).

J.E. Randall
M. Snyderman

127. Brown stingray *(Dasyatis latus)*

Identification: Rhomboid disc, with nearly straight anterior and posterior margins; disc margin is smooth even in adults, larger specimens with three large tubercles on middle of disc; snout produced and rounded; no dorsal finfold or keel on tail, ventral finfold long and narrow and ends in a keel which terminates at the tip of the tail (not visible in photo); tail has tubercles on top and sides with a pair of large tubercles in front of sting; tail pre-sting length shorter than 110% of disc width, tail length about twice disc length; dorsum color olive-brown, no markings. A little known but wide ranging stingray, Bennett's stingray *(D. bennetti)*, also lacks a dorsal tail finfold or keel, but has a long ventral finfold, a long snout (longer than 25% of disc width), a disc with straight anterior and convex posterior margins, and a pre-sting length of 120% of disc width (see figure in Pictorial Key to Families). This stingray is reported from the Indian, Pacific, and Atlantic Oceans. *Size:* Maximum disc width about 1 m (3.3 ft). *Range:* Hawaiian Islands and Taiwan. *Biology:* Found on sand and mud bottoms, sometimes near coral reefs.

128. Longtail stingray *(Dasyatis longus)*

Identification: Rhomboid disc, disc margins close to straight; snout blunt; row of small tubercles on shoulder; tail at least twice as long as the disc; long, low ventral tail finfold and a keel, not a finfold, on the dorsal surface of the tail starting just behind the sting; eyes small, eye diameter much less than 1/3 of interorbital width; dorsum uniform brown, reddish-brown, or grayish. *Size:* Maximum disc width to over 1 m (3.3 ft). *Range:* Sea of Cortez to the Galapagos Islands. Common off coast of Costa Rica and in southern Sea of Cortez. *Biology:* Rocky and coral reef dweller.

129. Blue stingray *(Dasyatis marmorata)*

Identification: Rhomboid disc; disc is smooth; short dorsal keel and a long ventral finfold on tail; snout slightly rounded; tail less than twice disc length; dorsal color, bright blue reticulations on a golden background. *Size:* Birth 15 cm (5.9 inches) disc width, maximum disc width 75 cm (29.5 inches). *Range:* East and west coasts of Africa. Depth range from intertidal zone to 50 m (165 ft). *Reproduction:* Litter number one to four; gestation period about 1 year. *Biology:* Occurs inshore on sandy bottoms, sometimes near rocky reefs. Feeds on crabs, mantis shrimp, amphipods, worms, and fishes. Migrates from inshore waters in winter to deeper offshore areas.

R. Van Der Elst

130. Common stingray *(Dasyatis pastinaca)*

Identification: Rhomboid disc, anterior margin straight, posterior margin convex; snout slightly produced; short dorsal tail finfold present, ventral finfold also short and deep and originates at the level of the sting; tail not twice as long as disc; disc is smooth; dorsum gray to brown, ventrum white with brown or gray margin. Similar sympatric species, Tortonese's stingray *(D. tortonesei)* has a more pointed snout and a dorsal keel, not a finfold, on the tail. *Size:* Maximum disc width 60 cm (23.6 inches). *Range:* Madeira north to Baltic, including Mediterranean and Black Sea. Depth range from intertidal zone to 200 m (660 ft). *Reproduction:* Litter number four to seven; gestation period 4 months. *Biology:* Found on sand and mud bottoms, sometimes in estuaries and near rocky reefs. Feeds on crustaceans, gastropods, cephalopods, and benthic bony fishes.

A. Purcell
R.H. Kuiter

131. Bluespotted stingray *(Dasyatis kuhlii)*

Identification: Rhomboid disc, anterior and posterior margins are slightly convex; snout short and not produced; dorsal tail finfold short, ventral finfold length 70% of disc width; tail equal to or slightly longer than disc; eyes large, slightly smaller than interorbital width; dorsal color reddish-brown to olive drab, with blue spots and smaller black spots, sometimes with white rather than blue spots, tail with black and white bands. *Size:* Maximum disc width 50 cm (19.7 inches). *Range:* From Indian Ocean and Red Sea to Samoa, Japan, and Australia. Depth range from intertidal zone to 50 m (165 ft). *Biology:* Found on sandy bottoms near coral and rocky reefs. Usually in deeper parts of the lagoon or on the reef face, moves onto reef flat and into shallow lagoon waters at high tide. Solitary. Feeds on crabs and shrimp. Difficult to approach underwater.

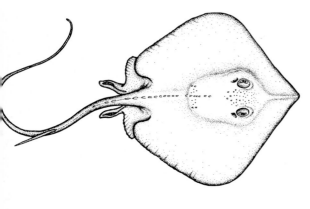

R.H. Kuiter

132. Atlantic stingray *(Dasyatis sabina)*

Identifcation: Rhomboid disc; anterior disc margin concave, outer and rear margins rounded; snout long and pointed, the length from the tip to the eyes is longer than the distance between the eyes; row of turbercles down middle of back; dorsal and ventral tail finfolds low, dorsal finfold inconspicuous (especially in juveniles); brown or yellowish-brown dorsum, paler toward the edges of the disc; ventrum white. The bluntnose stingray *(D. say)* is a sympatric ray that can be separated from *D. sabina* by its short, rounded snout, which is weakly convex, and its well developed dorsal finfold on tail. The bluntnose stingray attains a maximum disc width of 91 cm (36 inches). *Size:* Birth 10 cm (3.9 inches) disc width, maximum disc width 49 cm (19 inches). *Range:* U.S.A., from Chesapeake Bay to Florida and the Gulf of Mexico. Depth range from intertidal zone to 20 m (66 ft). Most common in shallow coastal areas. *Reproduction:* Gives birth in late summer in Florida. *Biology:* An inshore species, often observed in estuaries and lagoons. Ascends rivers, having been caught 320 km (200 mi) up the Mississippi river. Digs holes in sand and mud by undualting the disc margin. The ray usually faces into the current while feeding in this manner, so the current carries the sediment away from the feeding depression. Feeds on surface, infaunal, and tube dwelling species, including tube anemones, polychaete worms, small crustaceans (amphipods, mole crabs, pistol shrimp), clams, and serpent stars.

133. Thorntail stingray *(Dasyatis thetidis)*

Identification: Rhomboid disc; in adults large tubercles are present down the midline of the back, between eyes and on the tail; long ventral finfold, no dorsal finfold on tail; tail thick at base but more whip-like towards the end; one or two stings on tail; dark green to black dorsal coloration, no markings. *Size:* Maximum disc width 2 m (6.6 ft). *Range:* South Africa, Australia, and New Zealand. Depth range from intertidal zone to 380 m (1,254 ft). *Biology:* Occurs near coral reefs, in lagoons, and on the reef flat, rocky reefs, in estuaries and also reported to enter rivers in Australia. Observed to aggregate in caves and in rocky reef archways in New Zealand. Gatherings reported in shallow water in summer, possibly mating groups. Reported to feed on crabs, mantis shrimp, worms, clams, and conger eels.

134. Tahitian stingray *(Himantura fai)*

Identification: Rhomboid disc; skin is smooth; snout bluntly pointed; tail long (when intact it can be almost three times the length of disc), slender with no spines and one functional sting; color of dorsum uniform tan to brown. The sharpnose stingray *(H. gerrardi)* is a closely related species that differs from *H. fai* in having a more sharply pointed snout, a row of enlarged denticles in the middle of the back, and light and dark brown transverse bands on the tail (these bands may fade in adults). The sharpnose stingray occurs in the Indian and western Pacific Oceans. *Size:* Maximum disc width 1 m (3.3 ft), possibly larger. *Range:* Society Islands, Thailand, and India. Occurs from intertidal zone to at least 20 m (66 ft). *Biology:* In Rangiroa, French Polynesia, they are abundant in the lagoon and aggregate in shallow water to feed at night.

135. Caribbean stingray
(Himantura schmarde)

Identification: Disc oval with a short median snout lobe, the anterior margin is nearly straight; upper surface of disc covered with small tubercles, one enlarged tubercle on each shoulder; spiracle two times as long as the eye; longest gill opening 0.75 to 1 times as long as the eye; tail about two times as long as disc, two stings usually present; color of dorsum dark brown or dirty olive with disc margins darker, tail black, ventrum yellowish or creamy white with dark margin. A similar species, *H. pacifica,* occurs along the Pacific coast of Costa Rica and can be distinguished from *H. schmarde* by its longer spiracles (3 times as long as the eye), its longer gill openings (two times as long as the eye), and its inconspicuous shoulder tubercles. *Size:* Maximum disc width 1.2 m (4 ft). *Range:* Cuba to Dutch Guiana, including all of Caribbean. Common near Cuba. *Biology:* Found on sandy bottoms, sometimes near coral reefs. Also reported from rivers in Venezuela. Little is known about the biology of the Caribbean stingray. The closely related Pacific stingray *(H. pacifica)* enters shallow water at night to feed on snapping shrimp, mantis shrimp, and bivalves.

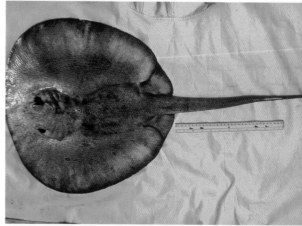

D. Watson

136. Honeycomb stingray
(Himantura uarnak)

Identification: Rhomboid disc; tail about three times length of disc; one sting usually present; flat tubercles on back; tail black and white banded; dorsal color dark spots on tan dorsal surface, in larger specimens the spots are often interconnected, forming a reticulated pattern. Young specimens often without markings on disc, but with banded tail. A similar species, the reticulated stingray *(H. fava),* has an oval disc, an elongate median snout lobe, and is dark brown overall with dull yellow reticulations. That species has only been reported from India. *Size:* Birth 20-40 cm (7.9-15.7 inches) disc width, maximum disc width 2 m (6.6 ft). *Range:* Indo-West Pacific from the Red Sea to South Africa, east to the Philippines, Australia, Melanesia, and Polynesia. Recent immigrant to Mediterranean via the Suez Canal. Depth range from intertidal zone to 75 m (248 ft). *Reproduction:* Litter number one to five; gestation about 1 year. In Japan and South Africa, gives birth in summer. *Biology:* Feeds on both benthic and neritic prey, including bony fishes, crustaceans (crabs, mantis shrimp, alpheid shrimp), molluscs (squid, bivalves, and snails), and jellyfishes.

N. Coleman

137. Roundnose stingray *(Himantura sp.1)*

Identification: Rhomboid disc, slightly wider than long; pectoral fins rounded; snout rounded with a small projection at tip; disc smooth, except for a row of denticles in the middle of the back; tail length over twice, and as much as three times, the length of the disc; color black or grayish-blue. This species may be synonymous with *H. fai,* and has been misidentified as the mangrove stingray, *H. granulata* (see Coleman 1981). In the mangrove stingray, the disc is oval, the median snout lobe is short, the distance from the tip of the snout to the eyes is less than twice the distance between the eyes, the margins of the disc and pelvic fins are white, and the stings (there are usually two), and tail posterior to them, are also white. The mangrove stingray is known from Australia, New Guinea, India, and Micronesia (Ponape), and attains a disc width of about 1 m (3.2 ft). *Size:* Maximum disc width to at least 1 m (3.2 ft). *Range:* Reported from South Africa and, based on this photo, Australia (Queensland), and Lord Howe Island. It is very common around Heron Island on the Great Barrier Reef. *Biology:* Solitary or forms aggregations of 10 or more. Moves into tidal flats at flood tide to feed, often associated with white-spotted shovelnose ray.

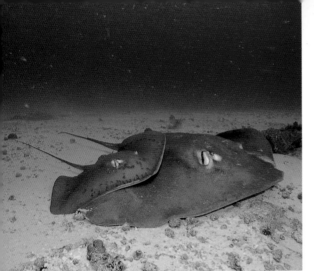

M. Strickland

138. Smalleye stingray *(Himantura sp.2)*

Identification: Rhomboid disc; snout round with small projection at tip; distance from eyes to the tip of the snout greater than the distance between the eyes; eyes very small and not prominent; spiracles large, eight times larger than the area of the eye; tail one to two times disc length; tail whip-like; usually a single large sting; skin smooth, without large denticles; dorsal color dark brown, with lighter area around spiracles and eyes. Another large member of this genus, Alcock's stingray *(H. alcockii)*, has a pointed snout, much longer than the distance between the eyes, a long, cylindrical tail, not twice as long as disc length, usually one sting on the tail, and a olive-brown dorsum with purplish disc edges and pale spots on the disc and base of tail. It occurs around India, and possibly Thailand. *Size:* Maximum disc width to at least 2 m (6.4 ft). *Range:* Thailand. *Biology:* This ray has been observed near coral reefs and is regularly observed by divers near Phuket Island, Thailand. Solitary individuals and small aggregations have been observed.

M. Bacon

139. Feathertail stingray
(Hypolophus sephen)

Identification: Disc rhomboid, anterior margin is nearly straight, posterior margin is convex; tail not twice as long as disc, with no dorsal finfold or keel and a long, broad ventral finfold; stings on tail further back than in many rays; dorsal color brown to black, ventrum white. *Size:* Birth 20 cm (7.9 inches) disc width, maximum disc width 1.8 (5.9 ft). *Range:* Wide ranging in Indian and western Pacific oceans; Japan, Philippines, New Guinea, Australia, to South Africa. Depth range from intertidal zone to 50 m (165 ft). *Biology:* Occurs near coral reefs in lagoons, reef flats, and reef faces. Also in estuaries and commonly ascends rivers into freshwater (reported to occur and breed more then 1,600 kilometers, 1,000 miles, up the Ganges River). Feeds on tidal flats at flood tide. Dominant food items include bony fishes (gobies, ponyfishes, threadfin bream, flatfishes), worms, shrimp, and crabs. It also eats snails, bivalves, and sea squirts. Young specimens feed more on invertebrates than adults. Usually solitary. One specimen that I observed returned to the same spot to bury at ebb tide for several days in a row. I have observed this species being cleaned by the bluestreak cleaner wrasse.

140. Bluespotted ribbontail ray
(Taeniura lymma)

Identification: Oval disc; yellow-brown with bright blue spots. *Size:* Maximum disc width 90 cm (35.4 inches). *Range:* East coast of Africa, including Red Sea, east to Philippines, Australia, Melanesia and Polynesia. Depth range from intertidal zone to 20 m (66 ft). *Reproduction:* Litter number up to seven. *Biology:* Common in lagoons, on tidal flats, and on sand patches on the reef face. At flood tide, moves into tidal zone to feed on worms, shrimps, hermit crabs, and small bony fishes. Feeds during day and possibly also at night. Seeks refuge under table corals, staghorn coral beds, and ship wreck debris; it rarely is observed to bury under the sand. Aggregations of mature males observed in shallow waters, gatherings possibly related to reproduction. Often visits cleaning stations to be cleaned by wrasses. Shy and difficult to approach underwater. Usually does not do well in aquariums.

141. Marbled ribbontail ray *(Taeniura melanospilos)*

Identification: Round disc; tail slightly longer than disc; dorsum gray with darker marbling, ventrum white. *Taeniura grabata* is a similar, possibly synonymous, species that occurs in the southern Mediterranean, East Africa, and, possibly, the Red Sea. *Taeniura meyeni* is a smaller species, with a narrower disc, a shorter tail, and a blackish brown dorsum. It has been reported from Mauritius. *Size:* Maximum disc width 1.6 m (5.3 ft). *Range:* Wide ranging in Indian and west Pacific oceans, including Red Sea, also occurs around the Galapagos Islands and Cocos Island (where it is very common) in the eastern Pacific. Depth range 3-500 m (10-1,650 ft). *Reproduction:* Litter number up to seven. *Biology:* Occurs near rocky reefs, estuaries, coral reef faces, and in lagoons. Lays on sand, rock and coral bottoms. Voracious predator; feeds on bivalves, crabs, shrimps, and benthic fishes. The related *T. grabata* feeds on worms, snails, nudibranchs, crustaceans, cephalopods (mainly squid), bony fishes (hake, goatfish, mackerel, sole), sharks (catsharks) and skates. Solitary or aggregates, sometimes in large groups. Jacks (e.g., big-eyed jack) and cobia commonly associate with this species, swimming just above or below ray as it moves over the bottom. Report of diver being stabbed by sting and killed when he tried to ride one of these rays. Average aquarium specimen (reported longevity record 81 days).

J.E. Randall / M. Strickland (inset)

142. Porcupine ray *(Urogymnosus africanus)*

Identification: Disc oval; tail sting is absent; tail approximately the same length as disc and with no folds or keels; adults with large, conspicuous thorns on trunk and pectoral fins; dorsum white to light gray. A second species, named *U. laevior*, was described from India and differs from *U. africanus* in that the pectoral fins are covered with small rounded denticles, not large thorns. A species, which may prove to be *U. laevior*, has been observed off of Thailand (inset photo). It has no thorns on the pectoral fins, has thorns on the trunk, and is grey above with white and black spots. *Size:* Maximum disc width 1 m (3.3 ft). *Range:* East Africa to Australia and the Marshall Islands. *Reproduction:* One female *U. laevior* reported with 12 pups. *Biology:* Observed on sand bottoms in reef lagoons and near reef faces, and sometimes in caves. A bold species that often allows divers to approach very close.

FAMILY UROLOPHIDAE (ROUND STINGRAYS or STINGAREES)

Round stingrays and stingarees are similar in morphology to the preceding group and considered by some to be in the same family. The most conspicuous difference between the two is the well developed caudal fin in the stingarees, which is lacking in whiptail stingrays. Also, the urolophids are smaller (the largest species reaching about 80 cm or 31.5 inches, in length) and have shorter, broader tails. There are currently three genera recognized in the family Urolophidae. The two most likely encountered by reef watchers are *Trygonoptera* and *Urolophus*. Members of the genus *Trygonoptera* are apparently restricted in distribution to Australia, Tasmania, and the East Indies. There are 34 species in the family and most occur in temperate areas; a number of these frequent rocky reefs. They are most abundant near Australia, and several species that occur there have yet to be described. The stingarees have one or two stings on the tail and they are responsible for injuring many bathers each year with this defensive weapon. Some species have been observed to swim backwards at a potential threat and successfully use the sting! Due to their small size they are probably not responsible for any human fatalities. Females also use their sting to ward off amorous males; there is a report of a sandyback stingaree *(Urolophus bucculentus)* that had the broken sting of a conspecific embedded in its back (the sting had been there long enough to have barnacles growing on it). These rays are ovoviviparous; the lining of the uteri exude uterine milk during pregnancy to aid in nourishing the developing embryos (uterine viviparity). Males of at least two species have longer tooth cusps than females, apparently to hold a mate during copulation. The stingarees are preyed upon by large teleosts and other elasmobranchs (e.g. tiger sharks, other stingarees). These rays do well, some species even reproducing, in public and large home aquariums.

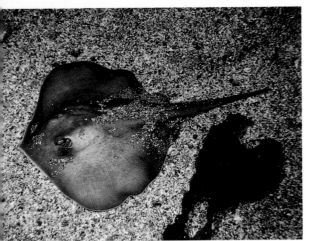

143. Sepia stingaree
(Urolophus aurantiacus)

Identification: Tail length less than disc length; no dorsal fin; disc wider than long; snout and pectoral tips rounded; back smooth, no enlarged denticles; dorsal color brown, no markings. *Size:* Birth about 8 cm (3.1 inches), maximum length 40 cm (15.7 inches). *Range:* Japan to East China Sea. *Reproduction:* Litter number up to four; gestation period about 1 year. Male grasps female pectoral fin and lies over the rear margin of the female's dorsum during mating. In one report, copulation lasted 14 minutes. *Biology:* Found on sand and rock bottoms.

144. Bulls-eye stingray
(Urolophus concentricus)

Identification: Dark rings around the edge of the disc, dark reticulations on dorsum, no dark spots. *Size:* Maximum length to at least 60 cm (23.6 inches). *Range:* Sea of Cortez, probably south to Panama, also the Galapagos Islands. Depth range from intertidal zone to 20 m (66 ft). *Reproduction:* Mating behavior of this species has been observed in the wild (similar to round stingray). *Biology:* Occurs on sandy and rocky bottoms, in bays, and around reefs. More often observed on rocky reefs than the sympatric round and spotted stingrays. Feeds on small crabs and worms.

145. Crossback stingaree
(Urolophus cruciatus)

Identification: Disc longer than wide; tail shorter than disc; lateral tail skin folds absent; small dorsal fin sometimes present in juveniles; banded pattern, including cross-like markings on the back. The spiny stingaree (*U. armatus*) is a similar species that has spines on its back, large tubercles on each shoulder, and a brown dorsum with darker spots. This spiny stingaree occurs around New Ireland in the Bismarck Sea. *Size:* Birth 13 cm (5.1 inches), maximum length 50 cm (19.7 inches). *Range:* Australia (New South Wales to Tasmania). Depth range from intertidal zone to 160 m (528 ft). Usually deeper than 25 m (83 ft) in Victoria, common in shallow water in Tasmania. *Biology:* Occurs along sandy coastlines, near estuaries, and rocky reefs. Usually buried in sand or mud during day. Feeds on crustaceans, molluscs, and worms. Said to raise and hold its tail and sting over its disc, like a scorpion, when threatened.

146. Giant.stingaree *(Urolophus gigas)*

Identification: Disc round in juveniles, oval in adults; small dorsal fin; tail shorter than disc; length of eye half the spiracle length; dorsum color dark brown to black with white spots and rings. A similar species, the circular stingaree *(U. circularis)*, can be separated by the ring of white or blue centered spots in the middle of the back and the size of the eye, which is about equal to space betweeen spiracles (see figure in Pictorial Key to the Families). The circular stingaree is only reported from western Australia and attains a maximum length of 60 cm (24 inches). *Size:* Maximum length 60 cm (24 inches). *Range:* Australia (south and western Australia). Depth range from intertidal zone to at least 35 m (116 ft). *Biology:* Occurs in estuaries, sea grass beds, and near rocky reefs. This species is not as aggressive as some of the other Australian round stingrays (e.g. sparsely-spotted stingray).

R.H. Kuiter

147. Round stingray *(Urolophus halleri)*

Identification: Tail shorter than disc length; no dorsal fin; back smooth, no tubercles; color variable, often plain brown with yellow spots and vermiculations. *Size:* Birth 13 cm (5.1 inches), maximum length 56 cm (22 inches). *Range:* Northern California to Panama. Depth range from intertidal zone to 91 m (300 ft). *Reproduction:* Litter number one to six. Females segregate in deeper offshore areas than males, move into shallows to mate (in late winter and spring in the Sea of Cortez), and, 2 to 3 months later, to give birth. Male grasps female by disc margin, flips under her and inserts a single clasper. Mating lasts about 5 minutes. *Biology:* Usually on sand and mud bottoms, sometimes around rocky reefs (especially in the Sea of Cortez). Feeds almost exclusively on worms, bivalves, and crustaceans (as many as 50 small shrimp have been found in the stomach of one ray); juveniles feed most on crustaceans and annelid worms, with few bivalves being consumed by this smaller size class. Adults bite off the extended siphons of certain bivalves and crush thin and moderately thick shelled clams. Digs large holes in the mud looking for prey (up to 13 cm or 5 inches, deep) and picks prey off eel grass. Forages during the day. Responsible for many stings to humans along California coast. Good aquarium fish.

M. Bacon

148. Yellow stingray *(Urolophus jamaicensis)*

Identification: Tail length not as long as disc; no dorsal fin; low tubercles occur along the back from the front of the eyes to the tail spine (not present in juveniles); pointed snout; disc slightly longer than wide in adults; dorsal color dark reticulated pattern and yellowish spots on a pale background. *Size:* Maximum length 67 cm (25.6 inches). *Range:* North Carolina, Gulf of Mexico, throughout the Caribbean, to Trinidad. Depth range from intertidal zone to at least 20 m (66 ft). *Reproduction:* Litter number two to four. During copulation, male grasps disc margin of female, swings under her, and inserts a single clasper. Other males will swim around and nudge the mating pair. Mating period includes spring. *Biology:* Occurs in harbors, bays, and lagoons, often near coral reefs. Excavates holes in the sand by undulating the anterior disc margin and exposes buried prey. Reported to feed on shrimp, but probably also eats small fishes, clams, and worms. Lifts front of disc and remains motionless, forming a "pseudo-cave" to attract potential prey. Good aquarium fish.

149. Cortez round stingray
(*Urolophus maculatus*)

Identification: Similar to the round stingray, but with conspicuous black spots on back and ventral surface. Tumbes round stingray *(U. tumbesensis)* has been reported from shallow water near Peru. It has a vermiculated color pattern with spots equal to the eye diameter, and denticles and thorns on the dorsum and tail. *Size:* Maximum length 42 cm (16.5 inches). *Range:* Magdalena Bay on the west coast of Baja California, Mexico to Sea of Cortez. Depth range from intertidal zone to 20 m (66 ft). *Reproduction:* I observed a female of this species being bitten and held by two male round stingarees. The female thrust her sting at the two courting males and escaped their grasp. *Biology:* Occurs on shallow sand and mud bottoms, in sea grass beds, near rocky reefs, and in bays. Feeds on worms and crustaceans (amphipods). Forages during the day.

D. Gotshall

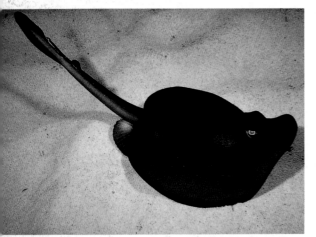

150. Oval stingaree *(Trygonoptera ovalis)*

Identification: Disc oval; small dorsal fin present; tail length 75-100% of disc length; dorsum color gray to grayish brown with two dark patches at the center of the disc, dark lines from patches to tail. *Size:* Maximum length 61 cm (24 inches). *Range:* Western Australia. Depth range 4-43 m (13-142 ft). *Biology:* Occurs near reefs, sea grass beds, and sandy beaches. Observed resting exposed on the sea bottom or buried under the sand.

R.H. Kuiter ▲ ▼

151. Sparsely-spotted stingaree
(*Trygonoptera paucimaculatus*)

Identification: Disc round; tail as long, or nearly as long, as disc; lateral skin folds present on tail; no dorsal fin; dorsum pale gray or sandy brown with or without ring of white spots. *Size:* Maximum length 57 cm (22.4 inches). *Range:* Australia (New South Wales to western Australia, including Tasmania). Depth range 5-150 m (17-495 ft), deeper in northern parts of its range. *Reproduction:* Litter number two to six, with larger females having larger litters. Two peaks in reproductive activity, August and September, March and April. *Biology:* Occurs on sand, shell, and mud bottoms, in bays and estuaries and often in deeper offshore habitats. Juveniles feed primarily on small crustaceans (amphipods and isopods), while adults consume worms, crabs, shrimp, and small bony fishes. This ray is preyed upon by sharks and other stingarees. Reported to be more aggressive than other round stingrays, stinging without much provocation.

152. Common stingaree
(Trygonoptera testaceus)

Identification: Disc more rhomboid, slightly broader than long; tail as long, or nearly as long, as disc; lateral skin folds on side of tail; small dorsal fin usually present; dorsum brown to black, tail sometimes black and white. The Javanese stingraee *(T. javanica)* is apparently closely related to this species. It differs in having black spots on the dorsum and more papillae behind the lower jaw (13 compared to 6 in *T. testaceus*). The javanese stingaree occurs near Indonesia. *Size:* Maximum length 92 cm (36.2 inches). *Range:* Australia (Queensland south to south Australia). Depth range from intertidal zone to 130 m (429 ft). *Biology:* Occurs on sand and mud bottoms in bays, estuaries, and near rocky reefs. Feeds on worms, crustaceans, bony fishes, and other stingarees.

R.H. Kuiter

153. Banded stingaree *(Trygonoptera sp.)*

Identification: Disc slightly wider than long; tail equal to or as long as disc; dorsal fin present; lateral skin folds on side of tail; base color gray to brown with darker banded color pattern. Often mistaken for cross-back stingaree. *Size:* Maximum length 40 cm (15.7 inches). *Range:* Southern New South Wales, Australia. Usually deeper than 15 m (50 ft). *Biology:* Observed on sand bottoms near rocky reefs.

FAMILY MYLIOBATIDAE (EAGLE RAYS)

These rays are similar in appearance and behavior to cownose rays. They differ morphologically in the form of the snout (it is a single projecting lobe in eagle rays). Like the two preceding ray families, these batoids also possess tail stings (sometimes up to five are present on a single individual) that are used for self defense. There are 23 species and four genera in the family. The genus *Myliobatis* has a rostral lobe that is connected to the side of the pectoral fins, while this lobe is not contiguous with the pectoral fins in *Aetobatus, Pteromylaeus* and *Aetomylaeus*. The Japanese bat ray *(Myliobatis tobijei)* is known from reef areas near Japan, but is not included in the species accounts. This species has an elongated snout, a narrow subrostral lobe, and rounded pectoral fin tips. The adults are light brown dorsally, while the juveniles have pale and reddish spots. The eagle rays swim in the same manner as the cownose and devil rays and can move at great speed and jump clear of the water's surface. They commonly rest on the sea floor, raising themselves up on their pectoral fins and pushing off the bottom if danger threatens. They sometimes school, but usually not in massive numbers like the cownose rays. They are ovoviviparous (uterine viviparity). Courtship and copulation has been reported in two species and the spotted eagle ray has bred in a large oceanarium. Apparently females leap out of the water and slam down on the water's surface to facilitate birthing. Estuaries serve as nursery grounds for some species. By excavating large holes in the substrate and grubbing with their elongated, flexible snouts, eagle rays capture invertebrates that they masticate with their dental plates. Bat rays, and possibly other eagle ray species, are often followed by bony fishes that consume the small invertebrates the rays expose when feeding. In the wild and in aquariums, myliobatids, especially young specimens, are commonly eaten by sharks and there is at least one report of an individual being preyed upon by a killer whale. Eagle rays are usually difficult to approach underwater (the underwater photographer is best to stay still and let the ray approach), and they fare well in public aquariums.

M. Snyderman

R. Van Der Elst
M. Francis

154. Bat ray *(Myliobatis californicus)*

Identification: Subrostral lobe short, rounded; pectoral fins with broad, rounded tips; small dorsal fin positioned just behind the tips of the pelvic fins; dorsal coloration olive to brown with no markings. *Size:* Birth 29 cm (11.4 inches) disc width, maximum disc width 1.8 m (5.9 ft). *Range:* Oregon to the Sea of Cortez. Occurs near or over rocky reefs and kelp beds. Depth range from the surface to 46 m (152 ft). *Reproduction:* Litter number up to 10; gestation is about 1 year. Form large mating aggregations. One or more males will follow close behind a female with their rostrums near her vent. Male moves under the female so his back is against her belly, rotates a clasper up and to the side, and inserts it into her cloaca as the pair swims with synchronous beats of the pectoral fins. *Biology:* Dig out invertebrates from the sand and mud with the snout and also digs large depressions by lifting body on its pectoral fin tips and moving up and down. The suction generated by this behavior pulls the sand out from under its body, exposing buried prey. Clams are a major food item of juveniles; as they grow, echiuroid worms become more important in their diet. Also eats polychaete worms, abalones, oysters, snails, shrimp, crabs, and bony fishes. When eating molluscs, it ingests the animal whole, crushes the shell, spits it all out, and reingests the soft body parts. Swim off the bottom and rest on the substrate or on the kelp. Solitary or schooling (large schools containing thousands of individuals reported); sometimes form mixed schools with spotted eagle rays. Major food of broadnose sevengill shark, small specimens sometimes eaten by California sea lion.

155. Bull ray *(Myliobatis aquila)*

Identification: Subrostral lobe short and round; head flat; pectoral fin tips narrow and rounded; dorsal fin behind pelvic tips by one to three times its base length; dorsal color brown to black with no markings. *Size:* Birth 25 cm (9.8 inches) disc width, maximum disc width 1.5 (4.9 ft). *Range:* Southern North Sea to South Africa, including entire Mediterranean. Depth range from the surface to 300 m (1,089 ft). *Reproduction:* Litter number three to seven; gestation 6-8 months. Males of this species have large spines, or tubercles, above each eye that may jab into the female's ventrum during mating (i.e. if they mate like the bat ray); this may aid the male in maintaining his position as the pair swims through the water. *Biology:* Occurs in shallow bays and estuaries, occasionally near rocky reefs. Feeds on clams, snails, crabs, worms, sea squirts, and small bony fishes (gobies, codlets, flounders, eels). Reported to flap its pectoral fins over the substrate to expose buried prey and to dig out prey with its snout.

156. Southern bat ray *(Myliobatus tentuicaudatus)*

Identification: Subrostral lobe short, narrow, and round; pectoral fin tips narrow and pointed; dorsal coloration gray-green with blue bars and blotches (more apparent in smaller individuals). Rare individuals are bright orange with gray-green blotches. *Size:* Maximum disc width 1.5 m (4.9 ft). *Range:* New Zealand (Kermadec Islands to northern South Island), Australia (southern Queensland around southern coast to western Australia). Depth range from intertidal zone to 110 m (360 ft). *Biology:* Occurs in bays, estuaries, and near rocky reefs. Often observed lying motionless on the bottom. Excavate infaunal prey by pulling water through their spiracles and jetting it out of the mouth and gills toward the bottom. This results in a depression in the sand or mud as deep as 20 cm (7.9 inches). In northern New Zealand, they feed mainly on Cook's turban top shell; they are reported to crush them in specific areas, where large piles of shell fragments are found. They also feed on clams, oysters, worms, and crabs. Usually solitary.

157. Barbless eagle ray (Aetomylaeus nichofii)

Identification: Subrostral lobe long, narrow, and rounded; tail sting is absent; disc width twice the length; origin of dorsal fin opposite the pelvic fin axil; dorsum smooth; dorsum bronze with approximately seven transverse pale blue bands. The genus *Aetomylaeus* contains three other species. *Aetomylaeus milvus* (Red Sea, Indonesia, and China) has ocelli on the rear part of the disc with greenish-brown edges, and a disc that is less than twice as wide as it is long. *Aetomylaeus maculatus* (Indonesia) has a dorsal fin that originates behind the pelvic fin axil, small spines on the middle of the back, and is similar in color to *A. milvus*. *Aetomylaeus vespertilio* (Indonesia) has a smooth back, a disc that is nearly twice as wide as it is long, a dorsal fin origin behind pelvic fin axil, and black, transverse bands on the rear portion of the disc. *Size:* Maximum disc width 35 cm (13.8 inches). *Range:* Indo-West Pacific. *Biology:* Occurs in coastal waters, including areas near coral reefs. Feeds on worms, snails, crustaceans, and bony fishes.

CSIRO

158. Spotted eagle ray (Aetobatus narinari)

Identification: Subrostral lobe long, narrow, and rounded; two to five stings at the base of the tail; dorsal coloration black or bluish, most often with numerous, small, white spots. A spotless form, known as *A. flagellum*, is usually considered synonymous with this species. *Size:* Birth 50 cm (19.7 inches) disc width, maximum disc width 3.5 (11.5 ft). *Range:* Circum-tropical. Depth range from intertidal zone to 24 m (80 ft). *Reproduction:* Litter number one to four; gestation about 12 months. One or more males follow a female and rasp her dorsum with their upper dental plates. One male then grasps the edge of female's pectoral fin and flips under her, so they are venter-to-venter, and inserts a single clasper. Mating lasts from 30 sec to 1.5 min. In a short time period (e.g. 1 hour), a female may mate with up to four different males. *Biology:* Occurs in most reef habitats, and in the open ocean. Probes the sand with its snout to locate food items. Feeds on clams, oysters, snails, worms, shrimp, octopuses, squid, sea urchins, and bony fishes (with adults feeding heavily on bony fishes). Groups move from reef channels and the reef face during flood tide to feed and, possibly, to avoid predators. Single individuals, pairs, or large schools (200 individuals) observed. It is important prey for several large sharks. Sharks are reported to follow eagle rays during the birthing period and feed on the newborns. Known to breach; one report of a leaping specimen landing in a small boat! Usually shy and difficult to get close to underwater.

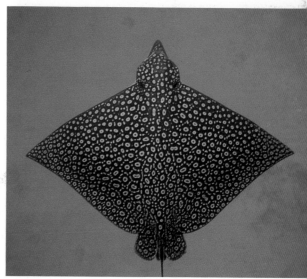

D. Perrine

FAMILY RHINOPTERIDAE (COWNOSE RAYS)

This family has 10 species that have a divided subrostral lobe or fin, a broad head, a concave forehead, a single dorsal fin near the base of a long whip-like tail, and one or two stings at the base of the tail. Another characteristic useful in differentiating species within this family is the number of tooth rows in each jaw and the shape of the teeth. The two species covered in this book have seven rows of pavement-like teeth in each jaw. These rays are strong swimmers that swim by flapping their large angular pectoral fins up and down. They occasionally rest on the sea floor and have been known to breech clear of the water's surface. The cownose rays are ovoviviparous (uterine viviparity); mating has been reported in one species in captivity. The flaccid subrostral fins of these rays are used to probe the substrate in search of bivalve prey and may serve to detect water expelled from a clam's siphon or the weak bioelectric field generated by a bivalve. To excavate their prey, they dig deep depressions (up to 40 cm or 15.7 inches in depth) in bottom sediment by flapping the pectoral fins and by sucking sediment through the mouth and expelling it out of the gill slits. The flat tooth plates, present on both jaws, are used to grind their hard shelled prey. Several species form massive schools that can number in the thousands! These groups stir huge clouds of silt that may extend as far as 2 km (1.2 miles), as they forage. At least one species (*Rhinoptera bonasus*, the cownose ray) forms segregated schools; juvenile bisexual groups segregate by size, while the adults form unisex schools. There is a reported fatality of a fisherman stabbed in the stomach by the sting of a flapnose ray. They do well in large public aquariums, with one species known to mate in captivity.

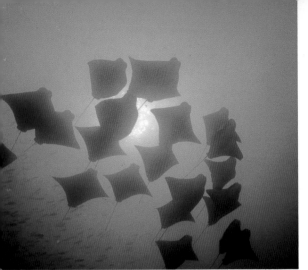

159. Pacific cownose ray
(Rhinoptera steindachneri)

Identification: Subrostral lobe has a median notch; tooth morphology set this ray apart from the flapnose ray; dark brown dorsally, creamy white ventrum; only species in this genus known from eastern Pacific. *Size:* Maximum disc width 71 cm (28 inches). *Range:* Mexico and the Galapagos Islands. Occurs over sandy bottoms, often near rocky or coral reefs, also near reef dropoffs. *Biology:* Observed in large schools; sometimes associates with the spotted eagle ray. Will jump clear of the water's surface.

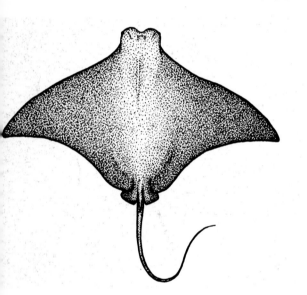

160. Flapnose ray *(Rhinoptera javanica)*

Identification: Subrostral lobe has a median notch; tooth morphology set this ray apart from the Pacific cownose ray; Brown to blackish-green dorsally, white ventrum. *Size:* Birth 38-47 cm (15-18.5 inches) disc width, maximum disc width 1.5 m (4.9 ft). *Range:* Japan to Indonesia, west to South Africa. *Reproduction:* Litter number one. Courtship similar to spotted eagle ray. Males nip the female's dorsal surface during courtship. Mating occurs with the rays in venter-to-venter orientation, with one or both claspers inserted. The mating pair usually rests on the substrate with the female on top of the male. During copulation, as many as three other males may mount the female and nip her back. Mating lasts about 30 seconds and one female may mate with several males in a short time period. In Japan, breed in late summer and fall. *Biology:* Occurs in bays, estuaries, and near coral reefs. Usually in large schools (as many as 500 individuals reported in a school). Feeds on clams, oysters, and crustaceans. Does well in captivity (longevity reports of over 2 years).

FAMILY MOBULIDAE (DEVIL RAYS)

These spectacular rays are often encountered around rocky and coral reefs in tropical to warm temperate seas. The family contains two genera, *Mobula* and *Manta*. The genus *Mobula* consists of nine species distinguished from *Manta* by the ventral mouth, the presence of teeth in both jaws, and a narrow head. The genus *Manta* consists of one wide- ranging species, although until recently, a number (i.e., *M. alfredi, M. ehrenbergii, M. hamiltoni*) were considered to be valid. Some of the manta species were differentiated on the basis of color pattern, which is quite variable even in a single geographical area. The *Mobula* spp. can be distinguished from one another by the presence or absence of a tail sting, size, pectoral fin shape, cephalic fin length, tail length and shape, and color pattern. The serious student of devil rays should consult Notarbartolo Di Sciara (1987), which is a paper revising the genus. The mobulid rays have large, complex brains and well developed behavioral repertoires. The rest of the chondrocranium is filled with an intricate network of arteries (known scientifically as the arterial rete mirabile cranicum), the function of which may include cooling the brain, supporting and protecting the brain, and, possibly, enhancing blood monitoring. These rays are ovoviviparous (uterine viviparity), usually producing one or two offspring per litter. What was presumably mating has been observed in one species and possibly another. In one case, the pair swam in tandem during copulation and in the other report the rays mated on the sea floor. Several of the mobulids (e.g., manta ray Japanese devil ray, sickelfin devil ray) are most often encountered in the summer months. Mating and birthing occur in shallow water, as is the case with many elasmobranchs, and juveniles remain in these areas. During winter devil rays may migrate to warmer areas, to deeper water, or disperse offshore. The devil rays are filter feeders that consume primarily planktonic crustaceans and, in some species, small schooling fishes. They swim by flapping their large pectoral fins and are usually observed cruising near the ocean surface. However, they also spend time resting on the substrate as indicated by one observation of a group of 12 devil rays resting on the sea floor. These rays seek the services of cleaner wrasses and often hang over or swim near "cleaning stations," sometimes in groups. All the mobulids will leap from the water (smaller species are known to clear the water's surface by several body lengths) and oftentimes jumps are made in quick succession. Several leaping behaviors have been described for mobulid rays. These rays sometimes launch vertically into the air and land on their bellies causing a loud clap. Larger mantas will lift their bodies part way from the water and fall backward or forward, or slide sideways back into the ocean. Smaller devil rays will somersault in the air, from one to three times, before falling back into the sea. There is one report of a devil ray being attacked and killed by a killer whale. Divers are usually excited when a manta ray appears, but it is a poor practice to pursue and try to hitch a ride on these giants. In areas that are frequented by divers, mantas have become wary and have ceased to approach divers if regularly chased. On rare occasions, individual mantas will solicit the attention of humans, possibly "enjoying" the tactile stimulation given by the diver. On numerous occassions, I observed that mantas approached or grasped from above quickly rolled on to their backs, exposing their bright white underbelly, and sank toward the depths (dubbed "dorsal roll"). When some distance separated the manta and the observer, the ray would upright itself and swim away. Another unusual behavior pattern was the "S-curve display"; the manta curled one fin toward its belly and the other toward its back and tilted on its side (in cross section the ray forms the letter S), so its dorsum faced the observer. This display occurred when I approached the ray from the side. The mobulid rays adapt poorly to captivity, although the manta ray has been successfully maintained for short periods (average survival time at Okinawa Expo Aquarium is 36 days).

161. Manta ray *(Manta birostris)*

Identification: Mouth terminal; head broad; cephalic fins long; dorsal coloration black or reddish brown, sometimes black morph with white shoulder patches; one albino specimen reported. *Size:* Birth about 1.2 m (3.9 ft) disc width, maximum disc width 6.7 m (21.9 ft), possibly larger. *Range:* Circumtropical. *Reproduction:* Litter number one or two. One harpooned specimen expelled a pup when it breached and it may be this behavior is part of "normal" birthing. *Biology:* Occurs most often in nearshore waters (occasionally over deep water), near coral and rocky reefs. When feeding the cephalic fins are uncurled, spread apart, and the animal moves about in various directions and sometimes somersaults in the water column. Feeds on planktonic crustaceans and small schooling bony fishes. Solitary individuals or loose aggregations (of 50) observed, never seen in true schools. Observed in association with other marine vertebrates, including: dolphins, sea birds, sharks and other rays (spotted eagle ray). They often are hosts to one or more discfishes. Mantas breach, but adult specimens do not completely clear the water surface. Instead they drive their bodies part way out of the water and fall back into sea, with individuals sometimes performing several consecutive jumps.

D. Gotshall

162. Lesser devil ray *(Mobula hypostoma)*

Identification: Tail sting absent; base of tail laterally compressed; distance between the first gill slit margins 14% of disc width; dorsal coloration dark brown to black. *M. rochebrunei* is a similar species and is the only member of the genus known from the eastern tropical Atlantic. *Size:* Birth 55 cm (21.7 inches) disc width, maximum disc width 1.2 m (3.9 ft). *Range:* North Carolina to Argentina, including Gulf of Mexico and Caribbean. *Reproduction:* Litter number one. Copulation has been reported to take place in a venter-to-venter orientation as the copulating rays continue to swim at the water's surface. The duration of mating reported to be 10 minutes. *Biology:* Occurs in shallow coastal waters, often with tips of pectoral fins breaking the water's surface. Feeds mainly on planktonic crustaceans (mysids), but also consumes some small schooling fishes (killifish). Solitary, small groups, or schools.

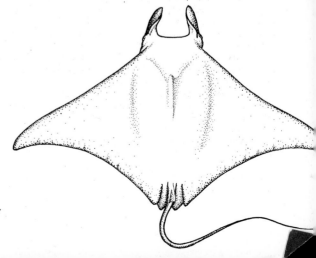

163. Japanese devil ray *(Mobula japonica)*

Identification: Tail sting present; tail very long (whip-like) with a row of white denticles on each side; dorsal coloration blue, with white-tipped dorsal fin and white shoulder patches in newborns and juveniles and sometimes on adults. Probably synonymous with *M. mobular* from the North Atlantic and Mediterranean. *Size:* Birth 85 cm (33.5 inches) disc width, maximum disc width 3.1 m (10.2 ft). *Range:* Tropical and warm temperate seas. From the eastern tropical Pacific, west to the east coast of Africa, south to northern New Zealand, and north to Japan. Occurs in inshore surface waters. *Reproduction:* Litter number one. Mating probably occurs in spring and summer in Sea of Cortez. *Biology:* Feeds almost exclusively on krill. Solitary, small groups, sometimes, but rarely, schools (that can number over 100 individuals).

D. Perrine

164. Pygmy devil ray *(Mobula munkiana)*

Identification: Tail sting absent; base of tail laterally compressed; dorsal coloration purplish to gray, ventral surface white with gray pectoral fins. *Size:* Birth about 35 cm (13.8 inches) disc width, maximum disc width 1 m (3.3 ft). *Range:* Sea of Cortez to Ecuador. *Biology:* Occurs in shallow, inshore, surface waters. Feeds on mysids near the sea bottom. Usually observed in large schools. This mobula jumps as high as two disc widths clear of the water, sometimes somersaulting as it falls back into the sea. I observed a group in the Sea of Cortez in which up to five individuals would breach simultaneously. These animals were observed to leap from the water for 5 minutes. *Biology:* Occurs in shallow coastal waters, often with tips of pectoral fins breaking the water's surface. Feeds mainly on planktonic crustaceans (mysids), but also consumes some small schooling fishes (killifish). Solitary, small groups, or schools.

T. Hobson
M. Snyderman

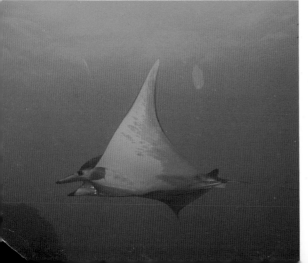

165. Sicklefin devil ray
(Mobula tarapanaca)

Identification: Tail sting present; tail shorter than disc; moon-shaped (lunate) rostral margin; pectoral fins strongly falcate; dorsal coloration brown to olive green, dorsal fin not white-tipped, ventral surface demarcated, white anteriorly, gray posteriorly. *Mobula eregoodootenkee* is another stingless devil ray known from the north Indian Ocean, the Red Sea to southeast Asia, Indonesia, and tropical Australia (see figure in Pictorial Key to Families). It is easily separated from other mobulas by its long-necked appearance and its very long cephalic fins (greater than 16% of disc width). This is a small species, reaching sexual maturity at a disc width of less than 1 m (3.3 ft.). *Size:* Birth just over 1 m (3.3 ft) disc width, maximum disc width 3 m (9.8 ft). *Range:* Circumtropical. Occurs in inshore areas, but apparently a more pelagic devil ray. *Reproduction:* Litter number one. *Biology:* This ray feeds on pelagic crustaceans and bony fishes (anchovies, small jacks, pufferfish). Most often solitary, occasionally forms groups; one report of a group of nine swimming in a tight circle at the water's surface.

166. Bentfin devil ray *(Mobula thurstoni)*

Identification: Tail sting absent; cephalic fins short (less than 16% of disc width); pectoral fins with double bend to front margin; dorsal color dark blue with white-tipped dorsal fin, ventral surface white with silver pectoral fin tips. *Mobula kuhlii*, which ranges from east Africa to Indonesia, is a similar species but the anterior margins of the pectoral fins are straight or slightly convex. This species reaches a maximum disc width of around 1 m (3.3 ft). *Size:* Birth 63 cm (24.8 inches) disc width, maximum disc width 1.8 m (5.9 ft). *Range:* Sea of Cortez and southern Mexico, west to South Africa, north to the Red Sea. Most abundant in shallow nearshore waters, usually at the surface, but down to at least 100 m (328 ft). *Reproduction:* Litter number one; gestation about 1 year. Reproduction occurs in shallow water, with mating in spring in the Sea of Cortez. The pectoral fins of the pups are folded up against the back before and during parturition. *Biology:* Feeds almost exclusively on planktonic crustaceans; juveniles (1.3 m disc width, 4.3 ft) consume both krill and mysids, while larger specimens feed only on krill. Solitary or in small groups (two to six individuals). Leaps clear of the water, sometimes somersaulting in the air. Will rest on the sea floor. Also floats at the surface with the pectoral fin tips protruding from the water.

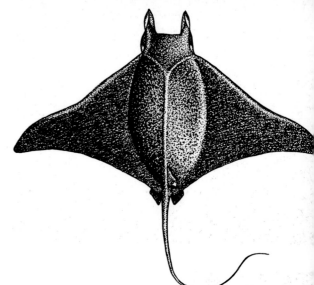

REFERENCES

Ainley, D.G., R.P. Henderson, H.R. Huber, R.J. Boekelheide, S.G. Allen, and R.L. McElroy. 1985. Dynamics of white shark/pinniped interactions in the Gulf of the Farollones. Mem. S. Calif. Acad. Sci. 9:109-122.

Allee, W.C., and J.C. Dickinson, Jr. 1954. Dominance and subordination in the smooth dogfish, *Mustelus canis* (Mitchill). Physiol. Zool. 27:356-364.

Annandale, N. 1909. Report on the fishes taken by the Bengal fisheries steamer "Golden Crown". Part I:Batoidei. Mem. Ind. Mus. 2:1-60.

Arnbom, T., and V. Papastavrou. 1988. Fish in association with whale sharks, *Rhiniodon typus*, near the Galapagos Islands. Noticias de Galapagos, 46:13-14.

Ayling, T., and G.J. Cox. 1982. Colins Guide to the Sea Fishes of New Zealand. W. Collins Publ. Ltd., Auckland, 343 pp.

Babel, J.S. 1967. Reproduction, life history, and ecology of the round stingray, *Urolophus halleri* Copper. Calif. Dept. Fish Game, Fish Bull. 137:104 pp.

Backus, R.H., S. Springer, and E.L. Arnold, Jr. 1956. A contribution to the natural history of the whitetip shark, *Pterolamiops longimanus* (Poey). Deep-sea Res. 3:178-188.

Baldridge, H.D. 1974. Shark Attack. New York, Berkley Corp. 263 pp.

Bane, G.W. Jr., 1966. Observations on the silky shark, *Carcharhinus falciformis*, in the Gulf of Guinea. Copeia, 1966:354-356.

Bass, A.J., J.D. D'Aubrey, and N. Kistnasamy. 1973. Sharks of the east coast of southern Africa. 1. The genus *Carcharhinus* (Carcharhinidae). Invest. Rep. Ocean. Res. Inst. Durban, 33:168 pp.

——. 1975. Sharks of the east coast of southern Africa. 2. The families Scyliorhinidae and Psuedotriakidae. Invest. Rep. Ocean. Res. Inst. Durban, 37:63 pp.

——. 1975a. Sharks of the east coast of southern Africa. 3. The families Carcharhinidae (excluding Mustelus and Carcharhinus) and Sphyrnidae. Invest. Rep. Ocean. Res. Inst. Durban, 38:100 pp.

——. 1975b. Sharks of the east coast of southern Africa. 4. The families Odontaspidae, Scapanorhynchidae, Isuridae,

Cetorhinidae, Alopiidae, Orectolobidae, and Rhiniodontidae. Invest. Rep. Ocean. Res. Inst. Durban, 39:102 pp.

——. 1975c. Sharks of the east coast of southern Africa. 5. The families Hexanchidae, Chlamydoselachidae, Heterodontidae, Pristiophoridae, and Squatinidae. Invest. Rep. Ocean. Res. Inst. Durban, 43:50 pp.

Baughman, J.L. 1955. The oviparity of the whale shark, *Rhincodon typus*, with records of this and other fishes in Texas waters. Copeia, 1955:54-55.

Beebe, W., and J. Tee-Van. 1941. Eastern Pacific expeditions of the New York Zoological Society. 25. Fishes from the tropical eastern Pacific. Part 2. Sharks. Zool., N.Y. 26:93-122.

——. 1941. Eastern Pacific expeditions of the New York Zoological Society. 26. Fishes from the tropical eastern Pacific. Part 3. Rays, Mantas and Chimeras. Zool., N.Y. 26:245-279.

Belbenoit, P. 1986. Fine analysis of predatory and defensive motor events in *Torpedo marmorata* (Pisces). J. Exp. Biol. 121:197-226.

Bigelow, H.B., and W.C. Schroeder. 1948. Sharks. Mem. Sears Found. Mar. Res. 1(pt 1):53-576.

——. 1953. Sawfishes, Guitarfishes, Skates and Rays. Mem. Sears Found. Mar. Res. 1(pt 2):1-514.

Bray, R.N., and M.A. Hixon. 1978. Night shocker: predatory behavior of the pacific electric ray *(Torpedo californica)*. Sci., 200:333-334.

Breder, C.M. Jr., and D.E. Rosen. 1966. Modes of Reproduction in Fishes. The Natural History Press, Garden City. 941 pp.

Brightwell, L.R. 1953. Further notes on the hermit crabs, *Eupagrus bernhardus*, and associated animals. Proc. Zool. Soc. Lond. 123:61-64.

Brockman, F.W. 1975. An observation on mating behavior of the southern stingray, *Dasyatis americana*. Copeia, 1975:784-785.

Cadenat, J., and J. Blache. 1981. Requins de Me diterrane e et d Atlantique. Fauen Tropical No. XXI. Paris: Office de la Recherche Scientifique et Technique Outer Mer (ORSTOM), 330 pp.

Capape , C. 1985. Donnies giﾐirales sur le rigime alimentaire des Myliobatidae (Pisces, Selachii). Archs. Inst. Pasteur

Tunis, 62:421- 427.

———. 1985. Donnies ginirales sur le rigime alimentaire des Dasyatidae (Pisces, Selachii). Archs. Inst. Pasteur Tunis, 62:299-304.

———. 1985. Propos sur la sexualiti des Poissons Silaciens. Archs. Inst. Pasteur Tunis. 62:429-464.

Capapé, C., and J. Zaouali. 1979. Etde du rigime alimentaire de deux Silaciens communs dans le gole de Gabis (Tunisie): *Rhinobatus rhinobatus* (Linni, 1758) et *Rhinobatus cemiculus* (Geoffroy Saint-Hilare, 1817). Archs Inst. Pasteur Tunis, 56:285-306.

Carey, F.G., J.G. Casey, and H.L. Pratt. 1982. Temperature and activities of a white shark, *Carcharodon*. Copeia, 1982:254-260.

Casey, J.G. and H.L. Pratt. 1985. Distribution of the white shark, *Carcharodon carcharias*, in the western North Atlantic. Mem. S. Calif. Acd. Sci. 9:12-14.

Casey, J.G., H.W. Pratt, and C. Stillwell. 1980-1983. The Shark Tagger. Newsletter of the Cooperative Shark Tagging Program, (1)1980, (2)1981, (3)1982, (4)1983. Narragansett, Rhode Island: Nat. Mar. Fish. Ser.

Casey, J.G., H.W. Pratt, C. Stillwell, and N. Kohler. 1984-1987. The Shark Tagger. Newsletter of the Cooperative Shark Tagging Program, (5)1984, (6)1985, (7)1986, (8)1987. Narragansett, Rhode Island: Nat. Mar. Fish. Ser.

Castro, J.I. 1983. The Sharks of North American Waters. College Station, Texas A&M Uni. Press, 180 pp.

Clark, E. 1963. The maintenance of sharks in captivity, with a report on their instrumental conditioning. In: Sharks and Survival, P.W. Gilbert (ed.). Boston, D.C. Heath and Co, 115-149 pp.

———. 1975. The strangest sea. Nat. Geo. 148:338-343.

Clark E., and E. Kristof. 1990. How deep do sharks go? Reflections on deep sea sharks. Amer. Littor. Soc. Spec. Publ. 14:79-84.

Clarke, T.A. 1971. The ecology of the scalloped hammerhead shark, *Sphyrna lewini*, in Hawaii. Pac. Sci. 25:133-44.

Cliff, G., S.F.J. Dudley, and B. Davis. 1989. Sharks caught in the protective gill nets off Natal, South Africa: 2. The great white shark, *Carcharodon carcharias* (Linnaeus). S. Afr. J. Mar. Sci. 8:131- 144.

———. 1990. Sharks caught in the protective gill nets off Natal, South Africa. 3. The shortfin mako shark, *Isurus oxyrinchus* (Rafinesque). S. Afr. J. Mar. Sci. 9:115-126.

Coles, R.J. 1910. Observations on the habits and distribution of certain fishes taken on the coast of North Carolina. Bull. Amer. Mus. Nat. Hist. 38:337-348.

Coleman, N. 1981. Australian Sea Fishes North of 30° S. Doubleday Australia, Sydney, 297 pp.

Compagno, L.J.V. 1973. Interrelationships of living elasmobranchs. In: Interrelationships of Fishes, P.H. Greenwood, R.S. Miles and C. Patterson (eds). J. Linn. Soc. (Zool.), 53 Suppl. 1:37 pp.

———. 1984. Sharks of the World. FAO Species Catalogue. FAO Fisheries Synopsis No. 125, vol. 4, part 1 and part 2. Rome: United Nations Development Programme, Food and Agriculture Organization of the United Nations, 655 pp.

———. 1990. Alternative life-history styles of cartilaginous fishes in time and space. Env. Biol. Fish., 28:33-75.

Compagno, L.J.V., D.A. Ebert, and M.J. Smale. 1989. Guide to the Sharks and Rays of South Africa. New Holland Ltd. London, 158 pp.

Cressey, R.F., and E.A. Lachner. 1970. The parastic copepod diet and life history of diskfishes (Echeneidae). Copeia, 1970:310-318.

Crow, G.L., J.C. Howe, S. Uchida, S. Kamolnick, M. Wisner, and J.N. Caira. 1990. Protrusion of the valvular intestine through the cloaca in sharks of the Family Carcharhinidae. Copeia, 1990:226-229.

Davies, D.H. 1963. The story of Sally the sawfish. Bull. S. Afr.

Ass. Mar. Biol. Res. 4:10-13.

Dempster, R.P., and E.S. Herald. 1961. Notes on the hornshark, *Heterodontus francisci*, with observations on mating activities. Occ. Pap. Calif. Acad. Sci. 33:1-7.

Devadoss, P. 1978. On the food of rays, *Dasyatis uarnak* (Forskal), *D. alcockii* (Annandale), and *D. sephen* (Forskal). Indian J. Fish. 25:9- 13.

Dingerkus, G., and T.C. DeFino. 1983. A revision of the Orectolobiform shark Family Hemiscyllidae (Chondrichthyes, Selachii). Bull. Am. Mus. Nat. Hist. 176:1-93.

Dodd, J.M. 1983. Reproduction in cartilaginous fishes (Chondrichthyes). In: W.S. Hoar, D.J. Randall and E.M. Donaldson (eds.). Fish Physiology, Vol. 9A, Academic Press, New York, 31-95 pp.

Dral, A.J. 1981. Reproduction en aquarium du requin de fond tropical Chiloscyllium griseum Müll. et Henle (Orectolobidés). Rev. Fr. Aquariol. 7:99-104.

Edwards, R.R.C. 1980. Aspects of the population dynamics and ecology of the white-spotted stingaree, *Urolophus paucimaculatus* Dixon, in Port Phillip Bay, Victoria. Aust. J. Mar. Freshwat. Res. 31:459-467.

Eibl-Eibesfeldt, I. 1965. Land of a Thousand Atolls. The World Publ. Co., New York, 195 pp.

Eley, T.J. 1988. The food habits and behaviour of the graceful shark, *Carcharhinus amblyrhynchoides* (Whitely, 1934), in western province, Papua New Guinea. Sci. New Guinea. 14:15-21.

Euzen, O. 1987. Food habits and diet composition of some fishes of Kuwait. Kuwait Bull. Mar. Sci. 1987:65-85.

Feder, H.M., C.H. Turner, and C. Limbaugh. 1974. Observations on fishes associated with kelp beds in Southern California. Calif. Dept. Fish and Game Fish Bull., 160:144 pp.

Francis, M.P., and J.T. Mace. 1980. Reproductive biology of *Mustelus lenticulatus* from Kaikoura and Nelson. N.Z. J. Mar. Freshwat. Res. 14:303-311.

Garman, S. 1913. The Plagiostomia (Sharks, skates, and rays). Mem. Mus. Comp. Zool., Harvard Coll., 36:515 pp.

Garrick, J.A.F. 1982. Sharks of the genus *Carcharhinus*. NOAA Tech. Rep. NMFS Circ. 445:194 pp. - 1985. Additions to a revision of the shark genus *Carcharhinus*: synonymy of *Aprionodon* and *Hypoprion*, and description of a new species of *Carcharhinus* (Carcharhinidae). NOAA Tech. Rep. NMFS Circ. 34:26 pp.

Gilmore, R.G. 1990. The reproductive biology of Lamnoid sharks. Amer. Litt. Soc., Spec. Publ. 14:64-67.

Grant, E.M. 1982. Guide to Fishes. Brisbane, Queensland Dept. of Primary Indust., 472 pp.

Gruber, S. 1981. Lemon sharks: supply-side economists of the sea. Oceanus, 24:56-64.

Gruber, S., and R. Keyes. 1981. Keeping sharks for research. In: Aquarium Systems, A.D. Hawkins (ed.). Academic Press, New York, 373- 402 pp.

Gruber, S., D.R. Nelson, and J.F. Morrissey. 1988. Patterns of activity and space utilization of lemon sharks, *Negaprion brevirostris*, in shallow Bahamian lagoons. Bull. Mar. Sci. 43:61-76.

Gudger, E.W. 1915. Natural history of the whale shark, *Rhincodon typus* Smith. Zool., N.Y. 1:349-89.

Hagiwara, S. 1989. Reproduction of Chondrichthyans in captivity at Shimoda Floating Aquarium. Abstr. Am. Elasmobranch Soc. Mtngs., San Francisco.

Hutchins, B., and R. Swainston. 1986. Sea Fishes of Southern Australia. Swainston Publ., Perth, 180 pp.

Iwamasa, H. 1981. Fisheries biology of the wobbegong, *Orectolobus japonicus* Regan. Rpt. Jap. Grp. Elasmobranch Stud. 12:93-97.

Johnson, R.H. 1978. Sharks of Polynesia. Papeete, Tahiti, Les Editions du Pacifique, 170 pp.

Johnson, R.H., and D.R. Nelson. 1973. Agonistic display in the gray reef shark, *Carcharinus menisorrah*, and its relationship to attacks on man. Copeia, 1973:76-84.

_____. 1978. Copulation and possible olfaction-mediated pair formation in two species of Carcharhinid sharks. Copeia, 1978:539-542.

Johannes, R.E. 1981. Words of the Lagoon. Univ. of Calif. Press, Berkeley, 245 pp.

Jones, B.C., and G.H. Geen. 1977. Food and feeding of spiny dogfish *(Squalus acanthias)* in British Columbia waters. J. Fish. Res. Board Can. 34:2067-2078.

Kauffman, D.E. 1950. Notes on the biology of the tiger shark *(Galeocerdo arcticus)* from Philippine waters. Res. Rep. U.S. Fish Wildl. Serv. 16:10 pp.

Kerstitch, A. 1992. Socorro. Freshwater and Marine Aquarium Magazine, 15:32-36.

Keyes, R.S. 1982. An unusual example of cleaning symbiosis. Copeia, 1982:225-227.

Klimley, A.P. 1980. Observations of courtship and copulation in the nurse shark, *Ginglymostoma cirratum*. Copeia, 1980:878-882.

_____. 1981. Grouping behavior in the scalloped hammerhead. Oceanus, 24:65- 71.

_____. 1985. Schooling in *Sphyrna lewini*, a species with low risk of predation: a non-egalitarian state. Z. Tierpsychol. 70:297-319.

_____. 1987. The determinants of sexual segregation in the scalloped hammerhead shark, *Sphyrna lewini*. Env. Biol. Fish. 18:27-40.

Lal Mohan, R.S. 1986. Can a sawfish (*Pristis* sp.) kill a dugong? Sirenews, 6:7.

Last, P.R., and M.F. Gomon. 1987. New Australian fishes. Part 15. New Species of *Trygonoptera and Urolophus* (Urolophidae). Mem. Mus. Vict. 48:63-72.

Limbaugh, C. 1963. Field notes on sharks, In: Sharks and Survival, P.W. Gilbert (ed). Boston, Heath and Co. 63-94 pp.

Lyle, J.M. 1987. Observations on the biology of *Carcharhinus cautus* (Whitley), *C. melanopterus* (Quoy and Gaimard) and *C. fitzroyensis* (Whitley) from Northern Australia. Aust. J. Mar. Freshw. Res. 38:701- 710.

Marliave, J. 1984. Six gill shark, a primeval visitor from the abyss. Skin Diver, 34(9):40-41.

Martin, L.K., and G.M. Cailliet. 1988. Aspects of the reproduction of the bat ray, *Myliobatis californica*, in Central California. Copeia, 1988:754-762.

McConnell, R. 1978. Mating yellow spotted stingrays. Skin Diver, 27:33.

McCormick, H.W., T. Allen, and W.E. Young. 1963. Shadows in the Sea: the Sharks, Skates and Rays. Philadelphia, Chilton Books, 415 pp.

McCosker, J.W. 1987. The white shark, *Carcharodon carcharias*, has a warm stomach. Copeia, 1987:195-197.

McCourt, R.M., and A.N. Kerstitch. 1980. Mating behavior and sexual dimorphism in dentition in the stingray, *Urolophus concentricus*, from the Gulf of California. Copeia, 1980:900-901.

McKay, R.J. 1966. Studies on western Australian sharks and rays of the Families Scyliorhinidae, Urolophidae, and Torpedinidae. J. R. Soc. West. Aust. 49:65-82.

McKibben, J.N., and D.R. Nelson. 1986. Patterns of movement and grouping of gray reef sharks, *Carcharhinus amblyrhynchos*, at Enewetak, Marshall Islands. Bull. Mar. Sci. 38:89-110.

McLaughlin, R.H., and A.K. O'Gower. 1971. Life history and underwater studies of a heterodont shark. Ecol. Monogr. 41:271-289.

Medved, R.J., and J.A. Marshall. 1983. Short-term movements of young sandbar sharks, *Carcharhinus plumbeus* (Pisces, Carcharhinidae). Bull. Mar. Sci. 33:87-93.

Moss, S.A. 1984. Sharks - An Introduction for the Amateur Naturalist. Englewood Cliffs, New Jersey: Prentice-Hall, Inc. 246 pp.

Myrberg, A. 1987. Shark behavior. In: Sharks, J. Stevens (ed.), Facts on file, New York, 84-93 pp.

Myrberg, A.A., and S.H. Gruber. 1974. The behavior of the bonnethead shark, *Sphyrna tiburo*. Copeia, 1974:358-74.

Natanson, L.J., and G.M. Cailliet. 1986. Reproduction and development of the Pacific angel shark. Copeia, 1986:987-994.

Nelson, D.R. 1981. Aggression in sharks: is the gray reef shark different? Oceanus, 24:45-55.

Nelson, D.R., and R.H. Johnson. 1970. Diel activity rhythms in the nocturnal, bottom-dwelling sharks, *Heterodontus francisci* and *Cephaloscyllium ventriosum*. Copeia, 1970:732-739.

_____. 1980. Behavior of the Reef Sharks of Rangiroa, French Polynesia. Nat. Geo. Soc. Res. Rpt. 12:479-499.

Nelson, D.R., and R.H. Johnson, J.N. McKibben, and G.G. Pittenger. 1986. Agonistic attacks on divers and submersibles by gray reef sharks, *Carcharhinus amblyrhynchos*: antipredatory or competitive? Bull. Mar. Sci. 38:68-88.

Nishida, K., and K. Nakaya. 1990. Taxonomy of the genus *Dasyatis* (Elasmobranchii, Dasyatidae) from the North Pacific. NOAA Tech. Rpt. NMFS 90:327-346.

Norman, J.R. 1926. A synopsis of the rays of the family *Rhinobatidae*, with a revision of the genus Rhinobatus. Proc. Zool. Soc. 62:941-982.

Notarbartolo-Di-Sciara, G. 1987. A revisionary study of the genus *Mobula* Rafinesque, 1910 (Chondrichthyes, Mobulidae), with the description of a new species. Zool. J. Linn. Soc. 91:1-91.

_____. 1988. Natural history of the rays of the genus *Mobula* in the Gulf of California. Fish. Bull. 86:45-66.

_____. and E.V. Hillyer. 1989. Mobulid rays off eastern Venezuela (Chondrichthyes, Mobulidae). Copeia, 1989:607-614.

Parin, N.V., and A.N. Kotlyar. 1985. Electric rays of genus *Torpedo* in the open waters of the southeastern Pacific Ocean. J. Ichthy. 25:1- 12.

Parker, F.R. Jr., and C.M. Bailey. 1979. Massive aggregation of elasmobranchs near Mustang and Padre Islands, Texas. Tex. J. Sci. 31:255-265.

Perrine, D. 1989. Reef shark attack! Sea Frontiers, 38:31-41.

_____. 1989. Reef fish feedings: amusement or nuisance? Sea Frontiers 38:273- 279.

Pratt, H.L. Jr. 1979. Reproduction in the blue shark, *Prionace glauca*. Fish. Bull. U.S. 77:445-470.

Pratt, H.L. Jr., J.G. Casey, and R.B. Conklin. 1982. Observations on large white sharks, *Carcharodon carcharias*, off Long Island, New York, Fish. Bull. 80:153-157.

Rancurel, P., and A. Intes. 1982. Le Requins Tigre, *Galeocerdo cuvieri* Lacepede, des eaux Neocaledoniennes examen des contenus stomacaux. Tethys, 10:195-199.

Randall, J.E. 1963. Dangerous sharks of the western Atlantic. In: Sharks and Survival, P.W. Gilbert, J.A.R. Garrick and L.P. Schultz (eds). Boston, D.C. Heath and Co. 339-361.

_____. 1967. Food habits of reef fishes of the West Indies. Stud. Trop. Oceanogr. 5:665-847.

_____. 1977. Contribution to the biology of the whitetip reef shark. Pac. Sci. 31:143-164.

_____. 1986. Sharks of Arabia. London: Immel Pub. 148 pp.

Randall, J.E., and G.S. Helfman. 1973. Attacks on humans by the blacktip reef shark *(Carcharhinus melanopterus)*. Pac. Sci. 27:226-38.

Rodgers, C., C. Roden, R. Lohoefener, K. Mullin, and W. Hoggard. 1990. Behavior, distribution, and relative abundance of cownose ray schools, *Rinoptera bonasus*, in the northern Gulf of Mexico. N.E. Gulf Sci. 11:69-76.

Rudloe, J. 1989. Captive maintenance of the lesser electric ray,

Narcine brasiliensis, with observation of feeding behavior. Prog. Fish Cult. 51:37-41.

Russo, R.A. 1975. Observations on the food habits of leopard sharks *(Triakis semifasciata)* and brown smooth-hounds *(Mustelus henlei)*. Calif. Fish Game, 61:95-103.

Salini, J.P., S.J.M. Blaber, and D.T. Brewer. 1990. Diets of piscivorous fishes in a tropical Australian estuary, with special reference to predation on penaeid shrimp. Mar. Biol. 105:363-374.

Schwartz, F.J. 1983. Occurrence, abundance, and biology of the blacknose shark, *Carcharhinus acronotus*, in North Carolina. N.E. Gulf Sci. 7:29-47.

Sciarotta, T.C., and D.R. Nelson. 1977. Diel behavior of the blue shark, *Prionace glauca*, near Santa Catalina Island, California. Fish. Bull. 75:519-528.

Smith, B.G. 1942. The Heterodontid sharks: their natural history and the external development of *Heterodontus japanicus* based on notes and drawings by Bashford Dean. In: Bashford Dean memorial volume; archaic fishes. New York, Amer. Mus. Nat. Hist. 649-770 pp.

Smith, J.W., and J.V. Merriner. 1982. Association of cobia *Rachycentron canadum*, with cownose ray, *Rhinoptera bonasus*. Estuaries, 5:240-242.

_____ . 1985. Food habits and feeding behavior of the cownose ray, *Rhinoptera bonasus*, in lower Chesapeke Bay. Estuaries, 8:305-310.

Springer, S. 1963. Field observations on large sharks of the Florida-Caribbean region. In: Sharks and Survival, P.W. Gilbert, J.A.F. Garrick and L.P. Schultz (eds). Boston, C. Heath and Co. 93-113 pp.

_____ . 1967. Social organization of shark populations. In: Sharks, Skates and Rays, P.W. Gilbert, R.F. Matthewson and D.P. Rall (eds). Baltimore, Johns Hopkins Press, 149-174 pp.

Standora, E.A., and D.R. Nelson. 1977. A telemetric study of the behavior of the angel shark, *Squatina californica*. Bull. S. Calif. Acad. Sci. 76:193-201.

Stead, D.G. 1963. Sharks and Rays of Australian Seas. Sydney, Angus and Robertson, 211 pp.

Stevens, J.D. 1974. The occurrence and significance of tooth cuts on the blue shark *(Prionace glauca* L.) from British waters. J. Mar. Biol. Assoc. U.K. 54:373-378.

_____ . 1984. Biological observations on sharks caught by sport fishermen off New South Wales. Aust. J. Mar. Freshw. Res. 5:573-590.

_____ . 1984. Life-history and ecology of sharks at Aldabra Atoll, Indian Ocean. Proc. R. Soc. Lond. B. 222:79-106.

Stillwell, C.E., and N.E. Kohler. 1982. Food, feeding habits, and estimates of daily ration of the shortfin mako *(Isurus oxyrinchus)* in the Northwest Atlantic. Can. J. Fish. and Aquat. Sci. 39:407-414.

Stratsburg, D.W. 1958. Distribution, abundance, and habits of pelagic sharks in the central Pacific Ocean. Fish. Bull. U.S. Fish. Wildl. Serv. 58:335-361.

Strong, W.R. 1989. Behavioral ecology of the horn shark, *Heterodontus francisci*, at Santa Catalina Island, California, with emphasis on patterns of space utilization. Masters Thesis, C.S.U., Long Beach, 255 pp.

_____ . 1990. Instruments of Natural selection: How important are sharks? Amer. Littor. Soc. Spec. Publ. 14:70-73.

Strong, W.R., F.F. Snelson, and S.H. Gruber. 1990. Hammerhead shark predation on stingrays: an observation of prey handling by *Sphyrna mokarran*. Copeia, 1990:836-840.

Talent, L.G. 1976. Food habits of the leopard shark, *Triakis semifasciata*, in Elkhorn Slough, Monterey Bay, California. Calif. Fish Game, 62:286-298.

_____ . 1982. Food habits of the grey smooth-hound, *Mustelus californicus*, the brown smooth-hound, *Mustelus henlei*, the shovelnose guitarfish, *Rhinobatus productus*, and the bat ray, *Myliobatis californica*, in Elkhorn Slough, California. Calif. Fish Game, 68:224-34.

Talwar, P.K. 1981. The electric rays of the genus *Torpedo* Houttuyn (Rajiformes: Torpedinidae) of Indian seas. Bull. Zool. Surv. India, 3:185-189.

Tasaka, S. 1986. Mating behavior of rays in captivity. Alley in the sea. Shimoda Floating Aquarium, 2:6.

Tricas, T.C. 1979. Relationship of the blue shark, *Prionace glauca*, and its prey species near Santa Catalina Island, Calif. Dept. Fish and Game Bull. 77:75-82.

_____ . 1980. Courtship and mating-related behaviors in myliobatid rays. Copeia, 1980:553-556.

_____ . 1981. Diel behavior of the tiger shark, *Galeocerdo cuvier*, at French Frigate Shoals, Hawaiian Islands. Copeia, 1981:904-908.

_____ . 1982. Bioelectric-meditated predation by swell sharks, *Cephaloscyllium ventriosum*. Copeia, 1982:948-952.

Tricas, T.C., and E.M. LeFeuvre. 1985. Mating in the reef whitetip shark, *Triaenodon obesus*. Mar. Biol. 84:233-237.

Tricas, T.C., and J.E. McCosker. 1984. Predatory behavior of the white shark *(Carcharodon carcharias)*, with notes on its biology. Proc. Calif. Acad. Sci. 43:221-238.

Uchida, S., M. Toda, and Y. Kamei. 1990. Reproduction of elasmobranchs in captivity. NOAA Tech. Rpt. NMFS 90:211-237.

Uyeno, T., and T. Tsutsumi. 1991. Stomach contents of *Latimeria chalumnae* and further notes on its feeding habits. Env. Biol. Fish. 32:275-279.

VanBlaricom, G.R. 1982. Experimental analyses of structural regulation in a marine sand community exposed to oceanic swell. Ecol. Mongr. 52:283-305.

Wass, R.C. 1971. A comparative study of the life history, distribution and ecology of the sandbar shark and the gray reef shark. PhD Thesis. Univ. of Hawaii, Honolulu.

Wetherbee, B. 1990. Feeding biology of sharks. Amer. Littor. Soc. Spec. Publ. 14:74-76.

West, J.C., and S. Carter. 1990. Observations on the development and growth of the epaulette shark, *Hemiscyllium ocellatum* (Bonnaterre), in captivity. J. Aquaric. Aquat. Sci. 5:111-117.

Whitley, G.P. 1940. Fishes of Australia. Part 1. The Sharks, Rays and Devilfish, and other Primitive Fishes of Australia and New Zealand. Royal Zool. Soc. of N.S.W. 280 pp.

_____ . 1967. Sharks of the Australasian region. Aust. Zool. Vol 14:173-188.

Wolfson, F.H. 1986. Occurrences of the Whale Shark, *Rhincodon typus* Smith. In: Indo-Pacific Fish Biology: Proceedings of the Second International Conferance on Indo-Pacific Fishes. T. Uyeno et al. (eds.), Ichthy. Soc. Jap. Tokyo, 208-226 pp.

Appendix   Courtship and Mating in Sharks and Rays

Courtship behavior in the epaulette shark. The pair moves along the bottom, as the larger male grasps the left pectoral fin of the female in his mouth. Photo by author.

Mating in the eqaulette shark. The male lyes on top of the female, still holding her left pectoral fin in his mouth, and inserts his left clasper into her cloaca. Photo by author.

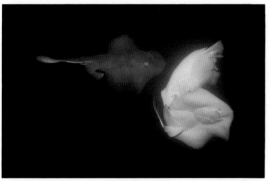

Courtship in the round stingray. One male (upper right) grasps the pectoral fin of the female (lower right) in his mouth, while another male (left) interferes. Photo by author.

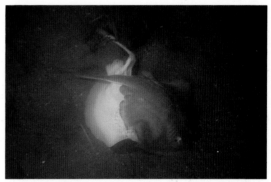

Round stingray mating. The male lays under the female and holds her disc margin in his mouth as the pair copulate. Photo by author.

Yellow stingray mating. Mating in this species is similar to that in the round stingray. The male is under the female, is grsping her disc margin in his mouth, has his right clasper rotated forward and inserted into her cloaca. Photo by William J. Arzbaecher.

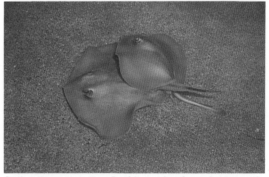

Sepia stingray mating. In this species the male grasps the disc margin of the female, lyes over the posterior part of the female's disc, and curls his pelvic region under her's in order to insert a clasper. Photo by Soichi Hagiwara.

INDEX TO COMMON NAMES

INDEX TO SCIENTIFIC NAMES